Find It In Five Seconds

Gaining Control In The Information Age

Greg Vetter

HARA
PUBLISHING GROUP

Published by
Hara Publishing
P.O. Box 19732
Seattle, WA 98109
(425) 775-7868

Vetter, Greg.
    Find it in five seconds/Greg Vetter. -- 1st ed.
    p. cm.
    Includes index.
    ISBN: 1-883697-07-7

    1. Business records--Management. 2. Paperwork
(Office practice)--Management.   I. Title

HF5547.15.V48 1999   651.5
                        QBI99-1196

        Library of Congress Number: 99-95531

        Manufactured in the United States
            10 9 8 7 6 5 4 3 2

Editing: Vicki McCown
Cover Design: Bill Fletcher
Graphics: John McLaughlin
Index: Nancy Ball

Dedicated To

This book is dedicated to my family, the greatest gift anyone could have ever received. To the best dad and mom, who used to say, write it down and let the paper do the worrying for you and my brother, John, the model of success.

Acknowledgments

I am very appreciative to the following group of friends:

Carol Hacker, who encouraged me regarding my writing skills and assisted me with her own book writing experiences.

Rex Kelly, who guided me to a book concept.

Cheryl Lezovich, who spent many hours editing the writings of a speaker.

Cornelius Washington, Mike Landry, David Greenberg, Jeff and Diane Justice, Doug and Gayle Smart, Barbara Pagano, Tricia Molloy, Dr. Andrew Linial, David Chambers, Dr. Allen Clark, and members of the Georgia Speakers Association who helped guide me in preparing the book.

Matt Huet, Mark Joyner, and Bill Pamplin for their computer knowledge.

Dr. Frank Meaux, Jim Frost, and Thom Hartmann, who advised me about the psychological concepts.

Mike Semarau, who years ago, by allowing me to come in and work with him and my first Fortune 100 company, jump-started my business into corporate America.

Martha Wiederhold, who was always there for me and with me during the personal-growth years.

All of my wonderful and courageous clients who, through their training experiences, have helped me create the system I use today.

And most of all, the unknown fellow who wrote an article in 1974 in an Orlando newspaper about what to have on your desk, who first made me aware that there was such a thing as an office organizer. I hope you get to read the book and see what you inspired me to create.

Contents

Part 4—Your Day

Part 5—System Set Up

Appendices

"It must be remembered that there is nothing more difficult to plan, more doubtful of success, nor more dangerous to manage than the creation of a new system. For the initiator has the enmity of all who would profit by the preservation of the old institution and merely lukewarm defenders in those who would gain by the new ones."

—Machiavelli
"The Prince" (1513)

Introduction

Who knew?

I was just 17 when I first tried putting some basic organizational principles into practice. I was working as a lowly stockboy at the local 7-Eleven and decided to reorganize the cooler section. I hoped my initiative would impress my boss.

Instead, I got fired.

Not the most auspicious beginning to a career, but then I didn't know then I would eventually become an organizational consultant. Back in 1968, there was no such thing. Still, ever since I could remember, I had loved analyzing a situation and asking myself if there was a better way to accomplish various tasks.

When it came time to go to college, I still didn't know what I wanted to be when I grew up, so I decided to study what I enjoyed and majored in psychology. Here I broadened my analytical skills by learning the "why" behind people's actions and behavior when confronted with a variety of situations.

When I entered the work force, I worked in some psychology-related positions, but I found myself gravitating more towards business. I held a number of positions in sales, including regional sales manager, and became involved in the food service industry, eventually owning my own restaurant. All the while, I continued to analyze workers and their environment and devise systems to help them do their job better.

Finally, in 1989, I realized that no matter what job I had—whether I was the boss or an employee, out in the field or sitting behind a desk—what I really enjoyed doing, and seemed to have talent for, was creating organizational systems that increased productivity. And, so, I officially began my career as an organizational consultant by starting my own company, Vetter Productivity Inc.

System? What system?

I think I first realized the need for organizational systems when I made the transition from blue-collar to white-collar work. One of my first jobs was in the family construction business, where there were very specific ways to perform each task required in the building process. They didn't give me a bag of cement and a mixer and hope I would come up with a way to make concrete; I had to follow a proven, step-by-step process.

But when I took a job in an office, I was given very few instructions. I was shown my desk, the lunch room, the supply cabinet, maybe a job description, and then expected to get to work. There was no company-wide system in place that I could follow to organize my work and immediately become a productive employee. As a result, they had a company full of people who had worked out their own systems, some good, some not-so-good, but all of them different.

I found this practice to be consistent, no matter what job I held in corporate America. Is it any wonder that most companies—and their employees—function in an atmosphere of chaos and crisis, reacting to what's urgent rather than controlling their work flow? It doesn't have to be that way.

This might hurt a little

Some years ago, my doctor sent me to visit a physical therapist who put me through a series of brutal exercises. When I complained about the pain, he told me, "I'm not concerned about your pain now. My job is to help you achieve a pain-free lifestyle for the future."

I had to laugh, for I had said virtually those same words to every one of my clients.

Trying something new is always difficult, and setting up the system I suggest in this book is no different. Like anything worthwhile, it requires commitment and hard work. But once it is in place, I guarantee that the benefits you will reap will far outweigh the few hours of work you put in. And you only have to go through the process once. Then, whether you're at work or at home, you can use this system to coordinate every aspect of your life—now and for as long as you want.

What's it all about, Alfie?

Here's a brief outline of the five sections you will find in the book.

Part One, Drowning In A Sea Of Information, examines what's happening in the workplace today, explains how to deal with the effects of the Information Age, and gives some enlightening background on addiction to work and clutter.

Part Two, Processing, teaches you a new system for categorizing, sorting, prioritizing, storing, and accessing information.

Part Three, Producing, discusses a new way of working in the Information Age so that you can perform your tasks more efficiently and thereby realize better results.

Part Four, Your Day, looks at how to set up your daily schedule, eliminate interruptions, and improve how you communicate and work with your administrative assistant.

Part Five, System Set Up, gives you a specific, detailed, step-by-step procedure for putting the system into action.

As you go through the book, I'd like you to keep two things in mind. First, as you learn the concepts, remember that you will be using them to create your own system—one that works for you and your office. Second, notice how many times making a decision enters into the process—that is a key element to the success of this system.

When you put this system in place, you will work less, produce more, reduce stress, and regain control of your work day. Thousands of people across the country can tell you that it works—but the only way it will work for you is for you do it.

Make that decision to use this system, and watch your life change for the Vetter.

1.1

Drowning In A
Sea Of Information

The Information Age
- This Is The Dawning Of The Age Of Information
- I Am A-Frayed I Am At The End Of My Rope
- Not With My Space You Won't
- There Is Something Rotten In Your Office In Denmark

The Deadline Approacheth
And It's Closer Than You Think!
- The Good Old Days
- Gulp! Their Faces Were Flushed!
- The Distinguished Medal For Bravery Under Fire
- More, Please

What To Do
- The Solutions

I'm Organized, Aren't I?
- Born To Organize

What Do You Want To Accomplish?
- Shredding The Myths Of The Office
- Bennys
- You Can Pay Me Now Or You Can Pay Me Later

What You Will Learn In This Chapter
- Why you feel so overwhelmed and out of control
- How the Information Age will affect your life
- Seven solutions to working in the Information Age
- The organizational myths of the office
- Benefits you will receive by using this system

💣✶ Myths of the Office

If I file it away, I'll never find it.

The Information Age

This Is The Dawning Of The Age Of Information

Ladies and gentlemen, you are about to drown in a sea of information.

Historians tell us we're in the forefront of the third great age. The first was the Age of Hunters and Gatherers. The second age was the Industrial Revolution. Currently we're in the Information Age.

In the first age, we hunted for our food. We were simply trying to survive. In the second, the Industrial Age, we revolutionized how we worked by introducing machinery that enabled us to manufacture and produce at a much more rapid rate via the mechanized assembly line.

Currently, we are in the third great age, where information is king. Information is sold and transmitted at dizzying speeds. Many people are experiencing an unsettling shift in their world. Some feel as if they are drowning in a sea of paper, technology, and information. It's a whole new way of life, both personally and professionally.

1-1
Drowning
In A Sea Of
Information

The next age, which some feel is already here, will be The Age of Globalization. Your own country's economy and market will be replaced with one worldwide market. There will no longer be many economies but rather just one in which you will participate through the Internet.

Studies state the amount of information that will come into our lives in the next five to six years will double every six months. It is estimated that one week-day edition of today's *New York Times* contains more information than the average person in seventeenth-century England was likely to come across in an entire lifetime. A recent study shows Americans are swamped with 190 electronic messages a day. A recent Gallup poll shows that the average Fortune 1000 worker receives 83 messages (electronic, voice, and written) a day. Annually, more than 6 trillion e-mail messages are being received.

I Am A-Frayed I Am At The End Of My Rope

Are you really ready to be engulfed in this massive sea of information and be interrupted at every turn? Are you able to handle the amount of information that is coming into your life now, or are you already in overwhelm? Consider all the pounds of junk mail hitting your mailbox, e-mail quacking on your computer, faxes invading your home, cellular phones disturbing your workout at the gym, beepers beeping, and call-waiting clicking to indicate a call. More and more new technology is being created every day, which means you'll have even more information sources to check in the future. More information sources simply mean more interruptions which mean less work accomplished.

One of the biggest problems, especially in the face of all this technology, is that people still don't even know how to set up their office and work in it. They don't know how to keep a paper-free desk, floor, and credenza, how to create a filing system, how to find things in less than five seconds, or how to take time to work on important rather than urgent things. They never learned the basics because the real basics were never taught. If anything was taught, it was in the form of the well-worn, time-management theories—theories that were really myths.

If you feel overwhelmed and out of control now, with way too much to do, imagine what your life will feel like in five years when information will be doubling every six months. Then again, maybe you'd rather not.

But what if you had a system that would allow you to find everything in your office in 5 seconds or less—and, what's even more important, take control of your day? This book introduces

The Vetter Way™, a powerful organizational tool you can implement right now that will show you how to do just that.

Not With My Space You Won't

I recently met with a client from a Fortune 20 company. Steve M. is a very sharp, capable systems manager. He had just been "cubisized," i.e., moved from a large, private office to a minuscule cubicle. He asked me to help him with the space layout of his cubicle. It was like trying to design a four-bedroom house in a shoebox. He politely mentioned the printer actually got more space than he did—its own private office. He was definitely not a happy programmer!

We started talking about all the different ways information was entering his work life. "I've got so many places to get information and check for its arrival, I know I won't get to some of it for a week," Steve said. The following are a few of the information sources he must deal with:

- Paper (memoranda, letters, notices)
- Newsletters
- Industry magazines
- Voice mail
- Beeper
- E-mail
- Intranet mail
- Lotus Notes databases such as:
  - Action items
  - Issues
  - Discussions
  - Scope of changes
- Meetings
- Faxes
- Overnight deliveries
- Telephone calls

And, of course, the pertinent information gathered while talking in important places such as the hall and restroom.

Years ago, Steve and the rest of the business world had only two sources of information in their offices: paper and the telephone. Now, because of so many information sources requiring attention, getting any actual work done has become impossible. Steve's manager didn't see it that way, however, and expected him to be more productive. I'm sure Steve couldn't wait for the next piece of technology that he would receive.

There Is Something Rotten In Your Office In Denmark

The following are some more interesting statistics I've found from various business sources to illustrate what is happening:

Via Fed Ex
Here is what happens in the typical office:
• Nineteen copies are made of each original document.

"Nineteen copies are made of each original document." Unbelievable! If Gale creates a document for her boss Allen, there will eventually be 19 other copies of that document created or copied in other departments. If you start a filing system in your company with 1,000 pieces of paper, you'll have copied those documents 19,000 times, creating 20,000 copies. Thank God some people actually throw things away!

Fed Ex also notes:
• About 8 percent of all paper documents are lost; 3 percent misfiled.
• For each document filed or retrieved, $20 in labor is spent.
• $250 in labor is spent finding a misfiled document.

If you work for yourself, it's easy to understand what $250 means. Imagine if you worked for someone else and every time you misfiled a document you'd be docked $250. I guarantee one of two things would happen rather quickly: You would never misfile again or you'd find yourself working somewhere else.

USA Today
• The average worker has 36 hours of work stacked up on his or her desk. (And on their floor and on their shelves and on their credenzas!)
• The average executive wastes 45 minutes a day searching for something lost on his or her desk. (That's only average, folks. Think how much more time is wasted if there is clutter around.)
• In the year 2000, U.S. businesses will file 120 billion new sheets of paper. (Ah. The paperless office. Paper consumption per capita in the U.S. tripled from 1940 to 1980 (from 200 to 600 lbs.) and tripled again from 1980 to 1990 (to 1,800 lbs.).

Nine To Five
- Many people spend 20 percent to 30 percent of their time looking for information that has been misplaced. Estimates of the cost of a single misfiling range from $61 to $73 according to management experts.

American Demographics
- Every day America wastes 79 million hours looking for lost or misplaced objects.

Didn't we learn "A place for everything and everything in its place"?

Coopers and Lybrand
- Of the 1.3 trillion documents in the U.S., 39 billion are misplaced at any given time.

Accountemps
Results of a survey of 200 executives of the nation's 1,000 largest corporations showed that they spent about:
- 32 minutes a day reading and writing unnecessary memos (128 hours a year)
- 1 hour and 12 minutes a day at unnecessary meetings (288 hours a year)
- 15 minutes a day on hold on the telephone

The same survey reveals that people waste six weeks a year trying to find mislabeled, misfiled, or misplaced items. That works out to approximately 50 minutes per day.

If you could find everything in your office in less than five seconds, you'd be able to save almost an hour a day, five hours a week, twenty a month, two hundred and fifty a year! And that's only one of the ways that you can save time.

I'm sure you get the point. Some of us are in real trouble!

The Deadline Approacheth
And It's Closer Than You Think!

The Good Old Days

Remember how slow and simple things were back in the 1950s? Gas cost only 25 cents a gallon. There were only three TV channels. Microwaves and VCRs weren't invented yet. Computers were the size of large rooms, but it really didn't matter since you hadn't heard of them and didn't even know what they were. There were no fax machines, copy machines, beepers, pagers, car phones, PDAs, voice mails, e-mails, nor cellular phones. If you wanted something copied, you'd use a black, messy piece of carbon paper. Things were slow, easy and simple. Words like *urgent, ASAP, rush, immediately*, and *emergency* were reserved for crises.

1-2
The Good
Old Days

Growing up in Riverhead, a small town on eastern Long Island, I very rarely heard the word *urgent* being used. The only emergencies we experienced occurred when the fire department was putting out a fire, a totally different kind of fire than the kind we put out nowadays.

Today, there is no down time and no escape from work or from other people. We have cell phones in our cars and beepers in our pockets, and we carry both everywhere. I'm constantly amused when I'm on line at the grocery store, and I hear a phone ringing. Is no place sacred? A lot of people are working 24 hours a day, seven days a week. They just haven't figured it out yet.

The high-tech revolution and the Information Age dictate you can never "get away from it all." Big Brother is watching and listening. We simply can't do business the way we used to because technology floods our consciousness with massive amounts of information and worse, interruptions.

Whatever happened to the good old days? When and why did things shift so dramatically? Why does everything have to be so rushed and urgent and have a deadline? The following phrases are now commonly heard:

"When can I have it?"	"Put a rush on it."
"I need it immediately."	"Fax it to me right now."
"It's an emergency."	"Overnight it."
"I need it now."	"I needed it yesterday."

Gulp! Their Faces Were Flushed

An old, established plumbing supply company in Chicago recently hired me to train two of their employees. While I was there, I couldn't help but notice that the company had some serious operational problems; but since I hadn't been asked to consult in that capacity, I kept quiet.

After I had finished the training and I was preparing to leave, the company president grabbed me by the arm. "As long as you're here," he said, smiling confidently, "I wonder if you would give us your opinion on the future of our company." He steered me down the hall to the meeting room where the company officers were all waiting to hear my sunny prognosis for their firm.

Now, I'm not a shy person, but I'll admit I felt a few butterflies at suddenly being put on the spot that way. How was I going to nicely tell them something they really didn't want to hear? (Congratulations, Mr. Jones. You are now the proud owner of a company that will soon be defunct.)

I told him (in so many words) that if he continued to run his business the way he had been, he could kiss that 150-year-old company goodbye. After everyone's mouths finally shut and the color came back into their faces, I explained that they couldn't do business in an environment where everything is treated as urgent—a mistake that most businesses make today.

Their must-do-it-right-now, don't-make-the-customer-wait mentality was killing the company. Products were promised immediately, although their production department was already a week behind. Deliveries were scheduled for the day after the order was placed, but, of course, that was impossible. Repairs, consultations, you name it and it was supposed to be done within 24 hours. Instantaneous customer service! More like how to go out of business quickly! They certainly could respond a lot quicker than any of their competitors could, at least in the short run. They believed, like many companies do today, that if everything weren't treated as an urgency, they'd lose their customers.

As I tell businesses, "You have to give up to get." You may lose business in the short run, but you still will be in business down the line, unlike many of these immediate-response businesses. Turning business away, as I well know owning my own company, is a bitter pill to swallow, but a necessary one. Companies need to understand that they are the ones who have to create and maintain boundaries they can live with, not the customer.

The Distinguished Medal For Bravery Under Fire

The corporate world's culture today rewards a reactive, firefighting type of behavior. When you manage the effect, i.e., when you put out the fire, you get rewarded much more enthusiastically than for finding out what the cause of the fire was and preventing it. Something is definitely wrong there.

Many companies have elaborate firefighting procedures in glorified fire departments yet have no fire prevention systems. It's kind of like our country's ICBM system. We have enough firepower to create a scorched earth for hundreds of years but no defense against another country's missile attacks. Who cares if we blow them to kingdom come, we'll be there with them. What we need is a preventive and defensive system to block their attack.

> Today, when you manage the effect, i.e., when you put out the fire, you get rewarded much more enthusiastically than for finding out what the cause of the fire was and preventing it.

1-3
The Wrong
People Are
Being
Rewarded

Where do all the fires and disasters come from anyhow? From doing business as usual, but also from the company's culture and its reactive mindset. The usual excuse for never getting caught up is having too many fires to put out. The vicious circle.

> *Be a fire marshal, not a firefighter. Spot the fires before they start.*

What about recognizing the same type of fires that keep breaking out and preventing them before they start? Heck no. How could we justify all the money we spent on our fire department?

More, Please

When you think of important issues, you think of proactive activities such as planning, working on your priorities, or tackling tasks that you don't have to work on yet, but if you do, will move you from point A to point B that much more quickly—such as pursuing self-improvement or developmental tasks, doing the budget, planning long-term, finding ways to improve efficiency, creating new systems in your business. These, of course, are not urgent—they are important. Getting an immediate buzz just won't happen, but these are the types of activities that will give you the big payoff later.

If you haven't already felt the heat, you will. More and more is going to be expected of you. Today, companies routinely ask employees to do the work of 1.3 people—for the same pay with less time off. Overtime is at an all-time high. Productivity among workers must be high, since so many people are being fired, laid off, and asked to retire early. Notice I didn't say they were being reengineered. American companies still treat our most valuable resource with the lowest concern. Employees today are much more productive than they were years ago, but at a terribly high price. Workers in corporate life today are dropping like flies. Too much stress, too many urgencies, too many expectations, too much invasion into their private life, being on call and having to take work home every night. The culture we have created is killing us.

What To Do

Solutions

As long as you continue to process everything from a time-based, reactive, deadline mentality rather than an importance-based one, you will always be behind and in trouble. There is absolutely no way you'll be able to keep up with the workload that will be thrown at you in the near future. The only answer is to learn a system of how to process information faster and learn a whole new way to work.

> *If you continue to operate in a time-based, tickler mentality, you will never be able to stay up with the flow of information.*

By doing this you will be able to survive the Information Age.

TIMES UP!

1-4
The
Deadline
Approacheth

What can you do to keep your head above water in the Information Age? Use any or all of the following:

1. Learn a whole new way to work
2. Be proactive 20 percent of your day
3. Learn and limit the amount of technology in your life
4. Understand the difference between Processing and Producing
5. Use one system
6. Learn how to process information
7. Limit your choices

1. Learn a whole new way to work

Anyone who has ever worked in a blue-collar job knows there is a very specific way to accomplish a task. I was fortunate enough to grow up in a family construction business. I'm proud to say after 43 years of my dad and mom running it, the business is still going strong with my brother, John, now in charge. When I started to work in the business, I was shown how to do things. Specific work processes were set up. I knew the steps and sequence to pouring a foundation, putting on a roof, and building a roof truss.

When I started in corporate life, it was nothing like that. I was shown the copier, the supply cabinet, the restroom, my desk, occasionally a brief job description and, a few times, the door. But I was never once shown a system of how to work.

Most people in white-collar jobs have never been taught a system of how to work. Many times they are thrust into their jobs with little or no training and expected to immediately perform and produce. This is especially true with administrative and sales people.

Unfortunately, many of us approach the way we work from an appointment-book, tickler-file, time-based, reactive, urgent, and deadline mentality rather than an importance-based one.

"Shut the barn door or the horse will get out" works if the horse is still in the barn. Mr. Ed is long gone. Shutting the door after the horse gets out doesn't do much good. Feeling like you get nothing done, are always behind, and never seem to have any time to work on important tasks typically means you are spending your time reacting rather than proacting. The answer is to recognize the need to learn a whole new approach on how to work in the office. This is exactly what we will cover in Part 3 under Producing.

2. Be proactive 20 percent of your day

You've all seen a hamster running on a wheel in a cage. Its only job seems to be to run on that wheel, the faster the better.

As time goes on, the hamster will get tired and be unable to run. Eventually the hamster will die and go on to wherever hamsters go when they die (Hamster heaven?).

1-5
Hamster
Running
On A
Wheel

Now imagine if the hamster built an electric motor that would turn the wheel. Granted, the hamster would probably take a long time to build the motor, perhaps needing to get an electrical or mechanical engineering degree. But think how happy the hamster would be in its cage, lying back in a hammock with its paws behind its head, sipping on a cold one, watching as the electric motor turned the wheel for him.

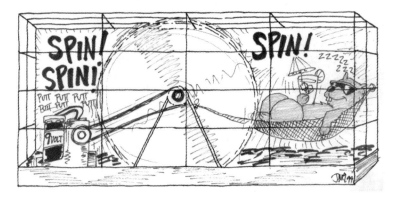

1-6
Hamster
Lying In A
Hammock

Your life is a lot like the hamster's. You get on your "wheel" every morning and start peddling. Information, data, and things to do are thrown at you at incredible rates of speed. You're running on that wheel as fast as you can, but it never seems to be fast enough. You feel out of control, overwhelmed, and always behind. Just once you would like to get ahead. You'll always be behind until you make time to build your own "electric motor."

Take 20 percent of your day, that's right 20 percent, and spend it working on important rather than urgent things. Do it in what I call a Quiet Time (QT). This is a specific, uninterrupted

**1-7
You
Running
On A
Wheel**

time you take daily with the door shut and the phone off the hook. If you're working an eight-hour day, you'll spend an hour and a half in a QT.

Is it realistic to expect that your QT slot will be open every day? Probably not. Meetings, urgencies, and other events will get in the way sometimes, but by taking your QT every day, you'll develop the habit of doing it; by taking it at the same time every day, others will honor your time slot.

The ideal situation is for an entire department or company to take a QT at the same time every day. From 1:00 p.m. until 2:30 p.m. is a great time, since most people who have just eaten lunch wish they were back in kindergarten about to take naptime. A few key administrative people or departmental receptionists can answer the phones. Make sure they get to participate in the QT the following day so they can benefit from it as well. When given a quiet, uninterrupted time, administrative people can produce a tremendous amount of work. One hour of uninterrupted time equals three to four hours of a regular day.

Imagine the results you will obtain when you take an hour and a half a day to work in your QT. It will be the equivalent of accomplishing the same amount of work that others would in four to six hours of a normal day.

If you find it difficult to block out a large period of time, break the time in half. Take half your QT in the morning and half in the afternoon or take an hour in the a.m. and 30 minutes in the p.m.

The Vetter Way™ system was created so you can save enough time during the day by having a clean desk, finding items in five seconds or less, and then using that time for a QT. A QT is the only real hope you have of getting ahead. You know the old saying: If you continue to do what you have always done, you will continue to get what you have always gotten. I disagree. With the Information Age upon you and the constant stream of data thrust upon everyone, you won't even be able to maintain and get what you've always gotten done. You'll get even less.

My experiences have shown me that less than 1 percent of the working population takes a QT, and I am being very generous with that number. Imagine if every employee was working daily on proactive work in a company QT. The company's productivity would literally double. Put that one in your stockholder's pipe and smoke it!

3. Learn and limit the amount of technology in your life

This may seem like blasphemy, but I suggest that you limit the amount of technology in your life. If you're going to use technology, learn it and learn it well. I don't own a cellular or mobile phone. I won't wear a beeper for all the money in the world. (Well, maybe if half of it were tax-free.) I have only one magazine subscription.

I want to keep as much of the noise out of my life as possible. I want to keep time open during the day while I am driving so I can think and plan and not feel like I have to handle the onslaught everywhere I go. I'm not suggesting that you avoid technology, but be aware that the more you have, the more often you will get interrupted and the less work you will accomplish. More is not always better; in this case it definitely isn't.

4. Understand the difference between Processing and Producing

The key to understanding why you feel so overwhelmed and out of control is knowing the difference between Processing and Producing. We'll cover this key concept in the next chapter, Processing and Producing.

5. Use one system

Think about the multitude of systems that you use to accomplish work. You may have:
- An appointment book to keep track of things to do and pieces of paper in it needed for certain dates
- A to do list on a separate piece of paper
- Tasks to work on in a contact manager such as ACT!
- A pile on your desk
- A pile on your credenza
- Stuff to work on in your briefcase
- A stack of business cards of people you need to call in a pile on your desk
- Projects to work on in a desk drawer

Systems you might use to store and access information are:
- ◆ A system for your paper in your file drawer
- ◆ No particular system for files on your hard drive
- ◆ Another system for your e-mail
- ◆ A different system from the rest of your department
- ◆ Various other systems in your secretary's file drawer, e-mail, and hard drive
- ◆ Yet another system in your central or long-term storage files

You get the picture. Most people are using five or more different systems to work from and store information. This might work now, but when information really starts pouring in and your workload increases, which it definitely will, most people won't be able to keep up. On the other hand, you could have one or two drawers for all the tasks you need to work on and the same system for storing everything everywhere.

6. Learn how to process information

You do lunch. You do movies. Why not do your In Box too? Most people "do" rather than process their In Box. Why? Because few, if any, of us have been taught how or what to do regarding processing paper and information. If at the end of the day you don't feel as if you got any of the real stuff done, you are probably doing your In Box. We will cover how to process information using the OATS system—which will allow you to empty your In Box in five minutes or less—in Part 2, Chapter 1. The OATS system can be used to process all of your information sources including paper, e-mail, computer, departmental, and Central Files.

7. Limit your choices

Imagine living in a third world country and then moving to the United States. Your first visit to a high-end department or grocery store would boggle your mind. Your choices would seem unlimited.

When I grew up things were different. I had to walk a mile to school in the snow—I know, here comes the story. Loved the walk and the snow. Hated carrying that enormous book bag. We played in the dirt with simple toys. We were lucky to get a couple channels on our old black-and-white television. We made do with what we had. My mom definitely didn't run a taxi service. There were more simple things to do. Family, church, and neighborhood played a big part in our activities. We had fewer choices.

As a client of mine, Rex Kelly, said, "The problem today is that we simply have too many options." Compare sitting around and listening to the radio versus participation in virtual reality. Today, we have a zillion different activities we can participate in and the list will continue to grow.

Simplify your life. You don't have to have one of everything. The more you have, the more you will want, and the more distracted, the less focused, the more indecisive, and the more confused you will be. The secret is to go back to the basics and have a simple life.

I'm Organized, Aren't I?

Born To Organize

Organized people aren't born. It's a skill that they learn just like everything else. Years ago, I remember hearing someone say salespeople are born. That is simply not true. Because somebody is able to talk a lot doesn't mean that he or she is a good salesperson. Some of the best salespeople are very quiet. Many have developed the skill of listening which is just as or more important than talking. The ability to organize is similar to the ability to sell. They're both specific skills that need to be learned. We're not born with them. Unfortunately, few of us ever learn how to acquire either of them.

How many time-management courses or seminars have you taken? Tape programs listened to? Different types of appointment-book systems used? PDAs tried? How many computer software programs, schedulers, PIMs, CIMs, and contact managers have you tried to keep you organized?

I was once asked to do a time-management class for a university. I politely stated I didn't feel there was anything new that people hadn't already heard before. Against my better judgement, I went ahead and taught it. The evaluations confirmed my belief: "Nice delivery but heard it all before." Yawn! So much for the proverbial time-management class.

I thought to myself there had to be a better way to work; thus, The Vetter Way™ system was born. Actually, it didn't happen that quickly. My background and education were in psychology, so I have always been interested in how people work. What really started the fire

> **Census taker:** And how many people work in your factory, sir?
>
> **Factory owner:** I'd say about one out of ten.

under me was when our Industrial Psychology class toured a John Deere plant in Dubuque, Iowa. As I watched the assembly lines and noticed the sectioned-off, yellow-painted areas on the floor, I thought of the amount of time that could be wasted when a worker took just one extra step. Multiply that one step every day by a thousand workers and some serious time could be wasted. If you think I'm kidding, consider how little work is done Monday mornings and Friday afternoons.

The second reason I created the system was that I have ADD. I needed a system that would keep me focused, since it always feels as if I have a million thoughts entering my mind a day and I have the concentration capacity of a cricket.

Through the years I've tried most time-management systems and they haven't worked for me. Using my educational background, work experience, and input from clients, I created not a time-management system, but rather a system of productivity and office organization—in other words, a system of how to work in the office and a way to store and access information, the two basic components needed to work.

What Do You Want To Accomplish?

Shredding The Myths Of The Office

I'm sure you've heard the saying, a clean desk is the sign of a sick mind. I believe the saying came about because someone couldn't figure out a system of how to get organized or needed an excuse or rationalization for their disorganization. From there it became a belief, which, of course, many people embraced since it was an easy way out.

The following test lists some commonly held beliefs about the office environment and organization. Choose true or false for each statement and learn whether you can tell the difference between fact and myth.

True   False

_____ _____   If I can't see something, I'll forget to do it.

_____ _____   I should touch a piece of paper only once.

_____ _____   If I throw away a piece of paper, I might need it later.

_____ _____ A clean desk is the sign of a sick mind.

_____ _____ If I file away a document, I'll never find it.

_____ _____ My computer files and paper files will never match.

_____ _____ When I make to do lists, I prioritize the tasks.

_____ _____ I put things to do in my tickler file a few days ahead of when they are due.

_____ _____ My entire calendar day should be blocked out.

_____ _____ I should keep my phone on the credenza behind me.

_____ _____ I can never get anything done because I'm interrupted all day long.

_____ _____ The harder I work, the more I'll get done.

_____ _____ I'm a salesperson. I'm not supposed to be organized.

_____ _____ I can never stay organized when I travel.

_____ _____ Multitasking is always productive.

_____ _____ A clean desk means I'm productive.

_____ _____ I can organize my office, but I can't organize my home.

_____ _____ I always have an open-door policy with my employees.

_____ _____ My employees can't do tasks as well as I can.

_____ _____ I'm creative. I need clutter around.

_____ _____ I don't have time to return phone calls.

_____ _____ My secretary can organize me.

_____ _____ In and Out Boxes should be on top of one another in the corner of my desk.

_____ _____ I work out of or from my In Box.

_____ _____ I can instantly find items in files that are called General, Miscellaneous, and Other.

All the answers are false. Now before you get your files in a flutter, please understand we will prove each are false in the following chapters. Unfortunately, many good people have bought into these fallacies for years.

Bennys

There will be many benefits if you choose to set up and use the Vetter Way™ system outlined in this book. A few of the benefits are:

- Have and be able to keep a clean and paper-free desk, floor, and credenza
- Be able to find everything in your office in five seconds or less
- Save between one and three hours per day. (Use the time doing something else. You can save time but you can't bank it.)
- Be able to use the system both at your office and at your home
- Be able to go through and empty your In Box in five minutes or less
- Align your computer, e-mail, and paper files with one another
- Adapt your system as your needs change
- Set up your office space for maximum productivity
- Create and set up your own personalized filing system
- Set up a paper flow with paper flowing out instead of staying in
- Learn a whole new way to work
- Use only one system rather than many for information storage
- And many more, but most important, you will be able to *stay in control*!

You Can Pay Me Now Or You Can Pay Me Later

Have you seen the TV commercial that features a mechanic trying to persuade you to get your oil changed and buy his company's oil filter? "You can pay me now or you can pay me later. It's up to you," he says.

The following chapters describe a proven system that has worked for many people throughout the United States. Will you read the book, avoid doing anything, and drown in a sea of information, or will you proactively prepare for the impending onslaught and do something about your life? I hope the latter. Through the years, as I have coached many successful and powerful people around the country, I've noticed there's just a slight difference between them and an average person. Successful people "do it" while average people simply "read it."

It's your choice. It's your life. I'll see you in five to six years when information is doubling at a rate too quickly to comprehend!

Remember These Concepts

- Be a fire marshal, not a firefighter. Spot the fires before they start.
- If you continue to operate in a time-based, tickler mentality, you will never be able to stay up with the flow of information.
- Ways to work in the Information Age:
  - Learn a whole new way to work.
  - Be proactive 20 percent of your day.
  - Learn and limit the amount of technology in your life.
  - Understand the difference between Processing and Producing.
  - Use one system.
  - Learn how to process information.
  - Limit your choices.

1.2

Processing And Producing

The Dilemma

- Oh Happy Day
- Two Information Sources
- More, More, More
- Never The Twain Shall Meet

Process and Produce

- The Battle Between Processing And Producing
- How To Process (Information)
- How To Produce (Results)

What You Will Learn In This Chapter

- How the Information Age is causing you to be unproductive
- How to tell the difference between processing information and producing work
- Why you shouldn't combine processing information with producing work

---

☀ <u>Myths of the Office</u>

Multitasking is always productive.

The Dilemma

Oh Happy Day

Another workday. Today will be different though. I will not allow myself to be pulled in a thousand directions, interrupted every eight minutes, and forced to leave work again at an ungodly hour, feeling as if I didn't get anything done. I have finally created some time in my office to work on that important project that I never seem to get to. Finally, some time to myself.

8:00 a.m.   I start working on the stack of papers on my right.

8:02 a.m.   Two minutes go by and the phone rings. I stop working on my project. (Of course I answer the phone; I have to.) Someone wants something, so I begin to assemble the information.

8:10 a.m.   Eight minutes later, a coworker walks in. I stop working on my mail-out from my phone call and start working with my coworker on a mutual project that we both started a week ago.

8:20 a.m.   Ten minutes later my vice president calls. She must see me immediately. I excuse myself and meet with her.

9:20 a.m.   An hour later I am finally back at my now covered desk of scattered files and papers when the phone rings. One of my biggest clients has an emergency, so I leave immediately.

11:20 a.m.   Two hours later I am back in my office working on one of the scattered files on my desk. I'm not sure which one.

11:30 a.m.   Ten minutes later another worker drops off something. Interrupted again. Finally, something fun that won't take long to do. It's not real important that I do it but hey, I need something fun once in a while.

The rest of my day continues the same way. I start working on something and I'm pulled off it by an interruption. Before I know it, it's time to leave. Somehow, I haven't been able to get back and finish that project. For that matter, I never seem to have any time to ever work on important things.

Why does it seem as if you can never complete a task? You start one thing and another interrupts you. Then you start working on that one and get interrupted again before you can finish it. You no longer dare dream of working on important tasks. You'd be overjoyed if you could just finish your routine tasks.

Two Information Sources

Years ago there were basically two sources of information in the office: the telephone and paper. If someone called on the phone, they either got you or they didn't. There wasn't any voice-mail or call waiting. A simple piece of paper was the other source of information. Things were fairly simple.

2-1
Two
Information
Sources

Today, think how many sources of information there are in your life—easily over a dozen. I'm talking about all those memos, newsletters, magazines, CDs, e-mails, faxes, beepers, cellular phones, PDAs, car phones, voice mail, computer files, overnight deliveries, contact managers, and who knows what other technology in the future that will cause even more information sources to drive you nuts.

2-2
Too Many
Information
Sources

The ratio of time we spent on Processing information in the past was fairly low and the time spent Producing work was high. Today, our Processing time is rising incredibly fast due to the many information sources from which we must Process information. More time Processing means less time Producing.

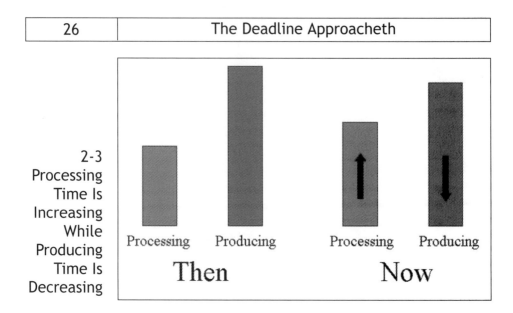

2-3 Processing Time Is Increasing While Producing Time Is Decreasing

More, More, More

The more technology you have, the more information sources you will have. The more information sources, the more interruptions. The more interruptions, the more time you will spend on Processing information. The more Processing time, the less Producing time. The less Producing time, the less you get done. The less you get done, well, you know what happens from here on.

> *The more information sources you have, the more interruptions you will have.*

By using more and more technology, we set ourselves up to be constantly interrupted. Each new piece of technology is a separate information source from which we need to Process information. This puts us into the Processing mode which means we aren't Producing which is how we get results, make money, keep our job, and sail into the sunset. Whew!

Here's the flow:

The more technology
⇩
The more information sources
⇩
The more interruptions
⇩

The more Processing time

⇩

The less Producing time

⇩

The less output

Less output simply means you produce less, which you will hopefully not list under your achievements on your next résumé. Less output provides the following work life choices.

    A. A rushed, hurried-up, frenzied, got-to-get-it-all-done-but-know-I-can't-get-it-done work life. (If you are lucky, you'll live to 50. If you are over 50, stay close to home.)

    B. Complete burnout, which allows you to start your new career as a piece of toast. (It's okay if your father is a baker.)

    C. Longer work hours including weekends. (I vaguely remember my family. Two or three kids, weren't there? A wife, too, I think.)

    D. Getting fired for lack of production. (I like to change jobs every six months anyway.)

    E. Losing your company. (There go my life savings!)

Great choices, aren't they? Have a nice work life.

By the way, how is your work life? Do you run your day or does your day run all over you? Do you feel in control or out of sorts? At the end of the day do you feel as if you really got something of importance done? Or do you feel like most people today: overwhelmed, out of control, too much to do with too little time to do it in, constantly interrupted. If you're not in control today, imagine what your life will look like in the next couple of years when information will be pouring into your life.

Never The Twain Shall Meet

The individuals who will succeed in the Information Age will be those who understand the delicate and subtle relationship between Processing and Producing, i.e., knowing when to Process information and when to Produce work and never combining the two. Many people combine the two and then wonder why they can't get anything done. They constantly shift back and forth from Producing to Processing. It's like trying to mix oil and water—it simply doesn't work.

Process and Produce

The Battle Between Processing And Producing

Let's look at the two key components around which your workday revolves: Processing and Producing. We Process information and we Produce work. Choose both at the right time and in the correct proportion and your day goes well. Process more than you Produce and your output is lowered considerably. Excessive Processing allows you to spend a lot of time and effort looking at a lot of information but not accomplishing much (Produce). Produce without Processing and you feel anxious about what you haven't done. Obviously, many tasks will slip through the cracks if you're not up with all of them. Recognizing the difference between Processing and Producing, not mixing them but balancing them are the keys to having a successful workday.

> *Your day is broken down into Processing and Producing.*

2-4
Processing
Versus
Producing

How To Process (Information)

What does Process mean? As I stated, we're now in the Information Age. Information enters our lives at dizzying speeds. Processing simply means examining, deciding on, categorizing, and prioritizing information. Information from all sources—

digital, paper, verbal, and any other crazy form that will be possible in the future. Processing allows you to see the big picture, the entire scope, the big show. It puts you in control and allows you to act proactively rather than always having to play catch-up. It can also sink you if you do it too frequently.

Back in the Civil War, armies depended on their cavalry to be their eyes and ears. If the cavalry didn't scout ahead, the army was at a great disadvantage. Imagine if one side had observation airplanes and had the advantage of seeing for miles around. The war would have been over almost before it had started.

When you have too much to do during the day or you're overwhelmed, what's the last thing you typically do? The action that's most important to take first, which is Processing information, such as going through your In Box, opening your e-mail and listening to your voice mail. Why don't you do it first? Because you feel as if you don't have enough time to do it. You already have too much to do. After all, haven't you been told year after year to produce?!

You're not paid on how much you Process but rather on how much you Produce and that's where the problem occurs. When you Produce before you Process, you are putting the cart before the horse. It still will work, the horse sometimes can push the cart, but generally the cart veers off to the side and the horse doesn't really much like it. It's a lot easier and quicker with the horse in front pulling. If you don't believe me, ask the horse.

When we're under the gun to get work done, especially regarding urgent tasks or tasks on deadlines, we tend not to take the time to Process the information. Instead, we jump right in and start working (Produce). As a result we feel out of control due to the fact that we haven't analyzed (Process) the information coming into our life. We don't know everything that we need to do. The rule is to Process first, then Produce.

> *Process before you Produce.*

The following are the ways to Process information.

Daily

✔ Go through your In Box, voice mail, and e-mail three times a day.

Process all information that comes into your office three times a day regardless of the technology or form it comes in. Open all your e-mails, listen to your voice mail, and go through everything in your In Box. Do this first thing in the morning, right after lunch, and late afternoon. Why do it three times a day?

◆ It allows you to handle urgencies. If something is urgent or time-sensitive, you have a window of three or four hours to get to it.

◆ It's easier. The bigger the pile, the less you want to do it. Aren't you more willing to go through two inches of paper than two feet of paper? Some of us have this interesting belief that if we don't do anything, the pile will just go away. Reality dictates the larger the stack, the less chance you will go through it.

Weekly

✔ Review everything in your Action Categories on your last workday of the week.

> *Processing includes:*
>
> • *Checking voice mail, e-mail, and In Box, three times a day.*
>
> • *Reviewing all your Action Categories, once a week.*

Once a week, generally Friday, you need to reacquaint yourself with every task you intend to do by reviewing work that will be in your Action Categories. (Action Categories will be covered in Part 3.)

Think how you feel when you are left out, when you don't know what's going on. Most people feel out of control and most people hate that feeling. When you look at all your tasks, it makes you aware which puts you back in control. The key is a shift in your thinking from looking at a day to an entire week. We will go into more detail in a later chapter on both of these.

How to Produce (Results)

The second component of your day is to Produce. What is Producing? To Produce simply means to accomplish work or create results. That's what you're paid for. Producing is not checking your e-mail or your voice mail. It isn't answering the phone. Producing means getting something done.

You need to work from each of the following three areas—To Do, Tickler, and Routine To Do—every day. The following is an overview, which will allow you to see the big picture.

✔ To Do
Characteristics:
- ◆ Important
- ◆ Impactful
- ◆ Big return for time spent
- ◆ One task
- ◆ Can be done before it's due
- ◆ Doing it increases your efficiency

Most people rarely work on these because they believe they don't have enough time to do them.

As part of the system you'll learn how to:
- ◆ Work on your top five items in your To Do Category in your QT (Quiet Time) every day.

✔ Tickler
Characteristics:
- ◆ Must be and can only be done today
- ◆ Follow-ups
- ◆ Reminders
- ◆ Tickets for a certain date
- ◆ Phone calls to be made on a specific date
- ◆ Urgencies
- ◆ Materials for an appointment or meeting on a specific date
- ◆ Items to take with you on your trip on the date you are leaving

The Tickler file is used very differently with this system than the way it's normally used.

As part of the system you'll learn how to:
- ◆ Work on all items in the today's date folder in your Tickler Action Category.

✔ Routine To Do
Characteristics:
- ◆ Repetitive tasks done either daily, every other day, every couple of days, weekly, or monthly
- ◆ Maintenance tasks
- ◆ Similar tasks that you can batch together

Most people hate to do boring, repetitive tasks. Many flit from one to another at an interruption's notice. Most would

> *Producing includes:*
>
> * *Working your To Do, Tickler and Routine To Do Action Categories every day.*

rather never do them. Similar tasks in your home life would be getting a good night's sleep, eating well, exercising, taking out the garbage. You know, those mundane activities you live for, that make your life complete.

As part of the system you'll learn how to:
◆ Look through every folder in your Routine To Do Category. Choose specific folders to work on with at least three tasks in the file so you can mass-produce whatever you are working on.

Remember These Concepts

- The more information sources you have, the more interruptions you will have.
- Your day is broken down into Processing and Producing.
- Process before you Produce.
- Processing includes:
  - Checking voice mail, e-mail, and In Box, three times a day.
  - Reviewing all your Action Categories, once a week.
- Producing includes:
  - Working your To Do, Tickler and Routine To Do Action Categories every day.

Things To Avoid
- Starting on one task, allowing yourself to be interrupted, then working on another.
- Processing and Producing at the same time.

The Psychology of Work and Clutter Addiction

Deep Down
- Causes Versus Symptoms

Higher and Higher
- What A Buzz
- Deadline

Addiction
- High Ho. High Ho. It's Off To Work, Uh-Oh
- This Drug Called Work
- Do Be, Do Be, Do Or Just Be
- The Addiction Of Clutter
- The Bottomless Hole

Later, Baby
- Can We Do This Later?
- I'm Not A Perfectionist. Wait, I Can Say That Better!

A.D.D.
- Attention Deficit Disorder

What You Will Learn In This Chapter
- Why we have addictions
- Why you have clutter in your life
- What workaholism is
- Why you procrastinate
- How this system will help you if you have A.D.D.

☢ **Myths of the Office**

A clean desk is the sign of a sick mind.

Deep Down

This chapter deals with the psychology of why we have too much clutter in our lives and why we work too much. I know, you may not want to read about the why—you just want to know the how. And that's fine. The system I outline in this book will work for anyone, whether they explore the psychology of their addiction to work and clutter or not. If you just want to learn how you can make your life more organized, more productive, and less stressful—without all the psychobabble—proceed directly to the next chapter (do not pass Go, and do not collect $200).

But if you'd like to understand some of the reasons why your life is disorganized, if you want to go beyond the superficial quick-fix and make some long-term changes, read on. I think you'll find this chapter fascinating.

Please be aware that I am not a psychologist or therapist. The following chapter is based on my background in psychology and my work with clients.

Causes Versus Symptoms

Most of my college classes put me to sleep, but one class was different: psychology. I remember one story my favorite teacher, Professor R. V. Sandven, told us about a man who started to have headaches. As time went on, they seemed to be getting worse, so he decided to go to a doctor. The first doctor couldn't find anything wrong but gave him a prescription for the pain. (Sound familiar?) The headaches persisted. The next doctor he went to prescribed another drug. Still no change (except a rise in the drug company's stock). The next treated him with yet another drug. The headaches still persisted.

After seeing most of the head and neck specialists he could find, the man went to see an old doctor. He wasn't a specialist as were the others, but simply an old-fashioned country doctor. He had a simple way to treat patients: Look at the person's entire body, and then treat the cause, not the symptoms.

For the first time in many years the man had a physical. None of the specialists took the time to get the overall view. They were too busy, and, besides, the rest of the body wasn't their specialty. (Your foot can't be that important, can it?)

During the exam, the doctor noticed a slight limp as the man walked. As he examined the man's foot he discovered an ever-so small-bump. An x-ray revealed a small, hidden metal splinter. After the doctor cut it out, the man could once again walk without the limp and, soon after, his headaches completely disappeared.

When I first started working with clients, I thought I was teaching them about paper and organization. Through the years, it dawned on me that it really had very little to do with paper. Paper or clutter or overwhelm were merely a manifestation of something else, something deeper psychologically that wasn't working in the person.

Often, as we attempt to solve problems, we deal only with the symptoms rather than the causes. Going on a diet is a classic example. When people are overweight (look around), many take the route of trying to lose weight by dieting. Ninety-six percent of all weight is gained back after dieting. Why? Because diets are a temporary fix. Avoiding certain foods or cutting down on portions for a specific period of time does not eliminate a basic need that is not being met. As soon as you get off the diet, you go back to gobbling food the way you used to. Your temporary behavior—your diet—hasn't changed your basic unfulfilled need.

ORGANIZATION ▬ = A System + Decision-Making

3-1
The Secret of Organization

In order to have long-lasting organization and productivity in your life, you need to understand that three elements are necessary:
  1. Having and using a system
  2. Being a good decision-maker
  3. Recognizing and meeting your unmet needs

1. Having and using a system
Think how much more work you get done and how much easier it is when you use a system.

Blue-collar workers know this; many white-collar workers don't. The IRS is a perfect example of a group who couldn't possibly have nor use a system as evidenced by all the paperwork they lose.

2. Being a good decision-maker
Think how you feel when you are in the middle of working on

something and your inability to make a decision holds you back from completing a task. Multiply that feeling by 20 uncompleted tasks, and you feel like you've got a big, black cloud hanging over your head.

> ## *Organization = A System + Decision-Making*

Now think back to when you had a lot to do and you made quick decisions and completed the tasks quickly. You felt great and your life worked well.

Many times the importance of fast decision-making is overlooked in time-management classes. They teach you systems, but not much about the importance of decision-making. Yet as you will see, almost everything you do in life is about making a decision. When you make a decision, your life works. This isn't to say you shouldn't spend time thinking about big decisions, but don't let thinking keep you from making the decision.

As you read through this book, you'll be creating your own personalized system. A large part of the system will be about how you make decisions.

3. Recognizing and filling your unmet needs
This will be discussed in the next couple of sections.

Higher and Higher

What A Buzz

Urgent activities come and go, but they'll never diminish. There will always be urgencies. This is the nature of life and business, especially at companies that are customer-service oriented.

Yet, half the time, urgencies are not necessary. They are created by people who seek a payoff. It's like getting a fix. When they complete the task, they get a high—a buzz, a sense of accomplishing the impossible.

Working on important tasks that may take a while to complete eliminates that buzz. There's a delay of gratification, and it's long-term, rather than instantaneous. In the big picture, however, these tasks are very important!

Who wants to wait? Little kids and adult kids want gratification now or even sooner. They'll wait until the last moment to handle tasks rather than do them early and put off gratification. They're too busy gratifying themselves. That's why so many people have a TV set in every room, but no money left over for their retirement account. Give it to me now, baby!

Deadline

The word deadline supposedly came from the Civil War or, as my southern friend Jackson H. calls it, "The War of Northern Aggression." During the war there was a prison camp in Andersonville, Georgia. It was basically an open-air camp walled in by a perimeter of pine tree posts. It was not one of the better examples of the humane side of man. There was an area that was cleared just inside the fence with a line delineating it. If you crossed over the line, you'd be shot dead, thus the "dead line."

3-2
The Dead-
line

Today, if you miss a deadline, doesn't it feel like you're going to get shot? Some deadlines create artificial boundaries for you when you're not disciplined enough to complete a task before it's due. You get your fix by leaving a job to the last moment; when you're out of time and you don't have a choice, you have to get it done. Your brain recognizes the pattern and teaches you to start experiencing that high when you leave these tasks to the end. The later it is, the more frenzied the work, the greater the high you will experience.

Addiction

High Ho. High Ho. It's Off To Work, Uh-Oh

The goal for many people at work is to get to the top as quickly as possible. Getting promoted to senior management is their dream. Power, prestige, money, control, and respect.

Once upon a time there was a young executive whose ultimate goal in life goal was to become a vice president. It was what he lived for. He was involved in a quick-start, leadership-training program for young, promising executives. He grabbed every possible assignment, worked late every night and every weekend. He lived and breathed work.

The years passed quickly. At the age of 65, he was finally promoted to a vice presidency. It felt great. At long last, the good life.

A couple of weeks later he started to feel very depressed. He could hardly fathom why. He was, after all, a vice president of a Fortune 100 company, part of an elite group of other vice presidents. And then it suddenly hit him. He was no longer a young man; he was 65. His life had passed him by. He could hardly remember enjoying it. He was so busy trying to get to the top that he never really experienced life.

Oh, well, he thought, probably just a temporary feeling that would go away. Three weeks later, a new corporate policy came out requiring mandatory retirement at age 65. He was in total shock. He'd be out of a job in less than a month. All that work for this? He couldn't believe it. Work was his life. He didn't even have a chance to enjoy his vice presidency. It wasn't fair.

His biggest shock was yet to come. When he was no longer working, he had a lot of time on his hands. He had never had any outside interests or real friends since his life was all about work. His wife was now a stranger. He no longer had any goals to keep him pumped up. What would he do? After a year of severe depression, he committed suicide.

This Drug Called Work

I'm constantly amazed that workers are as proud as they are about the number of hours they work. They think by working more hours, they will feel better. Never mind their lack of productivity or that it takes them twice as long to accomplish a task. The more they work, the more they wear their long hours as a badge of honor.

People are now working more than ever. Why are work hours on the rise? More is expected today. The Information Age is upon us and we have more demands on our time. Workaholism has become a socially accepted addiction.

Here's how the cycle works:

The harder you work, the more you get done.

⇩

The more you get done, the more you are rewarded.

⇩

The more you are rewarded, the better you feel.

⇩

The better you feel, the more you work.

A vicious, addictive cycle.

Workaholism is the most prevalent addiction in America today; however, rarely is it ever perceived as a problem. It's difficult for Americans, with their strong work ethic, to think of working in the same way they view gambling, doing drugs, watching porn or eating to excess. But, when men and women spend endless hours at work, making that the priority over all else, something is wrong.

Workaholism—like all our other behaviors, good or bad—is fueled by the desire for a certain payoff. When we drink or take drugs, we get a pleasant buzz; when we eat, we satisfy the taste buds; when we gamble, we think we will get rich. Working harder and longer promises us all sorts of payoffs: status, success, self-worth, money, a sense of beating the competition. Working for these payoffs isn't bad in and of itself; it's when working dominates our lives that we know we have succumbed to its addictive grip.

Unfortunately, just like all the other negative, addictive behaviors, working too much is a way to compensate for something that's missing in your life. If you are in constant motion, you won't feel that awful hurt—whatever that

> *Everything we do is for a payoff. Payoffs can be both healthy and unhealthy.*

might be for you. Work becomes a drug, a way to anesthetize your feelings so you don't feel your pain, shame, isolation, or fear.

If you work hard and long enough, you can numb that awful ache you shoved down into your gut so many years ago as a child—that horrible pain you never want to feel again. Most people are not even aware of it. They don't understand why they have an uncontrollable urge to save everything, to control every situation, to smoke, or to buy too much. Look around. Better yet, look in the mirror. We're an addicted society and becoming more and more so every day.

How can you tell if you're addicted to something? According to therapist Jim Frost, it's usually hardest for the person with the addiction to recognize the symptoms. That's the nature of the disease. Addictive behavior may include: excessive use, as in eating too much; habitual use, such as needing a drink no matter what time of day it is; an inability to stop, like a smoker who can only go without a cigarette for a short time or not at all; a need to up the dose, like a drug addict who can't get high with just one hit any more.

Shame, fear, and isolation are typically the underlying causes of addictive behaviors. Adults often seek to replicate situations that allow them to feel shamed—the same feelings they experienced as children. Some of the women who were beaten as little girls grow up to find a husband who will beat them. When the husband leaves, many women seek out another mate to beat them again. Human beings feel most comfortable in a setting that is familiar, even though it may be unhealthy.

Ever wonder why you constantly partake of such self-defeating behaviors? A basic need isn't being met, and instead of meeting that need, you disguise it with an addictive behavior that simply doesn't work. Ever wonder why you started eating so much after giving up smoking? You merely substituted another drug—food—for nicotine. The problem is the void can not be filled with any of the substitutes, only the real thing: good, honest inner-child work. You have to find out what basic need isn't being met and meet it, or you'll spend the rest of your life shifting from addiction to addiction.

> *The definition of insanity is doing the same thing over and over and expecting different results.*

Addictions are merely temporary ways to deaden the shame, never creating the solution. Getting recognition from the outside doesn't work; it must come from the inside. Individuals will work themselves silly to be at the top or make large sums of money; yet they still feel empty, thus creating the need for more money, more power, etc. Got to keep moving and producing. The old vicious cycle again.

Many people have to "bottom out" with their life before they recognize their addiction or get help. When their life becomes unmanageable, when the addiction suffocates them, when their spouse threatens to leave them, when they're fired, is when most people

> *The outside cannot fix the inside.*

finally bottom out and get help. Many never do.

Do Be, Do Be, Do Or Just Be

What contributes to our sense of workaholism is our belief in the West that our worth comes from producing. Who you are and what you do is highly important in our society. The first question you ask someone upon meeting is what they do for a living. Take this test: Think about a bank president and a waitress and their respective jobs. Which brings a more favorable image? There's an unwritten built-in prejudice, which fans the flames of workaholism. The higher the position, the more prestige, the more money, the more worth as a human being. By moving up to the big time and acquiring status or position, some people think they'll be happy. Yet think about the many rich, famous, prominent, successful people who self-destruct.

Back in the early '70s, when I was in college, there was a popular poster of a father holding his little son's hand as they walked through the woods. The caption on the poster was "Take Time." I liked that because it seemed I never took time for the really important things in my life. I was always busy running around, in a hurry, feeling the pressure to produce. Father Ed Murray, a friend of mine, would tell me that, in the West, we were human "doings." In the East, they were human "beings." The belief here in the West is that our worth comes from what we "do," how much of it we "do," and how well we "do" it.

3-3
Doing vs.
Being

Doing vs. Being. West meets East. The way to get ahead in the West is by doing; the way to "be" in the East is simply by being. Actually the Eastern philosophy works better. We are worth something simply because we "are."

In the West	In the East
Producing = Worth	Being = Worth
Being = Worthless	Nonproducing = Worth

As I told a very conscientious client of mine who was spending too much time trying to do too much, "Set boundaries for yourself. If you don't, the following will happen: First you'll get sick. Then you'll get divorced. Then you'll die." She kind of half laughed.

Three months later, I ran into her while walking down one of the hallowed halls of her company. Her face was ashen. She looked as if she were on the verge of total exhaustion. After saying hello, I looked her in the eye and repeated, "First you get sick..." A look of enlightenment crossed her face. She finally got it. She is one of the few who did.

The Addiction of Clutter

Saving things, pack-ratting, buying too many items, collecting and holding onto stuff, stockpiling, hoarding are all forms of being a Clutterholic. Those who are addicted to clutter feel a sense of security by having things.

Why are offices so cluttered? Because many people don't have a system, they're scared or reluctant to make decisions, or they're addicted to clutter. Clutter is as much an addiction as are drugs and gambling. Clutterholics tend to emotionally bond with their stuff. Having a lot of things allows them to fill that empty void, to stuff that empty feeling with something—in this case, clutter.

Many of us believe more is better. We are in America after all. Hey, the more stuff you have, the better you are and the more successful you are. The attempt to deaden the pain and fill up that hole with paper, information, and clutter is as real as it is with any drug.

The excuses used for a cluttered office are many. Two of the most common are not enough time to clean up or too busy working to spend time on trivial things, such as a clean office. "There are reasons and results. Only one of them matters." I like that saying because excuses are not even mentioned in the picture.

Remember, clutter is a way of trying to fill up that pain and emptiness. The real hurt

> *There are reasons and results. Only one of them matters.*

is buried so far down that most people never find it. Clutter is nothing more than a temporary security blanket to briefly warm you for the night. In order to truly free yourself, you must go back and deal with the issues you have ignored.

The Bottomless Hole

You'll never be able to fill up that hole until you go back and deal with your basic needs that were never met. You must revisit the pain in order to eliminate the pain. By now you're probably saying you've already had too much pain in your life and the last thing you want is to experience any more. Sorry. If you want to lose your pain, you must first own your pain.

In psychology there's a concept called Approach/Avoidance. Approach means we gravitate towards favorable, familiar, and comfortable things. Avoidance means we try to stay clear of uncomfortable, unpleasant, and unhappy situations. We'll engineer our behavior in such a way as to stay away from people or situations that are uncomfortable, such as that impossibly long report we keep putting off. That's why it's very understandable when you say no thanks to going back and revisiting your pain. Who in their right mind would want to be hurt again?

The best way around most things is through them. As you read this book, you'll discover the way to really be successful in your life is by addressing a problem, making a decision, and taking action instead of avoiding action. For example, take a situation where you must make a key decision at work. You know it will be painful, messy, and unpleasant Yet, rather than shoving it back into the corners of your mind or letting it stew for weeks, you jump right in and deal with it.

Many people never received real acceptance or unconditional love from their parents when they were very young. They grew up in what we call today a dysfunctional home. This is fairly typical. As a result, a void within them was created that they've

> *The best way around something is always through it.*

been trying to fill ever since. They stuff it with a variety of things: food, drugs, alcohol, tobacco, nicotine, sex, gambling, work, religion, shopping, buying, and clutter, among many others. The more they hurt, the lonelier they are, the more shamed they feel, the more they try to fill that bottomless hole.

Remember, the way you interact at work is the same way you interact at home, which is the way you interacted growing up. You can better understand this is by revisiting your childhood and reexamining the dynamics of your home life.

Later Baby

Can We Do This Later?

Procrastination is about a lack of decision-making or, as some people would say, the decision not to make a decision to do something. Procrastination is about the need to be gratified now rather than wait for the rewards in the future.

A way to deal with procrastination is to perform one small, easy part of a task. As the Chinese proverb teaches, a thousand-mile journey begins with one small step.

Think about doing your taxes. When do you get them done? Are they in the mail by February 1, or do you put them off until April? If you do put them off, how does it feel from January 1 through April 15?

Let's pretend it's a new year. You're feeling pretty good. This year will be different, or so you say. You're going to knock out your taxes early. January comes and goes, as do February and March. Suddenly it's April. As each month passes, you feel worse and worse. Procrastinating is like carrying a bag on your shoulder. In January, it's fairly light. February feels fifty pounds heavier, March feels a hundred pounds heavier, and April feels like you are crawling along the ground. As each month slips by, the weight or the heaviness gets worse. What a way to live life.

Why do people procrastinate? Here are some of the reasons:
- Being a perfectionist
- Too big to do
- Takes too long to do
- Too difficult to do
- Don't like to do it
- Fear of failure
- Not good at it
- Life is stuck
- Fear of being successful
- Need for instant gratification

Through the years, I've noticed many more people are afraid of being successful than of being a failure. Many people don't feel they are worthy of success, and so they use procrastination to keep from reaching success. The following are solutions to dealing with procrastination—but maybe you would rather go over these later...

✔ **Make decisions.**
Be decisive. Make quick decisions and a lot of them. Decisions cause action. Action produces energy. Energy causes results. If you're wrong, the worst thing that can probably happen is you'll get fired and, if you do, you were suppose to move on anyway.

✔ **Get a coach.**
Work with someone who will make you accountable. Get a mentor; use your boss or your overlooked secretary.

✔ **Have your buddy do the task with you.**
Remember studying together in high school? Synergy and peer pressure still work.

✔ **Hire someone else to do the task.**
If you make $50 an hour and an assistant only charges you $20 an hour, you still make $30 an hour and, best of all, don't have to do the work. You can hire a part-timer or set up a college practicum for credit hours with real-life, on-the-job experience for college students. Only in America, folks!

✔ **Delegate the task.**
You hire people to make your job easier. Let them!

✔ **Find someone who likes to do it.**
Believe it or not, there are actually people who like to work on taxes and put up insulation.

✔ **Break the task down into simple and easy tasks.**
The smaller the task, the greater the chance of you doing it. Limit the length of the task. The more of a buzz you get, the better the chance you'll do it.

✔ **Decide not to do the task.**
Remember the 80-20 rule. Lower your sights. Many tasks are unnecessary and unprofitable. After all, it probably wasn't really important anyway. No over-committing. Learn to say "No thank you."

✔ **Focus on the starting of the task.**
Focus all your energy on doing the first step rather than dwelling on the enormity of the project. Think about jump-starting a car. Once the car gets rolling, it gets a lot easier to push.

✔ **Differentiate between routine tasks versus tasks that need to be done well.**
Top-notch quality isn't necessary in every aspect of what you do. Some of the work you do can actually be average. Perish the thought!

✔ **Change how you talk about the task.**
"I have to," "I must," and "I should" all create an environment of dread and doom. How about: "I choose," "I want to," "I get to." Hey, I get to mow the lawn! And rake it too!

✔ **Be proactive.**
Work on the task before it's due, way before it's due. Allow enough time to do it. Do it in a Quiet Time daily. Limit the number of deadlines in your life.

✔ **Reward yourself. Reward yourself. Reward yourself.**
Think back to when you were a child. When you were a good little boy or girl, you got a lollipop. You were rewarded. When you grew up, you seemed to have forgotten that principle. The more you reward yourself, linking cause and effect, the less you will procrastinate. Rewarding yourself is the least used and most powerful solution to overcoming procrastination.

I'm Not A Perfectionist. Wait, I Can Say That Better!

A lot of people are perfectionists. They're very concerned about doing it exactly right or perfectly. The basis for this is rooted in various sources:

- overrestrictive religions (You'll go to Hell if you commit a mortal sin.);
- an overactive Critical Parent (in Transactional Analysis terms);
- low self-esteem which they attempt to boost by being perfect (Who, after all, can criticize someone who is perfect?);
- feelings, usually going back to childhood, of having little or no control; as adults, they have an overpowering need to control everything. If they can't do it perfectly, then they won't do it at all.

> *The more right decisions you want to make, the fewer decisions you'll end up making.*

At any given moment, if you've decided to do the very best that you can, then you're doing the very best you can. You may feel your actions or performance were "better" at other times when you compare them, but given the set of circumstances in your life at the present, you're doing the best that's possible now. You're always doing the very best that you can. If you could do better you would have.

Question: What is the name of the periodical published by the Procrastinators Club of America?

Answer: *Last Month's Newsletter.*

When it comes to making decisions, do you ever feel like you are damned if you do, and damned if you don't? Stop and think. Do you like to make decisions? Very few people do. You make the wrong decision and you lose the bid. You make the wrong decision and the woman of your dreams marries someone else. You make the wrong decision, investing with the wrong financial planner, and you lose thousands. So many of us avoid or are scared of making decisions.

There is a basic problem with procrastinating—you don't get any results.

A.D.D.

Attention Deficit Disorder

When I grew up, A.D.D. (Attention Deficit Disorder) wasn't a term that was used or even known. I was simply a child who had a high energy level, a very high energy level, one that wouldn't allow me to sit still or concentrate for long. As you can imagine, sitting in a schoolroom for endless hours was not my favorite thing to do. However, as I found out later, it was great training for all the corporate meetings I got to sit through.

I had the concentration capacity of a cricket. Math was always a tough subject, but I did enjoy geometry (which I later found out wasn't math). I had a hard time learning strictly by listening. I needed hands-on activities to really get it and plenty of breaks to keep me tuned in.

If you have A.D.D., the system that will be explained in this book will help you stay focused and in control. The system has helped hundreds of people both with and without A.D.D. The system was set up to minimize distractions and keep you on track so that when you are distracted, you know exactly where to jump back in. If this sounds familiar, this book is for you.

Remember These Concepts

- Organization = A System + Decision-Making.
- Everything we do is for a payoff. Payoffs can be both healthy and unhealthy.
- The definition of insanity is doing the same thing over and over and expecting different results.
- The outside cannot fix the inside.
- There are reasons and results. Only one of them matters.
- The best way around something is always through it.
- The more right decisions you want to make, the fewer decisions you'll end up making.

Things To Avoid
- Doing the same thing over and over and expecting different results.

2.1

Paper Flow

Paper Flow
- Where Does All The Paper Flow?
- Your Friend, The 3 x 5 Card
- Every Loose Piece Of Paper On Your Desk Represents A Decision Not Made
- Touch Me Once And Touch Me Twice

OATS
- "GRITS" Just Doesn't Work
- OATS Or HOATS?

Out Box
- Get It In, Get It Out; Move It In, Move It Out
- The Prime Directive
- Your Assistant's Part
- Route This!

What You Will Learn In This Chapter
- How to create a paper flow in your office
- What OATS is
- How important it is to make decisions
- How to get paper out of your office
- Why your Out Box is so important
- How to route materials
- Who is responsible for storing memos

☀ <u>Myths of the Office</u>

Touch a piece of paper only once.

Paper Flow

Where Does All The Paper Flow? (Sung To "Where Have All The Flowers Gone?")

Think about all the places you put paper during the course of a day. Thank goodness paper doesn't have a back that's sticky because some people's walls would be plastered. If there's an open space on your desk or floor, it may soon be not just covered but layered with paper. Why? Because it's an easy, convenient place to drop it. And, of course, you don't want to lose track of it.

> *Everything always goes into your In Box first.*

Paper generally goes everywhere except the one place it needs to go—your In Box.

The In Box is perhaps the most important tool in your office. Best of all, it's inexpensive to buy. That's right! For only a couple of bucks you, too, can purchase your very own, matching, deluxe In and Out Boxes.

Everything always goes into your In Box first. All loose paper, memos, books, tapes—you name it—always go into your In Box first. The following are some possible office scenarios. What would you do in these cases?

- You just got back from a sales appointment and you have a pile of stuff in your arms.

- You just returned from an out-of-town trip with a briefcase that is so overweight it's about to enroll in a Jenny Craig program.

- Your wonderful boss hands you yet another assignment to do, one of too many already.

- A courier drops off a packet.

- You write something down you think of to work on during a phone conversation.

- A fax suddenly appears.

- You have a customer's file out from a phone call you just finished.

📌 Your overzealous secretary brings items into your office every five minutes.

📌 You just completed a task and it can be filed away.

The answer is to dump away. When a piece of paper comes into your office or you have it in hand, it should always go into your In Box first. Why the In Box?

◆ It's a predesignated, centralized, specifically chosen location into which you drop everything. Think of it as a big vacuum cleaner sucking up all the loose information that is normally deposited in the most unlikely of places. Do not, however, think of it as a bottomless pit.

◆ If something goes into your In Box, it won't go anywhere else in your office. Placing everything into your In Box keeps your desk, floor, credenza, and walls clean.

◆ It gives you only one place to put things, which means you now have a system.

◆ Dropping something into the In Box allows you to eliminate interruptions (Processing) and continue to work (Producing) on what you were doing.

◆ It keeps items from getting lost.

Think about how many times someone asks you to look at something during the workday. Or think about how often manager Sluggo interrupts you and gives you a task. Typically, you stop what you are doing and start the new task. Now, you can drop all your interruptions into your In Box. That's right. You have permission to dump everything in one special spot all day long. It's fun to do. It's a lot easier to dump interruptions into your In Box than to stop and figure out what to do with them at the time.

A typical workday goes something like this. You're handed something and you stop working on what you're doing and look at it (Process). Then you probably start to work on it (Produce). Granted, some things have to be handled immediately, but the majority don't. They can simply be dropped into your In Box. What you want to avoid is constantly interrupting yourself while you are working (Producing) to look at and handle a new item (Processing).

From now on, thank the person delivering the item, immediately drop it in your In Box, and go back to what you were doing (Producing). The way to remember where everything goes first is easy if you think of your In Box as a hub within your office. Just as when you fly anywhere in the South, you are routed through the hub city of Atlanta first, so it is with your In Box. Everything always goes into it first.

1-1
Everything
Goes Into
The In Box

> *When you are interrupted and given an item, simply drop it into the In Box and finish what you are doing.*

Once you learn how to go through your In Box, it doesn't matter how much stuff you have in it. You'll be going through your In Box three times a day, so don't be concerned that the paper will build up. You'll usually be able to go through and process it all in less than five minutes.

Your Friend, The 3 x 5 Card

When you think of something you need to do during the day, simply write the action on a 3 x 5 card and drop it into your In Box. If you have the document or file at hand which you need to work on, use it to remind you rather than rewriting it on a 3 x 5 card. This allows you to stay focused on what you are doing (Producing), yet capture all the great ideas popping into your head during the day.

Many people file each item away after they finish with it. A better idea is to drop the items into your In Box. You'll be emptying your In Box and filing everything away three times a day. We'll be covering this more thoroughly in Part 2, Chapter 5. I've found that putting files into the In Box rather than filing them away saves a lot of time because it allows you to continue to focus on your task.

Think about coming into your office at night after a hard day. You are loaded with a lot of stuff and you are tired. Instead of going through it all and working on it, or stacking it on another pile on your desk, simply dump it into your In Box. It'll be there when you're fresh and ready to tackle it in the morning.

Every Loose Piece Of Paper On Your Desk Represents A Decision Not Made

A shuffle with a piece of paper is not merely a shuffle. Neither is a kiss a kiss, but that's another story. There's a lot more to it than that. Every loose piece of paper on your desk, floor, or credenza represents a decision that you didn't make. Why didn't you make it?

◆ You don't know what to do with it or where to put it (no system)

◆ You're scared to make a decision on it

◆ You're reluctant to make a decision on it

◆ You avoid making decisions

The key is to recognize that a cluttered office is generally not about paper. It is a manifestation of something deeper that is not working— your inability to make decisions. The solution is to simply make a decision rather than shuffle the paper away.

> *Every loose piece of paper on your desk represents a decision not made.*

Touch Me Once And Touch Me Twice

What happens when you walk out to your mailbox to get your mail? On the way back to your house, you open the interesting-looking, hand-printed envelopes. You pull out the contents, take a look at them, and then stuff them back into the envelope. When you get inside, you put the mail down somewhere on the kitchen counter or on your desk to look at them again later.

We are constantly touching paper over and over again. From now on, just drop all your paper into your In Box at home the same way you do at the office. Have an In Box and an Out Box and go through it once a week. Otherwise, you are going to waste an incredible amount of time every day fiddling around with paper, moving it from the kitchen counter to the coffee table to the computer room. If you have a home office, separate your personal mail from your business mail and use two sets of In and Out Boxes.

OATS

"GRITS" Just Doesn't Work

> *From your In Box, there are only four places a piece of paper can go: To your Out Box, Action, Trash or Support (OATS).*

I remember those cold wintry mornings up north when I was growing up. My mom used to feed me a good, hot helping of Quaker Oatmeal for breakfast, Quaker Oats for short. OATS is an easy way to remember that, from the In Box, there are only four places a piece of paper or an item can go.

Since I have moved to the South, I have tried to use GRITS instead of OATS, but I haven't figured it out yet. "G" could be for Garbage, "R" could be for

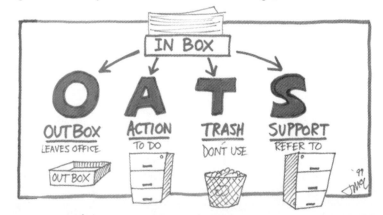

1-2
OATS

Reference, and "T" could be for Trash, but I can't figure out what to use the "I" for so I guess it will have to be OATS.

In OATS, the "O" stands for Out Box. The Out Box is where you place anything you want to move from your office or cubicle or room to another location. It could be to another employee, your secretary, or a storage area.

"A" stands for Action. Action means anything you want to take action on or work on. It's something you intend to do actively now or in the future. The operative word is "intend": you have plans to do something with it.

"T" stands for Trash. Trash is anything you no longer need or use, something you want to get rid of. The main reason you get cluttered with paper and hold onto trash is that you won't make a decision about it. As a result, the trash is shuffled over and over again and piles up in your office.

"S" stands for Support. Support indicates reference items—information in your office that's inactive or at rest—there simply as a resource of knowledge. Think of Support as a big reference library filled with enormous amounts of information. When you need it, it's available but you don't need to do anything with it other than refer to it. You have no intention of working on or doing anything with Support items. It's the opposite of Action.

From now on, when you pick up a piece of paper, a file, a book, or a disk from your In Box, there are only four places it can go: Out Box, Action, Trash, or Support. From your In Box, two kinds of items will be leaving your office: the Out Box and Trash. Action and Support will be staying.

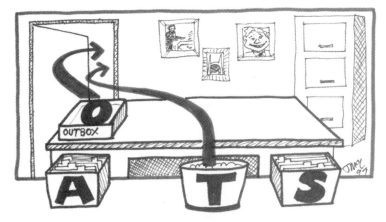

1-3
Two Going
And Two
Staying

In your Action and Support areas, you will need to have some type of a structure or system to locate things. Under Action and Support you'll be using Categories and Files to find things. Using Categories and Files as a system will allow you to find everything in your office in seconds. We'll talk about these in an upcoming chapter.

OATS Or HOATS?

If you have a secretary who picks up your Out Box contents, you may want to have a Home Box. A Home Box is a tray that sits behind you, generally on the credenza. Anything you want to take home, on a trip, to a meeting or an appointment that day goes into the Home Box. It acts as a reminder to take whatever is in it with you when you leave your office. This way, these important items won't be mixed with the general contents of the Out Box that your administrative person will be picking up. Your briefcase can also be used instead of the tray. If you use a Home Box, you may now have five places instead of four to send items from your In Box.

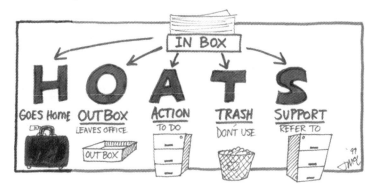

1-4
HOATS

Out Box

Get It In, Get It Out; Move It In, Move It Out

Years ago, when I was working with my family's construction business, I used to make my lunch the night before. The next morning I would pack it into my lunch box. The lunch box was a way to transport the food from one place to another. I was the youngest brother in my family, so on the job I got all the fun stuff to do, such as moving things with the help of a wheelbarrow. I would position the wheelbarrow in a specific spot during the day. Whenever I touched anything I needed to move to another location, I would drop it in the wheelbarrow. I wouldn't walk each piece separately, but would wait until the wheelbarrow was full and drop off the contents to various locations in one trip. The same principle works for your Out Box.

What is an Out Box used for and what goes into it? Anything that you want to move from your office, cubicle, or desk area to another location outside of your office goes into your Out Box. If you want something to leave your area and go through the doorway, it goes into the Out Box. Having an Out Box allows you to utilize a system by dropping items into a specified spot.

Some specific examples of items that would go into your Out Box:

♦ A file your boss requested
♦ An invoice you approved that must go to Finance
♦ A file that goes out to the Central Files
♦ Mail
♦ Long-term storage
♦ Something to send to another employee
♦ A delegated task for your secretary
♦ Information to be routed
♦ Items to reroute

If you don't have an Out Box, you might tend to get up when you have completed a task and make a drop-off at someone else's desk. Why? You don't want to clutter up your desk and you get a buzz from the recognition of completing a task. You can get quite a high from this and make a lot of trips during the day, interrupting not only you but also the other person. Instead, simply drop the item into your Out Box and deliver it only after you've gone through your In Box.

The Prime Directive

The goal for every piece of paper that comes into your office is to get it out as fast as you can. Many people think they should keep as much stuff as possible. Instead, your aim is to get as much out as quickly as possible, especially if you are in a management position.

> *The faster I move my paper from my In Box to my Out Box, the more I get done.*

Your Assistant's Part

If you are in a secretarial or administrative position, you need to have an Out Box for yourself and an Out Box for each person for whom you are responsible. If you have two bosses then you're going to have three Out Boxes—one for yourself and one for each of your two bosses.

> *The goal for every piece of paper that comes into your office is to get it out of your office.*

Your job is to pick up your boss's Out Box contents three times a day and deliver them to the appropriate place. You'll drop off all your boss's stuff to his or her In Box at one time rather than interrupt him or her every time you have something.

I've talked with many managers who complain that their secretaries are constantly bugging them. What they don't understand is that they themselves are causing the interruptions, because they haven't created a specific time for pick-ups and drop-offs. Another reason bosses are interrupted is that they never make any time to meet with their administrative people. It's vitally important that every morning the manager meets with his or her administrative person when he or she brings in the In Box contents. A quick, stand-up meeting works better than the typical, lengthy seated kind.

On the other hand, sometimes managers will bug administrative people to death. If you need to talk with your secretary, save the information for an In Box drop-off or pick-up, which should occur three times a day, rather than interrupting her or him every time you have a thought.

Route This!

Another article or magazine has paid you what should have been a brief visit but then somehow decided to settle in for a long stay on your credenza. Once again you're not sure if it's important. You already have three magazines on your credenza that you still haven't read. You really need to look at them, even though they're probably not that important. And you'd never consider initialing them without reading them for fear of missing something.

What can you do with people who route too much stuff to you?

🖈 **Be specific as to what it is you wish to receive**

If it is your boss, ask him if he would be more selective in what he sends. This obviously depends on your relationship with him. If it's from a coworker, specifically explain the only topics you wish to receive.

🖈 **Write "No thanks" in a red pen on the items.**

If you keep sending things back with a "No thanks" to the people (other than your bosses) who keep sending them to you, hopefully, after a while, they'll get the message. If you throw the stuff away, they'll never know the pain they are causing you and conclude you really must enjoy receiving their routings.

Managers take notice! You are driving your people crazy with all the stuff you route to them. Your intentions are good, but you are sending too many things to read and often the wrong information to the wrong people. Think of the story of the boy who cried "wolf" too many times. They can not tell what is important or not anymore. You can solve this problem by creating a new type of a routing slip using terms that you and your people understand.

Example

Status:	READ	SAVE	FYI
From:	Bobo		

Please check your name and send it onto the next person on the list.

Don S.	Charlie H.
Niles K.	Dave D.
Brian Z.	Glenn H.

READ: This means read it and know it.

SAVE: This means read it, know it, and save it.

FYI: This means I thought you might be interested in it. Read it, shred it, line the bird cage with it, do with it as you want.

Send along a short memo to your people explaining what the information will mean so they can quickly make a decision on it.

Speaking of memos, people always ask who is responsible for keeping information. A simple rule is "Whoever initiates and writes a memo keeps it." Unless, of course, you are the boss. Then the assistant keeps it. Paper obeys the laws of gravity—it flows downward.

> *Whoever initiates and writes it keeps it.*

Memos are another fun item to receive. The following is an example of a simple, clear way to write one. Include:

> To:
> From:
> Re:
> What I will do:
>
> What I need you to do:

Remember These Concepts

- Everything always goes into your In Box first.
- When you are interrupted and given an item, simply drop it into the In Box and finish what you are doing.
- Every loose piece of paper on your desk represents a decision not made.
- From your In Box, there are only four places a piece of paper can go: To your Out Box, Action, Trash or Support (OATS).
- The faster I move my paper from my In Box to my Out Box, the more I get done.
- The goal for every piece of paper that comes into your office is to get it out of your office.
- Whoever initiates and writes it keeps it.

Things To Avoid
- Routing information without checking whether the person wants to receive it.
- Excess routing materials.

Action or Support

Action or Support

- My Mother Never Let Me Play With Grenades
- General Science
- As Roy Rogers Would Say, "What Will Trigger You To Remember To Do That?"
- Stop All That Noise
- Library
- Status Is Everything
- Nag, Nag, Nag

What You Will Learn In This Chapter
- How to tell the difference between an Action and a Support

☀ Myths of the Office

I'm creative, I need clutter around.

Action/Support

My Mother Never Let Me Play With Grenades

When I was a kid, I used to love to play Army man. My two favorite weapons were the flame-thrower and hand grenades. I used an electric-company hose for the flame-thrower and made the grenades out of concrete. There was no doubt who had the maximum firepower and best weaponry on my street.

Speaking of grenades, I normally carry two with me (duds with no powder) when I conduct a training seminar. Taking them on an airplane is an adventure, though. Security gets very touchy when you try to board with grenades, even if they are duds.

People at the airport ask me why I have them. I love responding that it's a way to get from coach to first class in a heck of a hurry. They, of course, do not enjoy my comment or my grenades.

Imagine holding two live grenades in your hands, one in your left hand and one in your right hand. Now pull the pin and release the handle on the grenade in your left hand. What would happen if it were real? It would blow up. By pulling the pin and releasing the handle you are taking an action.

Now think about the grenade you are holding in your right hand. Don't do anything with it other than hold it. Just stand there and look at it. What will happen? Absolutely nothing. Why? Because all you did was hold it and look at it (And besides you are imagining this anyway.)

Now imagine you have two new grenades. With one you're in a combat situation, pulling the pin, releasing the handle and throwing it. You're taking action. There is movement, motion, an activity, and an intention of having the grenade blow up.

Now once again imagine the other grenade is stored in a wooden crate in an ammo dump. It's just sitting there doing absolutely nothing. Is there a difference between the two? Sure. With one you're doing something—throwing it—and with the other you're not.

2-1
Grenades

The grenade in your left hand is an Action. You have pulled the pin and it'll explode in seven seconds. The grenade in your right hand is a Support. You're simply holding it with no intention of doing anything with it. By the way, you never pull the pin with your teeth like they do in the movies unless of course your father is a dentist, you happen to be the character called Jaws in James Bond movies, or you no longer want teeth.

General Science

One of my clients, Tommy Gregory, pointed out an easy way to tell the difference between Action and Support. Think back to when you took general science in high school. Do you remember what two types of energy were studied? Kinetic (the state next to New York) and Potential (what all the waiters and waitresses out in Hollywood think they have).

Words to describe Kinetic are: activity, motion, movement, tasks to do, work, an intention of doing something now or in the future. This is what we call an Action. An easy way to identify an Action is when a verb is used in the same sentence, such as: I want to write a letter. I need to read this memo.

The opposite of Kinetic energy (Action) is Potential energy, those things you use for reference, information, or as resources. Potential energy includes anything at rest, passive items that have the potential to do something but need an action to make it happen. This is what we call a Support. For instance, all the information in your office supports you in your job.

Think of the grenades again. On one you pulled the pin (soon to blow up) and the other is stored in an ammo dump (doing nothing). Which grenade is Kinetic and which is Potential? At rest the grenade has potential and is a Support. The grenade has the potential to blow up if you take action and pull the pin. When you pull the pin, it becomes an Action, since your intention is to have it explode. So if you want the grenade to explode, the action you need to take is to pull the pin, release the handle, and change the energy from Potential into Kinetic.

Action (Kinetic Energy)	Support (Potential Energy)
• Active	• Passive
• Intention of doing	• No intention of doing
• Things to do	• Information
• Working on	• Resource
• Deciding to work on	• Stored
• Motion	• Reference
• Doing	• Refer to
• Any verbs used	• At rest

As Roy Rogers Would Say, "What Will Trigger You To Remember To Do That?"

Another glorious day. As you lie in bed fighting to open your eyes, a gazillion thoughts and things to do flood your consciousness. "Get gas. Buy a present for Charlie. Call to clarify the meeting time. Stop by to pick up the check from Michelle. Drop off a proposal with Ray." A normal day is bad enough. Think of those days when you're really overwhelmed, when the noise is almost deafening.

Do you ever wonder why you feel so overwhelmed with so much to do? It's because you do have a lot to do. How much you have to do is not as important, though, as to how to get rid of that bothersome voice in your head.

Most people don't know the difference between an Action and a Support. They have stacks of stuff to work on, to do lists, tasks on their contact manager. And, within each stack, they combine tasks to work on with reference materials. Knowing the difference between Action items and Support materials is critical since it is the foundation of all organization.

Imagine Moses coming into your cluttered office and separating the sea of white paper: "Let my Action go." On one side would be all the Action and on the other Support. What this would do is place everything you need to work on (Action) in one, easy-to-access location rather than having it spread all over your office intermingled with your Support stuff.

2-2
Moses
Separating
The Sea Of
Paper

Let's go through an example to see if you can tell the difference between the two. Say you have a copier brochure in your hand. You've already researched copiers and know which one you'll buy. You've decided to buy the copier on the brochure in your hand. You have not yet bought it. Is the brochure an Action or a Support?

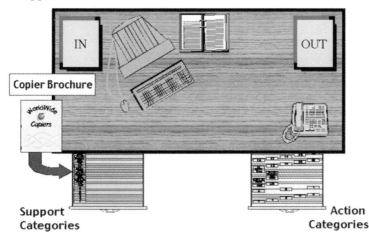

2-3
A Copier
Brochure
In Support

If you said it was a Support, you'd file the brochure in the Support side. If it were filed away in Support, what would trigger you to remember to buy the copier since Support materials have no action connected with them?

The only thing that would trigger you to buy it would be that little voice in your head. When I do a workshop, I often hear the answer "When the copier is broken, you will remember to buy it then." Down boy. The copier is fine. You simply want to buy a new one. Nothing is pressing you to buy it.

Nine out of ten people typically say it's a Support. They can't imagine a brochure or a piece of paper being an Action. They say the paper isn't the Action, the phone call is. Remember, you decided to buy the copier. Putting the brochure into the Action Category will remind you to take action, i.e., buy it. This is why most people are confused and overwhelmed in their office. They can't tell the difference between an Action and Support.

Stop All That Noise

If you file a piece of paper away in Support, the only way that you're going to remember to take action is by having that little voice in your head remind you over and over to do it. You know that little voice, the one that screams at you when you have too much to do. Instead of pumping up the volume of the voice, why not turn it down as low as it will go?

Believe me, you do have a little voice in your head. If you think you don't, listen to you ask yourself if you have one or

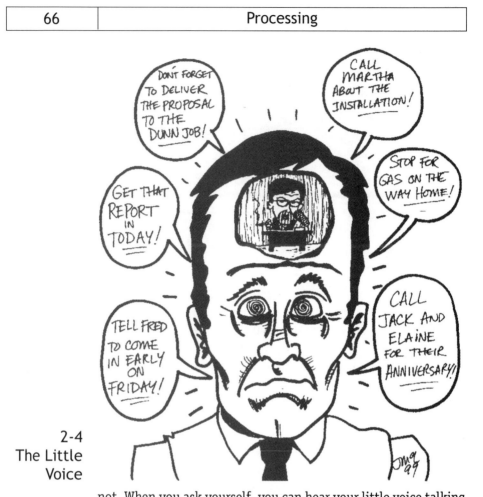

2-4
The Little
Voice

not. When you ask yourself, you can hear your little voice talking to you. It's like an early-warning attack system. It warns you something is not right. After a while the siren gets a little too loud.

This morning when you were getting ready for work, scrubbing away in the shower, your little voice was probably going crazy with all the stuff you needed to do. The goal is to quiet that voice. The way to do that is by knowing the difference between an Action and a Support and putting anything that you intend to work on in your Action section. Let your Action do the worrying for you and your fingers do the walking.

If you said it was an Action, do you mean to say that a piece of paper or brochure can actually be an Action? Absolutely. The copier brochure is an Action because it will trigger you to do something, that is, buy the copier, and that's what matters. Once you've ordered the copier, you may want to keep the brochure as a Support to refer to; or upon delivery of the copier, you might trash the brochure.

Library

2-5
The
Library

What do you call those big books in a library that you can look at but can't check out? Reference books. What do you do with a reference book? You look at it. You have no intention of doing anything with it other than looking at it. Now say you're in the middle of a course and you have a book that you're working in, perhaps making notes or filling in the blanks. What kind of book do you call that? A workbook.

Kinetic Energy	Potential Energy
Workbook	Reference book

Status Is Everything

Where do Actions come from? You either are given them or you create them. When your boss or someone else wants you to work on something, they magically appear in your In Box. When you think of something you need to do, simply write it down on a 3 x 5 card or grab the actual piece of paper or file and drop it into your In Box.

Many times things that become an Action originate from Support. Support is anything that is hanging out in your office doing nothing except minding its own business.

> *The secret is to understand the status of everything in your office.*

Say you have a report in your file drawer. If you need information from it, you refer to it, which makes it a Support.

Say you decide to add a paragraph to it. The Support now becomes an Action. If you keep it when you're done working (Action) on it, it again becomes a Support. If you need to give it to your boss, it becomes an Out Box. If you no longer need it, it becomes Trash.

Can anything be an Action and a Support at the same time? No, never. Imagine a tank. At rest it's a Support. It has potential to fire. The tank changes to an Action when it fires. Boom! Kinetic energy. After it has fired, it becomes a Support again since it has the potential to fire again. It will change back and forth, from an Action to a Support and from a Support to an Action, depending on when it fires. The only aspect that you need to remember is what the status is, whether it is an Action or a Support.

2-6
Two Tanks

No matter when you intend to work on something, the task is always an Action.

For that matter an Action can become an Out Box or Trash, not just a Support. There are four places everything in your In Box can go. OATS. Remember, if you have any intention at all of doing anything with an item, it always is an Action—no matter when you plan on doing it.

Nag, Nag, Nag

An easy way to tell if something is an Action is when you hear that little voice in your head remind you a second time to do something with it. It nags you. If you have a thought of something you need to do, it is merely a thought. If the same thought comes back and bothers you, it becomes an Action. All the nags you hear in your life are Actions. Of course, the first time you heard the nag, it was simply a wonderful idea.

Say the thought struck you to upgrade your computer, just one of the zillion thoughts that enter your mind. If the thought comes back and bugs you, it becomes an Action. Once you write it down on a 3 x 5 card and drop it into your In Box, you can let go of it. The system will take care of it for you.

Let's look at some other examples. The key is recognizing verbs as a telltale sign of an Action.

Say you intend to shoot someone. You shoot but you

> *Everything in your office is either an Action or a Support.*

miss. According to the law you were trying to kill. The fact that you were a bad shot really doesn't matter; your intention remains the same. The police will still lock you up. Of course, today they probably will only slap your hand a little.

Say you are going to buy a copier in six months. You're not going to buy it now but rather in the future. Is it an Action or a Support? Because it's not something you need to do right now many people feel it's a Support. It's, however, an Action. It's irrelevant when you plan on doing something. What's relevant is that you've decided to do it, regardless of when that takes place.

You have a form in your desk. A form is a piece of paper with blanks to be filled in. Is it an Action or a Support? It's a Support since you have no intention of filling it out. When you want to fill it out or are told to fill it out, it becomes an Action.

Everything that's in your office is an Action or a Support. If it is Trash, throw it away. If it can leave the office, send it packing in the Out Box.

Think about H_2O. It can be in the form of solid (snow or ice), liquid (rain or water), or gas (clouds or steam). Regardless of its form, it will still always be H_2O. The same is true with items in your office. A form can be waiting to be filled out, can be filled out, or can be filled out and ready to be given to someone. A form can change from a Support to an Action and an Action to a Support. Yet it will always be a form. It is its status that is constantly changing. The key is to understand the current status of the form.

Remember These Concepts

- The secret is to understand the status of everything in your office.
- No matter when you intend to work on something, the task is always an Action.
- Everything in your office is either an Action or a Support.

Things To Avoid

- Keeping Action materials with Support materials.

Trash

To Trash or Not to Trash

- Copy This, Good Buddy
- To Trash Or Not To Trash
- My Body Lies Over The Trash Can

Pack Rat

- Have You Ever Seen A Pack Rat Or A Rat Pack Anything?

Hoarding

- My Dog's Bigger Than Your Dog
- These Are A Few Of My Favorite Things
- When You Pass Your Desk, Collect $50

A Keeper

- Keep It If...
- Less Is More

Let's Talk Some Trash

- Words To Trash By
- Trash It If...
- Who Me?

Long-Term Storage

- File! File! The Gang's All Here
- Projects

Batting Cleanup

- The Great End-Of-The-Year Clean-Out

What You Will Learn In This Chapter
<ul>
<li>The more decisions you make, the less clutter you will have</li>
<li>What to keep and what to throw away</li>
<li>Why less is more</li>
<li>Words that will alert you to when something is Trash</li>
<li>The less you have the more you will get done</li>
</ul>

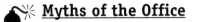 **Myths of the Office**

If I throw it away, I might need it.

To Trash or Not to Trash

Copy This, Good Buddy

Whatever happened to the paperless office? What about all the innovative technology that was supposed to eliminate the bothersome clutter we call paper? Guess what? It didn't eliminate paper; it created more.

Now, a zillion copies can be mass-produced in minutes. Paper is everywhere. When in doubt, make a copy and save it. Got a question about it? Copy it. Got a problem? Copy it.

3-1
Technology
Spitting
Out Too
Much
Paper

Our society produces incredible amounts of paper for a myriad of uses. Paperless office? Hardly. Ever since the Egyptians invented papyrus, it has been our destiny to fill the world with paper. We're not about to give paper up that easily, even with our so-called paperless computers. It's about time we learned what to do with all that paper before we drown in it.

To Trash Or Not To Trash

People save a tremendous amount of information out of pure fear. Knowing what to save or throw away indicates how good a decision-maker you are. It's human nature for us to want to hold onto things, especially emotional or sentimental items.

Why do you save paper? In some cases, it might be because you are scared to death to make a decision. Make the wrong decision with your investments and you lose the retirement money you worked so hard for. Make the

> *It takes more work to evade a task than to accomplish it.*

wrong decision at work and start looking for a new career. Make the wrong decision in your marriage and watch your spouse walk out on you. Many people falsely believe that it's easier to avoid something (procrastinate) than to deal with it (make a decision). Actually it takes more work to evade a task than to accomplish it. You waste a tremendous amount of time and energy avoiding what you need to work on and worrying about what you need to do.

When people finally decide to throw something away, they do so in a fascinating variety of styles. One type is the Crumpler. These people must crumple every piece of paper before it goes into the trash bin. You've all seen the Shooters. They can make it from anywhere in the office. Off the desk, off the ceiling, off the monitor. Basket! And then there are the Slashers. These folks must draw a line across it to signify it is trash. It absolutely, positively can not go into the garbage pail unless it has a line on it. When asked why they do this, Slashers haven't the slightest idea. Imagine the social stigma of being a piece of paper in the trash can without a line on it. Whatever would the other trash say?

Last year I finally met the Shredder. This client asked me to tear every piece of paper into tiny pieces. Talk about paranoid! I saved him hours a day by having him invest in a paper shredder and never allowing him to tear his trash by hand again. At the same time, he eliminated a time-wasting habit.

Think of all the things you have in your office about which you will not make a decision. What is holding you back emotionally? How important can these things really be if they have been there for so long?

3-2
Decision
Making

My Body Lies Over The Trash Can

The more decisions you make, the less trash you will have.

You would be amused and surprised if you could watch yourself on camera as you decided whether something was trash. I have stood a few feet away from hundreds of clients who were struggling with this decision. In fact, I can tell when a piece of paper is trash before my clients can just by the look on their face, how they move their bodies, and how they shift their weight.

Typically clients stand and shift their weight to one side. They shift because they are bothered and indecisive. Their head tilts over to the same side as the weight they are supporting, and they emit a low guttural sound: "Unnhhh." Then, still not sure, they shift their body weight to the opposite side, tilt their head again, and emit a pitiful moan. When I see clients exhibiting these characteristics, I instantly know it is trash. It is not a pretty sight. I hope most people will never be subjected to this type of horror in their lifetime.

If you notice yourself exhibiting any of these strange behaviors, immediately rush to the nearest trash can and throw away whatever you have in your hands.

I have seen some unbelievable clutter and trash in the span of my professional career. I thought 500 pounds of clutter from a financial planner's office was the worst I would see in my lifetime. I was wrong! Later I worked with a fellow, one on one, for more than 81 hours. He easily topped the 1,000-pound mark of trash. In just three years, he had saved almost all of his stuff. The scary part was that he still had nine more horizontal file drawers to clean out. "Hi, boys and girls. Can you say excessive trash?"

Your ability to throw out trash is directly related to your ability to make a decision.

Remember, the difference between being cluttered and being organized is making one simple decision.

Pack Rat

Have You Ever Seen A Pack Rat Or A Rat Pack Anything?

I still have my teddy bear packed away, along with a lead soldier of my dad's from the 1930s and my Gilbert erector set. I also have 1,000 comic books that I just found out are worth a lot of money. Despite all I know about getting rid of clutter, I like to save things. Do you know what an original Barbie doll goes for now? The amount is incredible. No, I do not have one.

It's okay to be a Pat Rack and save things. But would it make sense to keep your comic books, teddy bear, or Barbie doll in your bedroom or on your desk in the office? Let's hope not. Instead, you should label, categorize, date, and keep them in long-term storage far away from your bedroom or office.

There's a big difference between your garage, your overflowing closet, your basement, etc., and a specifically designated storage area where everything is neatly stored, categorized, and dated. Everything in my attic is labeled, dated, and categorized, so if I need anything, I can find it in minutes. If you have the storage space, go for it. Save away.

Most people have limited usable storage space in their office. Large amounts of old files or memorabilia you want to store need to go into Central Files or a long-term storage area. You can store as much as you want as long as you have made a decision about it, have the space, and can keep it away from your day-to-day stuff.

Hoarding

My Dog's Bigger Than Your Dog

We definitely live in a capitalistic society. Most of us think that the more we have, the better we are. I'm sure you have received the following communications through words and action:

- "I have more toys than you do."
- "I have more cars than you do."
- "I have more girlfriends than you do."
- "I have a lot more money than you do."
- "My house is bigger than your house is."

It's called keeping up with and outdoing the Hethermans.

> *The more secure you are, the less you will want.*

The belief that the more you have—i.e., more files, books, paper, software, information, technology— then the more secure, smarter, and better you'll be is really a bunch of baloney. Not that I have an opinion on it, though. Ironically, the truth is that the more secure you are, the less you will want things.

"The secret of happiness, you see, is not found in seeking more, but in the capacity to enjoy less."
—The Way of the Peaceful Warrior

Have you ever stepped inside an untouched, cluttered, older person's house? Yuck! It definitely doesn't feel very good. In fact, if you just stand there and experience it, you'll notice a heavy, uncomfortable feeling. Likewise, I believe the more junk you have in your office, the less energy you'll have for work. When you consider what you want in your office, think about the song "Bare Necessities" from the movie *The Jungle Book*.

> *Eliminating emotionally charged paper will free you up psychologically.*

Get everything you possibly can out of your office. Instead of having a lot of stuff, just keep a few key things around. You'll notice fewer distractions and you'll be able to focus much more easily.

These Are A Few Of My Favorite Things

The first time I worked in a Fortune 100 company, I consulted with an assistant vice president of Human Resources, Mike S. Fourteen boxes of paper and items went out to his secretary, Eileen. Everyone thought he was being fired and that I was a security guard watching to make sure he didn't take any of the company's property. I should have figured it was going to be a crazy career from that point on.

It's amazing what people stash away in their desks. One of my clients had 49 pen tops in his drawer. I, of course, had to ask why he needed 49 pen tops. He, of course, answered, "In case I need one."

Anybody have a pen? One client was stocking up on them in a "bic" way:
- 93 pens
- 26 pencils
- 12 markers

- 131 writing instruments. And he wasn't even a writer!

Try this: Remove all the pens or pencils from your drawer and clasp them in the hand you write with. Now try to write with all of them at the same time. It's a little hard to do. Why then do you need so many in your drawer?

Clean out the drawer so you have only one kind of each writing instrument and store the others. You'll be less likely to find a messy collection of pens, markers, and pencils scattered all over your desk at the end of the day. Sometimes the more pens or pencils you have, the harder it is to find one. When you only have one and keep it in one spot, you can find it a lot quicker.

A few other favorite things found at client sites:

- A garter belt in a trial lawyer's desk. I loved listening to his defense as to why he had it there. He also had a bottle of Jack Daniel's. He had just won a $4 million case, netting around $2 million. Oh! Now I understand why he had those things.

- Nine different colors of Liquid Paper: white, blue, canary yellow, ledger green, stock green, Just-For-Copies, stock pink, bond white, goldenrod, and Pen

& Ink. Either this individual made a heck of a lot of mistakes or her uncle owned an office supply store.

📌 Seven copies of the same piece of paper in one guy's desk. Maybe seven was his lucky number or he worked in the department of redundancy department.

📌 A slingshot that shot miniature marshmallows. I wonder if he ever lived dangerously, roasting them first, then shooting them like miniature meteors.

📌 Pink slips. One time a fellow I worked with brought in seven years' worth of office clutter he had stored at home that he never would go through. He had over 500 pink "While you were out" slips mixed in with his papers. I got the feeling he had been "out" for the last number of years and should have received another type of pink slip.

📌 Assorted bottles of spirits hidden away in drawers, a half of a lead airplane clock with propellers that actually spun, you name it. The list goes on. You probably wouldn't believe half of them anyway.

When You Pass Your Desk, Collect $50

Imagine you're walking down the sidewalk and right there, lying smack in front of you, is a $50 bill. Quickly, what do you do? Don't tell me you stand there looking at it, slowly circling it, putting your hands on your chin and saying, "Hmmm. I could possibly use 50 bucks." Of course not. You'd dive for it. In fact, you'd have an abrasion on your lip after diving down on the sidewalk to get that 50 bucks.

If you went through your In Box and saw a $50 bill, what would your first reaction be? You'd grab it. You wouldn't think about it. You'd simply react.

When you pick up a piece of paper in your In Box, think about your reaction to it. If you get a jolt from it like finding a $50 bill, then save it. If not, throw the paper away.

A Keeper

Keep It If...

Why do you keep any item in your office? For the simple reason that you use it. If you have something in your office that you don't use, throw it away, give it to your secretary, or send it to the Central Files or to long-term storage.

> *The main reason to save anything is because you are going to use it.*

Here are some other reasons to keep things:

📁 Legal
This information is very important to keep.

📁 Financial
Retaining these documents is very important due to the fact that the IRS is so disorganized. Consult with your accountant. Saving the correct information really comes in handy when the IRS comes-a-knocking at your door.

📁 Memorabilia
Sentimental items are very important to hold onto because we are emotionally tied to them. I still have the logo and stationery from my first business. Mind you, it's not lying out in my office. It's filed out of the way.

📁 Long-Term Storage
Anything that you want to keep can be stored in long-term storage, especially retention materials.

📁 Company Retention
A retention schedule simply dictates which items to save and how long to save them. It creates boundaries that help determine how long items need to be saved. If you don't have a retention schedule, it is vitally important to create one. Check with your accountant and lawyer.

Actual conversation with one of my soon-to-be clients.

Greg: "Do you have a retention system?"

Soon-to-be client: "Yes. We retain everything."

Less Is More

I've been saying "Less is more" for years. I wish I received a royalty for every time I use it. The less paper you have in your office, the less you have to look through. The less you have to look through, the more you can focus on your priorities and the more work you'll get done.

What percent of everything in your office do you think you use? Generally, I find around 20 percent of what's in someone's office is being used. This is the 80/20 rule, also known as the Pareto Principle. Take a company with 10,000 employees: 2,000 employees produce 80 percent of all the work being done while 8,000 produce only 20 percent. I love to go into companies and ask the group who among them is producing the 20 percent. It severely skewers the statistics when they all raise their hands.

Less is more.

The following is an example of how the 80/20 rule works in your office.

		100%	
• What you keep in your office		20%	
• That means 80% of what you have in your office is not being looked at or used. It needs to go somewhere out of your office.			
• What you get out of your office		80%	
• That which goes to my assistant, the Central Files, or long-term storage.			20%
• Trash			60%
EXAMPLE			
10 pieces of paper		100%	
2 pieces	I keep it.	20%	
2 pieces	My assistant keeps it or Central Files gets it.	20%	
6 pieces	I trash it.	60%	

Take a look at your bedroom closet. Count the total number of dresses you have. Not you, Klinger. Say you had 100 dresses in your closet (or 5,000 if you are reading this, Ivana). How many do you actually wear? Probably only around 20, if that many. You only wear your favorites. Why do you keep the others?

Yeah, I know because you never know when that little gold sequin number will come in handy.

Let's Talk Some Trash

Words To Trash By

When you are handling a piece of paper and you hear any of the following in your mind, trash the paper or item immediately:

- 🗑 Might
- 🗑 May
- 🗑 Possibly
- 🗑 Could
- 🗑 Maybe
- 🗑 What if
- 🗑 Someday
- 🗑 Perhaps
- 🗑 You never know
- 🗑 You can never tell
- 🗑 In case of
- 🗑 Who knows

3-3
Words To
Trash By

What if a workday like this **might** happen to you? **You never know. You can never tell** when, especially **in case of** an emergency, **perhaps**, say your boss **might** want something and it **could** be **someday** soon, **possibly** today. **Maybe** not though. Then again you **may be** hit by lightning or win the lottery. Notice how easily the "words to trash by" can be slipped into your daily vocabulary.

Let me assure you that you'll never throw anything away you really need.

Trash It If...

Whenever you make any of the following statements, trash the item:

🗐 *"It can be replaced."*

Generally an item can be replaced unless you are holding onto an original. Ask yourself if you have it on computer.

🗐 *"It's a duplicate."*

Birds have one. Bees have one. Everybody that you see has one. Let's do it, let's save another one. Bosses and secretaries will generally have many of the same documents. Let's face it, there are a lot of duplicates, triplicates, quadruplicates floating around.

A doctor from one of the local universities approached me to share her secret on throwing things out. "Make a copy before you throw it away." Oh, those higher educational centers of learning, how they help us so!

🗐 *"It's out of date."*

This is one of the biggest abusers. If a document is past the date, why continue to keep it, especially if you have a new copy? Once a year, preferably at the end of your fiscal year, you need to completely go through and clean out your entire system. In with the new, out with the old. Replace all those revisions that have been lying around.

🗐 *"It's a computer printout."*

Why keep printouts from your computer? If you're not sure you'll need a printout but can print out another copy, trash it. Every excess piece of paper keeps you from being productive. Decide. Be ruthless. Fill up that trash can.

🗐 *"Someone else can keep it."*

There have to be some advantages to being the boss. This is one of them. Paper flows downward. Your subordinates or administrative people get to keep any items you don't want in your office. When I was a boss, I gave the people under me information to hold onto. My job was to lead, to run the show. The less clutter I had, the more I could stay focused on what I was supposed to do.

📄 *"I will not decide on it."*

If you will not decide on a piece of paper, how important can it be? It can't.

📄 *"I no longer use it."*

If you haven't looked at a document in many a moon, why keep it? If it's that important, make a decision on it, clean it out, separate it and then put it in long-term storage. When you need it in the future, it will be where you stored it. I'm not asking you to throw everything away. What I am asking you to do is to make a good, clear, clean decision about everything. The less you have in your office, the more you'll get done.

📄 *"CYA"*

I have actually had clients create files labeled CYA: the initials for a euphemism for making sure they can document that whatever went wrong wasn't their fault. Something is very wrong if people work in an environment that creates that kind of fear. Please, no CYA or CYB files.

Who Me?

Ask yourself the following questions:

📄 *"When was the last time I used the item?"*

When do you remember using it last? If you can't remember, it's probably not worth saving. Adios!

📄 *"When was the last time I looked at the item?"*

If it has been more than a year since you last looked, chances are you aren't going to need it. If it is valuable, keep it and look at it again in a year and then decide again.

📄 *"Do I have a specific to do with the item?"*

If you do not have a definite action planned with it, chuck it. Listen for the "words to trash by" in the following sentences:
- I have been thinking about a project that I might do.
- You never know when you will need it.
- You can never tell when you'll have to look at it again.
- What happens if my boss...
- Someday I hope to do it.

Versus:
- I will be starting that project in one week.
- I need this for...
- I look at this regularly.
- My boss has assured me there is no need for this.
- I will work on this.

Notice the uncertainty in the former statements versus the certainty or specific actions in the latter.

I have a strong background in sales. I saved all my sales materials in a thick file because I figured I'd refer to them someday when I created a course on selling and organization. A couple of years ago I created the program "A Vetter Way™ To Manage Your Sales Day." When I was creating it, how many times do you think I referenced the file? Not even once, because I knew all the stuff. Why did I save the file then? That really hit home. Here I was, falling into the same trap I taught others to climb out of. But that was my only extraneous file. I swear. Hey! Everybody is entitled to at least one extra file.

▤ "What would happen if I threw the paper away?"

Years ago, I received a catalog from Day-Timers. I generally keep a copy of the catalogue for whenever I need to refer to it. I was thinking about throwing it away since I hadn't looked at in quite a while. I was very reluctant to. What if one of my clients wanted information from it? How professional would I look if I didn't have the catalogue? I worked myself up into a tizzy, worrying and wondering whether I should keep it or not.

Finally, three days later I threw it away. Guess what happened? I needed it. In retrospect I honestly believe that I caused that incident to occur because I was so concerned about it that I created that need for it. The simple solution was to call Day-Timers in Pennsylvania and three days later I received a catalog. Whoop-de-do. You can usually replace a trashed item without too much trouble.

Assuming that you don't have the Dead Sea Scrolls in your office, most of what you have can be replaced, probably from sources within your own company. Unless you have the only copy of a document, you can generally replace most items. If it's one of a kind or it's valuable by all means keep it. It's the gray area that gets you into trouble, when you refuse to make a decision.

▤ "Can I get it from someone else?"

Some people like to keep things—in fact, they love to keep

them. The more the better. Make them happy. Give them yet another copy to keep. As long as they don't have a paper conversion one day and throw everything away, your item will be safe.

📄 "I don't have it."

It's okay to say this. You won't be taken out and shot if you don't have something. At least most companies won't shoot you.

📄 "Someone else has it."

Typically, in every department there is always one person to whom everybody goes for information—in some cases everything that the company has ever printed. Unfortunately, this is how they get their warm fuzzies and attention. They generally have low self-esteem and need to get positive strokes from helping others. What better way than to come to their fellow employees' aid when they are in a jam? They realize that everybody will eventually have to come to them if they hold all the stuff. I see that happen all the time. If you are one of those people, please get your love in a different way. Don't do it through paper.

Long-Term Storage

File! File! The Gang's All Here!

The solution for too much stuff and not enough office space is a departmental or Centralized File. A departmental file, which should sit in a designated area of a common area, allows you to reduce the amount of paper in your office by shifting it there. One copy of everything can be kept here.

Instead of the same copy being duplicated and kept in everybody's office, only one will exist in your Centralized Files. Papers, binders, manuals, disks, books, and audio and visual tapes can be kept there. For paper, use hanging folders to maintain the integrity of the files. That way when someone takes out the contents of the file, the hanging folder will still be there. When someone takes the information out, they can leave a card with the date and their name in the hanging folder.

Just remember, the less clutter and materials you have in your office, the better you'll feel mentally and physically. A lot of people keep bills and paperwork in their kitchen. I'm a firm believer that your paperwork, financial information, and bills never should be kept in your kitchen, dining room, or if at all possible, in your bedroom. Store them in a room that you use as an office or in a spare room. Storing emotionally charged papers in the wrong room will negatively affect the energy in that room.

Projects

Where should those big, fat project files go when the projects are finally completed? You have worked on that project for six months and it's as wide as a city block. You have finally finished with the silly thing. What do you do with it now?

Pick one:

A. Nothing.
   Whatever you do, don't make a decision. Leave it alone. The file isn't bothering anyone. It just takes up valuable filing space and clogs your already log-jammed system just a little more.

B. Out Box it.
   Your secretary or administrative person probably doesn't have nearly enough paper in his or her desk nor enough work to do. Be generous and give it to him or her. After all, paper flows downward, doesn't it?

C. Leave it in your company will.
   That wiseacre junior executive who has been after your job all these years deserves it.

D. Put it into a continuous route.
   Route the file to every employee in the entire company who's ever worked on it or simply heard about it. You want to make sure everyone has a chance to look at it just one more time. Don't worry. You will have long since retired by the time it gets back to you.

When you have finished a project, what should you do with it? You want to save it because you've spent a lot of valuable time working on it. You MIGHT refer to it later. You don't want to throw it away, so you stuff that big, fat fella somewhere in the back of your file cabinet instead of going through it or throwing it away. After all, you MAY use it later.

A thunderbolt may hit you too. You never know. SOMEDAY it might happen. Instead of saving everything, go through the file when you're done with the project and pull out the unnecessary papers. Many times there are only a few sheets of valuable information that need to be saved. File them in a similar subject file in a Category, which we are going to talk about in depth in a future chapter.

Batting Cleanup

The Great End-Of-The-Year Clean-Out

After you create your organizational system, it's important to periodically go through it and clean it out. This gives you a chance to go back through your files, make adjustments and correct any file names that do not work. Obviously, this will be much easier and quicker to do after the initial setup.

Clean out your system at least once a year. A good time to take your first pass through it would be within three months after you set up the system. Then go through it within the next six months. If your fiscal year ends December 31, take that last week in December to clean it out. That means you get to make a decision on every single piece of paper in your office again. Why? During the

> *At the end of every fiscal year, go through everything in your office, including your computer and e-mail files.*

course of a year, you make a lot of quick decisions and save a lot more things than you really need. The end-of-the-year clean-out gives you a chance to eliminate all that bulky and unnecessary clutter in your office.

This annual cleaning and sorting is a lot easier if every Friday, on your review day of your Action Categories, (Part 4, Chapter 1), you pick out your biggest file and put it in your In Box. Then go through it, slim it down, and clean it out. That way, when you clean out your system at the end of the year, it will be that much easier since you have so much less stuff. It's a great way to give yourself a head start for the next year.

Remember These Concepts

- It takes more work to evade a task than to accomplish it.
- The more decisions you make, the less trash you will have.
- Your ability to throw out trash is directly related to your ability to make a decision.
- The more secure you are, the less you will want.
- Eliminating emotionally charged paper will free you up psychologically.
- The main reason to save anything is because you are going to use it.
- Less is more.
- At the end of every fiscal year, go through everything in your office, including your computer and e-mail files.

Things To Avoid

- Duplicates and triplicates.
- Hoarding.

2.4

Desk

Wax On

- Out Of Sight, Out Of Mind
- A Clean Desk Does Not Necessarily Mean You Are Productive
- Rolling, Rolling, Rolling, Keep That Paper Flowing
- Wax On, Wax Off
- Don't Stack Me Or There Will Be A Real Mess, Like In Elliot Mess
- A Trip To The Lawyer's

Boundaries

- Wild In The Streets (And The House)
- Clutter Not As I Do, Clutter As I Say Not To

Five Things On the Desk

- What! Only Five Things On My Desk?
- Lights! Camera! Action!
- Think Of Your Desk As A Workbench
- Oh, No! Not My Stapler Too!
- Credenzas Are An Unnecessary Evil
- Attack Of The Baby Papers
- Bill Me
- A Clean Desk Is A Happy Desk

What You Will Learn In This Chapter
- The only five items that belong on your desk

☀ Myths of the Office

Your In Box and Out Box should be on top of one another on the corner of your desk.

Wax On

Out Of Sight, Out Of Mind

Out of sight, out of mind. I hear it all the time. Once, when I was leading a workshop, I mentioned that it was possible to find everything in a desk in seconds even if it was hidden from view. A really big, hulking type of a guy stood up and voiced his opinion that the "out of sight, out of mind" principle proved me wrong. He believed if it wasn't out where he could see it, he could never remember where to find it.

I wondered how badly I wanted to make my point considering the size of the fellow. At 6 feet 1 inch and 210 pounds, I'm not small. Plus, I had recently purchased disability insurance so I was feeling a little braver than usual.

With his consent, I asked him a rather personal question in front of the group. "Do you wear underwear?" A dead silence hit the room with every head cautiously turning to hear his response. "Of course I do," he bellowed. I considered calling a break, but with a surge of courage said, "Then I assume your underwear is in plain sight all over your chest of drawers or bureau." (I was hoping the insurance company would honor my policy for what I guessed would be an impending accident). He said no, he kept them in a drawer in his bureau. (Drawers in a drawer. I like it!) I asked him how he could possibly remember where they were when he needed a pair if they were hidden from view. After a pause (it seemed like an eternity), he laughed and said it was because they were always where he kept them. He was in the habit of looking for them there. I wondered if the participants could see my lips moving as I silently said a prayer of thanks.

A Clean Desk Does Not Necessarily Mean You Are Productive

While I was working at one company, a fellow pulled me aside and asked me to take a look at his desk. I was very curious as to why he wanted me to take a look, since I wasn't even working with him. When I arrived in his office I understood why. His desk was more than spotless—it was perfect. I went over to his desk and asked if I might not look in his drawers. As I opened one up, he yelled, "Noooo." I found them stuffed with paper. They were a total mess.

Some people keep up the deception of being organized by maintaining a clean desk. A clean desk does not mean you are organized and being organized does not mean that you are productive. I was highly organized for years but not as productive as I thought I was. Organized means having and using a system while productive means getting the most out of what you do.

So the next time you see a clean and organized desk, don't be intimidated. The surface isn't always a true indicator of what's really going on inside. It's vitally important, however, to have a clean and paper-free desk.

Rolling, Rolling, Rolling, Keep That Paper Flowing

Where should your In Box and Out Box go? Many people put them on top of one another in the corner of their desk. Having your In Box on one top corner of your desk and your Out Box on the other top corner is a better way. The surface area that you lose from another box is more than made up by having a paper-free desk.

4-1
Desk With
An In Box
And Out
Box

Keeping the boxes on opposite sides of your desk creates a specific energy path or flow of information. "Paper in, paper out. Paper in, paper out." Paper flows into your office via your In Box, goes to you for a decision, and then flows out through your Out Box.

The blood in your body travels throughout a network of arteries, veins, and capillaries. It's pumped out from the heart and flows back carrying blood to your lungs to be cleansed. When blood no longer normally flows to a part of your body, trouble occurs. Say the blood flow to your arm is impaired. The end of your arm will become infected. The infection turns into gangrene. After gangrene sets in, you either cut off your arm or die, neither a very attractive choice.

The same is true in an office. When paper is stacked, piled, left in an In Box, or shuffled off into a corner, the natural flow or pathway will be clogged. A heavy, stuck feeling descends on the office. The more clutter and pending paper, the less work is produced and the lower the energy in the office.

Bosses are often the worst culprits when it comes to stashing away paper and impeding its natural flow out of their office. Never have so many done so much to cause so many others to get so little done. I'm never quite sure what their rationale is or if they even realize what they're doing. A few withhold information to maintain power and control. I believe most do not realize they are keeping their employees from being productive and getting work done. They have valuable information piled somewhere in their office that the employees desperately need. Picture a group of employees scratching on their boss's door like cats and dogs waiting for a handout. In this case, the handout is paper or information that they need to complete a task.

The solution is to make decisions and move the information out of your office. You'll be amazed at what a light and energetic feeling your office will have if you keep everything moving and how much work will be accomplished.

Wax On, Wax Off

Remember the movie, *The Karate Kid*? Mr. Miyagi had Daniel-san wax and polish his cars. "Wax on, wax off. Wax on, wax off." Mr. Miyagi was teaching Daniel-san a system or movement. Daniel-san, however, didn't quite understand his lesson and became impatient. He couldn't understand what waxing the cars had to do with learning karate.

4-2
Wax On.
Wax Off.

It really had nothing to do with Mr. Miyagi's cars getting waxed. The cars were simply the medium he chose to teach Daniel-san a karate movement, a technique in a system of defense. If you remember, Daniel-san also got to paint "defence" besides waxing "decars" and learning "desystem."

Wax on, wax off. Paper in, paper out. It's the same energy-flow movement. Think of the paper that comes into your office. The goal is for it to flow into your In Box on one side and out the other via your Out Box. You're creating a system for paper to flow out of your office instead of keeping it in to clutter your office.

Don't Stack Me Or There Will Be A Real Mess, Like In Elliot Mess

When you stack your In Box and Out Box together, you're hampering the energy flow from one side to the other. Reasons not to stack your In and Out Boxes:

📁 **Paper flow**
It may sound wacko but you want to create a free-flowing path of energy in your office. Paper in, paper out. Hey, could Mr. Miyagi be wrong?

📁 **Limited Out Box space**
If you keep your Out Box on the bottom of your In Box, the small area between the top and bottom box will limit the size of what you can put into it. When you place them on opposite sides of the desk, it's easier to drop items into them and also allows more vertical space.

If something is hard to do, you generally won't do it. You need to make your routines simple and easy to do. If it's easy to do, you'll do it. If it's hard to do, you probably won't. Think big, unlimited, vertical space for your In Box and Out Box contents.

> *If it's easy to do, you'll do it. If it's hard to do, you probably won't do it.*

📁 **Plenty of desk space**
The other reason you want to separate your In Box from your Out Box is because now you have plenty of space on your desk. They told you to put your In

Box and Out Box on top of one another to save space, since most people have so much other stuff on their desk. Your desk will be totally clear now so you won't have to worry about that.

A Trip To The Lawyer's

You desperately need the services of a lawyer. The one you picked charges $175 an hour. His secretary shows you into his office for your initial meeting. As you enter, you can't help but notice there is paper everywhere. Piles and piles and stacks and stacks on his floor, credenza, and desk. The man is drowning in paper.

As you begin your meeting he looks for your file. He looks but he can't find it. He looks from pile to pile and stack to stack. The clock is ticking. Every minute he spends looking costs you $3. If it takes this long to find something with you in the room, imagine how much time he'll spend when you're not there watching him trying to find it. Is this really the person you want representing you? At $175 per hour?

Have you ever walked into someone's office who was totally disorganized and wondered how much work they really got done? Imagine being someone else and walking into your office. What does your office say about you? What does it say about your productivity?

Now imagine walking into your ideal office. Your desk, floor, and credenza are completely paper-free. Your office has a clean, organized feeling about it and it really feels good to work in it. You know exactly what to work on and where everything goes. You can find everything in five seconds or less. For the first time in your life, you are really in control! You're now leaving work two hours earlier than you used to.

As you leave your office, you turn around and can't help but feel good. Your office is clean, organized, and paper-free. Your day tomorrow is already set. Life is good! Now pinch yourself and wake up. It's time to get to work.

Boundaries

Wild In The Streets (And The House)

Back in the 1970s, there was a movie called *Wild in the Streets*. Rebellious teenagers slipped LSD into the water supply. You can guess what happened to law, order, and the American way after that.

If you have kids, have you set any boundaries for them? How about your spouse? Any rules, regulations, or guidelines? Of course you have, but none that you want to admit to. If you hadn't set boundaries for them, what would happen? How would they behave? Pure chaos would reign. They'd run wildly all over the house, screaming at the top of their lungs, wreaking havoc in their path, creating wild disorder. Now, regarding the boundaries you set for your kids…

What are boundaries? Dr. Frank Meaux, a clinical psychologist, defines them as a way to limit ourselves. They limit us to how much we do, how often we do it, when we will do it, and with whom we do it. A boundary protects us. It creates a safe area, a comfort zone. When we honor our boundaries, our life works. When we don't, our life falls apart.

Clutter Not As I Do, Clutter As I Say Not To

Have you set up boundaries for yourself? If you create boundaries for your kids, thinking that's in their best interest, and expect them to follow them, why wouldn't you create them for yourself? Then, once created, why wouldn't you follow them?

Set them not only for your work life, but also your personal life—for the time you go to bed, how much you drink, how much you eat, on and on. How can you expect your kids to respond to boundaries if you won't? Monkey see, monkey do. Not monkey hear, monkey do. Think about how you'd perform at work if you didn't follow nor have any boundaries. There would be little "work" in your work life.

I don't believe most of us are very good at setting and observing boundaries. Remember the Lay's Potato Chip commercial? "Bet you can't eat just one!" The idea was that they were so good that if you ate just one you wouldn't be able to stop. You'd have to eat the entire bag. You were guaranteed to obliterate your boundaries.

Take for instance creating the boundary of saving money for retirement. The median income of an individual turning 65 today is $13,959. Over 90 percent of our population turning 65 have to rely on means other than retirement money. They either have to work, receive money from the government, or accept money from a family member. Why? Because they never set boundaries for themselves earlier in their lives and saved money. They did have lots of TV sets, new cars, and great vacations. Instead of saving their money in an IRA, they spent it.

Many of us live our life with an all-or-nothing-at-all attitude. The all is now. The nothing-at-all will come later at age 65.

Here are some examples of simple boundaries:
◆ Keeping your feet off the furniture
◆ Working out at the gym three times a week
◆ Saving $100 a month for your retirement
◆ Eating dinner with your family without the TV on
◆ Not running and screaming in the house
◆ Having only five items on your desk
◆ Taking a QT (Quiet Time) daily

Creating the boundary of keeping your desk clean and uncluttered is no different. The more boundaries you create, the more successful you will be. Everything should be off of your desk except the one item you are working on and the five items that are always there.

Five Things On The Desk

What! Only Five Things On My Desk?

4-3
Desk With
Five Items

There are only five items that should be on your desk. If you are an accountant or work in the financial industry, there will be six.

1. & 2. In Box and Out Box
Your In Box goes on either top corner and your Out Box on the other top corner. A lot of people want their In Box closest to the door so it's easier for items to be dropped in. Label both boxes so others know where to put things.

3. Telephone

Your phone goes on the left of the desk if you're right-handed and on the right if you're left-handed. It always goes on the desk in an easy-to-reach spot, never on the credenza, wall, or other crazy places, like in a drawer.

4. Calendar or appointment book

If you use one, your appointment book or daily calendar goes on the top middle of the desk, farthest away from you. I also keep a calendar with the entire year on the wall. It's the only business item that is on my wall.

5. Computer

If you have one, keep it close. The monitor can be set up off the desk with the keyboard sliding out from under the middle of your desk.

If you're in the numbers business, you'll obviously want a calculator on your desk too.

> The five items that stay on your desk are your:
> • In Box
> • Out Box
> • Telephone
> • Appointment book or calendar
> • Computer

Only five items sounds like a really boring desk. What else should go on your desk? Family pictures, your trophy, a plant, a paper-clip holder, pencils, your business-card holder, a rolodex, coffee cups, personal shopping list, calculator, disk holder, clock, tape dispenser, notebook, a clock radio, a big pen, and your favorite pencil sharpener.

Diagram 4-4 is what happens when you don't create boundaries for your desk and limit the number of items on it. The items are all legitimate but notice the difference.

4-4
Desk With
Too Many
Items

Exercise

Look at a desk that is full of clutter. What do you feel? Now look at a desk that has only five items on it plus the one item you are working on. How do you feel about this one?

Most people feel distracted, confused, and uneasy with the cluttered desk. When they look at the desk with only five items on it plus the one item they're working on, they have a strong sense of focusing all their energy on that one item.

Lights! Camera! Action!

If a hidden video camera were placed above you in the ceiling, recording how you worked during the day, you probably wouldn't believe what you saw. This is especially true if you were one of the many people who had a cluttered desk. Your head would be constantly moving from the left to the right, up and down, twisting and turning to look at all the paper on your desk reminding you to do this and do that.

Many people who complain about being constantly interrupted during the day have cluttered desks. If you asked an individual what they thought the source of their interruptions were during the day, very few would say their desk. Yet every piece of paper, book, file, business card, picture, plant, knickknack, trophy, to do list—every scrap on your desk—has the potential to and generally will interrupt you. Many of their interruptions are brought on by themselves. All you have to do is simply glance at your desk and that little voice in your head will remind you that there's still yet something else to do. And remind you and remind you and remind you. And each reminder is a distraction.

Think Of Your Desk As A Workbench

Think about a workbench. Now think about putting a 4- by 8-foot sheet of plywood on it and trying to cut it when it is cluttered with tools, nails, and blocks of wood. Trying to cut the plywood would be extremely difficult because of all the things that were in the way. Bob Vila wouldn't work on it, I can tell you that. Tim the Tool Man might. You'd have to clear off everything to properly make the cut.

Exercise

Place a business card on a cluttered desk. Now step back. Is it easy to see or does it blend in with all the other paper? Does all the other clutter distract you when you are trying to look at the business card? Now clear off the desk completely and put the same card down. Which way makes it easier to see the card? Obviously, the desk with only the business card on it.

Oh, No! Not My Stapler Too!

I can hear some of you now. "If there are only five items allowed on my desk, where's my stapler supposed to go? What about my scotch-tape dispenser? Surely my pictures get to stay. Is nothing sacred on my desk anymore?" They all leave the desk area and not necessarily quietly, either.

Where do you keep items such as your stapler, your ruler, and tape dispenser? Not on your desk where they slow you down and distract you, but rather in a Category called the Tool drawer. A Category is a grouping of similar or like items. The benefit is you can find everything very quickly

> *The less you have out on your desk, the less you'll be distracted.*

when it's in a Category. Another Category is your Office Supply drawer. Items such as your pen and pencils, sticky notes, and paper clips go into this. I often keep my Tool drawer slightly open when I'm using it so it's easy for me to pull tools out and put them back. My Tool drawer is the top right drawer on my desk.

All right, I will concede one more item to you. Administrative people can keep a message pad on their desk.

Credenzas Are An Unnecessary Evil

Sell your credenza, give it to charity, or choose to use it properly. Sometimes I think the only reason a credenza was built was for furniture companies to make more money. Just kidding. There go all my potential furniture clients. The only thing that goes on your credenza is one of your Categories such as Memorabilia or Knickknacks. Your pictures, your awards, your trinkets—all that stuff can go there. You never want any of your work, paperwork, books, or binders on your credenza. And keep your phone off of it too!

I once removed the credenza of a vice president of sales, Mark J., because whenever he had something he didn't know what to do with, he'd put it on his credenza. Quite an impressive stacking job too! I helped him create an organizational system, but he wouldn't break his habit of stacking. I finally said, "Mark, it's outta here!" So we took the credenza out of his office and he lived happily ever after.

Attack Of The Baby Papers

I have a theory about putting paper on your credenza. There's no problem if you put one piece on it. However, if you put two pieces of paper on it they have little baby pieces of paper and the stack grows. As soon as you get that second piece back there, you just can't help wanting to put another one back there, and another and another.

You're going to set your own boundaries as to what goes on your desk. If you're disciplined enough to keep just that stapler on and only that and not add more items, then that's what you'll do. I like to keep it off the surface of the desk because it's another thing you have to push out of the way, a distraction that takes up space and energy. If you're using your stapler for two hours straight, that's a different story. Keep it out. When you're done simply put it back into the drawer.

Bill Me

I once worked with a friend of mine, Barry Zipperman, who is an attorney. He was concerned that if his desk was clean and paper-free that his partners might think he wasn't doing anything. I told him all he had to do was let them look at his total billable hours and then look at theirs. Maybe he should be asking them why their desks are cluttered and they aren't billing more hours.

Some people's perception is that a clean desk means you aren't working or accomplishing anything. They couldn't be more wrong, and I believe after they watch how much you are producing, their belief will change.

A Clean Desk Is A Happy Desk

"A clean desk is a happy desk." From now on there will only be one additional thing on your desk and it will be whatever you're working on. When you focus only on that one item on your desk, you'll

> *The only other item on your desk should be the one thing you're working on.*

be that much more productive. Remember, if somebody hands you something, keep your desk clean and simply drop it into your In Box.

Remember These Concepts

- If it's easy to do, you'll do it. If it's hard to do, you probably won't do it.
- The five items that stay on your desk are your:
  - In Box
  - Out Box
  - Telephone
  - Appointment book or calendar
  - Computer
- The less you have out on your desk, the less you'll be distracted.
- The only other item on your desk should be the one thing you're working on.

Things To Avoid

- In Box and Out Box on top of one another.
- Paper on your desk, floor, or credenza.

2.5

In Box

In Box

- Mail Call
- You Do Lunch. You Do Movies. Why Not Do Your In Box Too?
- Once Upon A Time In A Far-Off Land
- At The End Of The Day, Do You Feel Like You Really Didn't Get Anything Done?
- Your Most Important Tool
- Touch Me In The Morning
- How To Abuse Your In Box, Let Me Count The Ways
- The Best Way Around Something Is Always Through It

The Decision Box

- The Five Steps Of The In Box
- A One And A Two
- Doing Versus Deciding
- Stand, Support, Forms, Duhhh
- First In Then Out
- Out To Lunch
- Habits Create Needs

What You Will Learn In This Chapter

- A five-step system on how to go through your In Box in less than five minutes

---

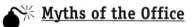 **Myths of the Office**

Work from or out of your In Box.

In Box

Mail Call

No doubt, at some time or another, you've seen a picture of a person in an old post office sorting mail into boxes on the wall. Each wall box was a street, area of town, or mail route. When the letters come in they were placed into a slot on the wall (just like an In Box). A person sorted them (Processing) by placing them into the appropriate wall box (Out Box). They followed this sorting procedure quite regularly. If they didn't, the mail would accumulate and end up taking a long time to go a short distance. (Oh! So that's why the mail is so slow.)

5-1
In The Post
Office
Sorting
Letter

You're doing the same thing in your office when you sort your mail or your information by going through your In Box. Instead of using mail routes to send it to its appropriate location, you can get it a lot quicker by using OATS (Out Box, Action, Trash, and Support).

You Do Lunch. You Do Movies. Why Not Do Your In Box Too?

I have always been amused to hear people say "Let's do lunch" or "Let's do a movie." Unfortunately, they "do" their In Box too! What happens when you "do" or work from your In Box? First, you're participating in a reactive activity. You react to what's on the top of the pile in your In Box and work on that versus being proactive and working on what's important, which is probably filed away in your drawer.

Another problem that arises when you "do" your In Box is you can never seem to empty it. If you do accomplish this Herculean task, it takes forever since you are interrupted so many times in the process. It can take days to finish when you've been on vacation or on the road or haven't regularly gone through it. With the amount of information that flows to you today, you could easily have a full-time job just working from, or "doing" your In Box.

Everyone who has ever come back from a vacation has known the terror of an In Box that has grown out of control. "Good morning, employees. We have some great news for you. Ginny has just returned from her vacation, and we are happy to announce that her In Box height has just surpassed the old record of 33 $1/2$ inches. Congratulations, Ginny! Tell her what she's won, Johnny." Not hardly. I know people who are afraid to take a vacation for fear of having to go through their In Box when they return.

5-2
The
Dreaded
Return

Once Upon A Time In A Far-off Land

Once upon a time there was a fair and just prince who spoke to the masses. The prince was away for two days in a far-off land giving a speech to Lady Lynn's subjects. On his return an evil dragon was waiting for him when he entered his castle, the dragon of The Neglected In Box. He wondered how so much parchment and debris could accumulate in just two days. Reluctantly, he emptied the contents of his pouch onto the enormous stack already in his In Box, adding even more height to the pile. On top was a 3 x 5 parchment with a reminder to thank Lady Lynn for the speech he had so fairly given in Charlestown. The prince began to scratch his thank-you letter to Lady Lynn. Ten minutes later he was finished. But an average prince is interrupted every eight minutes by serfs, and he was no exception. He had an unexpected visitor, a feudal lord who tied him up for 20 minutes, then had to rush off to a meeting at the Round Table. The rest of his day was tied up and he had no time to finish his In Box. Being away in a far-off land is very difficult since so many things can back up at the castle.

How much of his In Box was he able to go through and complete? Just that one little 3 x 5 parchment. Why just that one? He couldn't get to the rest of it for he was too busy! Meanwhile, during the day, his In Box mysteriously grew and grew so that when he got back to the castle, he shuddered to think of the dragon and how large and overpowering it had become.

The moral of the story is: Slay the evil dragon immediately upon returning to the castle or your days, knights, and In Box will drag'on!

At The End Of The Day, Do You Feel Like You Really Didn't Get Anything Done?

At the end of the day, if you feel like you really didn't get anything done, it may be that you're working from your In Box. We've been taught to do this over and over again. "Work from your In Box" is another of the myths of the office. The majority of items in your In Box are minutiae, junk mail, memos, insignificant items, and "squeaky wheels," i.e., urgent things to do. The more urgent the task, the more times requested, the higher up the boss, the more political the issue, the louder the squeak, the less important the task probably is to work on.

> *Process your In Box. Don't "do" it.*

Your Most Important Tool

Everything always goes into your In Box first. Some examples:
- an item brought in by your secretary
- a task dropped off by a fellow worker
- a file that you are finished with
- a note to yourself to do something
- handouts you've brought back from a meeting

Your In Box is the most important tool you have in your office. It enables you to stay organized, process information, and keep control—what most people want in today's hectic world. Your In Box is the most powerful tool that you have at your disposal, one that will guarantee you a paper-free desk, floor, and credenza and give you a centralized processing place. Plus, it is a sanctioned place for you to dump everything. What more do you want? And the best part is they only cost a few bucks each.

5-3
Your Most
Important
Tool

Touch Me In The Morning

"Touch a piece of paper only once!" You've heard it a million times. If you touch it, do something with it. Do not shuffle it or lay it down on the desk. Do not handle it more than once; do something with it right then. Otherwise you're wasting time and shuffling paper. Wrong!

What's wrong with touching a piece of paper only once and then taking action (Producing) right then? Or working (Producing) from your In Box while you go through it? The problem is you are combining Processing (going through your In Box) with Producing (taking action), an inefficient method.

What can happen is this: say you are working on (Producing) a task when someone hands you a another task. Instead of dropping it into your In Box to Process later, you interrupt yourself, stop working on your current task (Producing), Process the new task and then start working on (Producing) the new task. The original task you were working on becomes yet another incomplete task left by the wayside. This occurs repeatedly during the day, resulting in incomplete tasks strewn all over your desk and your life.

If you are trying to work out of your In Box, your chances are pretty slim of emptying it since most people are interrupted every eight minutes. You will be called out for a meeting, go on an appointment, handle an emergency, and then before you know it, the day will be over. So many people walk around all day with an In Box that is piled nearly to the ceiling and an overwhelming sense of too much to do, because they're trying to do (Produce) their In Box rather than make decisions (Process) on what's in it. They'll never get done with it.

How To Abuse Your In Box, Let Me Count The Ways

What are some of the misuses of the In Box? The following are common examples:

✔ The Pick and Chooser—Here a pick, there a pick, everywhere a pick-pick. Does extremely well picking out menus, checks, and fun things. Normal work and unpleasant tasks are mysteriously left in the In Box untouched.

✔ The Storer—Uses it as a place to store things. Could be a distant relative of the squirrel. Stores especially well during winter months, before vacations, or when procrastinating on really big and difficult projects. Contents of the In Box eventually overflow to the credenza, floor, and eventually the tree and nuthouse.

✔ The Never-Go-Througher—Does not or will not go through the In Box. Believes the less he goes through it and the longer the contents sit there, the greater the chance everything will magically disappear. Doesn't like to deal with reality.

✔ The Pender—Likes an extremely safe, visible, and close place for things she is waiting on. Keeps everything within arm's reach. Has a tendency to want to be in control.

✔ The Excuser—Has a million reasons why he can't go through the In Box: too busy, overworked, not enough time. For that matter, he doesn't have enough time to exercise or do anything else. A true victim having a great time in today's society of victims.

✔ The Doers (no, not the scotch)—Easily the largest group that's working out of or from the In Box today.

Their goal is to work on everything from the top to the bottom of it. Other than not going through the In Box at all, this is the worst way to abuse it, the most common and, unfortunately, the way we were all taught.

✔ The Undecider—Refuses to make decisions on difficult tasks and drops them back into the In Box. In a former life she probably worked for the IRS.

✔ The Piler—Believes more is better, as in "My pile is bigger than your pile." Has not yet quite caught on that he's supposed to deal with the contents of his In Box. Might be related to the Undecider.

✔ The Non-Exister—Does not have one and probably never will. She works from her desk, the credenza, or the floor, never an In Box. Often heard bragging that she doesn't have one, never had one, and never will have one. She enjoys living 50 years in the past.

I used to sell telephone equipment and I wasn't very technically minded. Once I picked up a part from a customer's phone thinking it was important. When I got back to my office, I didn't know what to do with it, so I put the part into my In Box. It was in there for a year. Why? I didn't know what to do with it so by storing it in my In Box, I never felt I had to make a decision on it.

The Best Way Around Something Is Always Through It

When you think about it, you spend incredible amounts of time in avoidance. When you make a decision and deal with whatever you want to avoid, you actually save time.

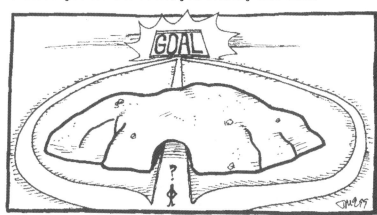

5-4
The Best
Way
Around
Something
Is Always
Through It

The easiest way to sabotage yourself is by avoiding going through your In Box. This is the most elementary part of the system, where it all begins.

> *You spend more energy avoiding doing something than just doing it.*

Once a client of mine, Robert C., a financial planner, had such a hard time making decisions that when I repeatedly challenged him to make one, he actually poked me fairly hard on my chest with his finger. I told him I was glad he made a decision—just not the one that involved poking me.

Another client of mine, Ann W., a VP of marketing for a hotel chain, had 2,046 e-mails opened with no decisions made on them. She also had 69 unopened e-mails for that day. Guess what she got to do in the training?

The Decision Box

The Five Steps Of The In Box

The following is a five-step process for going through your In Box.

Step 1. Stand up

Why stand when you go through your In Box? So it won't take more than five minutes to do. Sit down while going through your In Box and it will take you 20-30 minutes. Remember, your goal is to get through your Processing activities as quickly as possible since no production occurs when you're doing them.

Exercise

Try this. Lean back in your chair, put your hands behind your head, and pick up a piece of paper from your In Box. Now ever so slowly and deliberately, read it. This is how many people go through their In Box. Some actually do this with their legs crossed and their feet up on their desks.

Now stand up for a second. How do you feel when you are standing? What's the difference between standing and sitting? You're more comfortable, relaxed, and tend to work slower sitting down. You also have a tendency to want to work on tasks when you're sitting. When you stand up you're more energized, alert, and ready for action. Think about working out in a gym early in the morning. When you do, you create energy for the rest of the day. When you take action, you are creating energy from that action.

Remember years ago when you jump-started a car when the battery was dead? The cars were really built big in those days and were tough to push. While someone sat in the driver's seat, you got behind the car and pushed it. At first, getting the car going was very difficult since the car was starting from a complete stop. But once you got it moving, the task became easier as you overcame the initial inertia.

The same is true with decision-making. The more decisions you make, the easier they'll be to make. Once you get into the habit of making decisions, it will become a lot more comfortable as you go along.

If you stand up when you go through your In Box, you'll be done in five minutes or less. It shouldn't take you any longer unless you don't do it regularly or you've been out  *Action creates energy.* of town or on vacation and it has built up.

Standing up works in other areas. If you stand up when you're on the telephone, you will sound more alive, more vibrant, and will finish the conversation much quicker. Stand up in meetings. Take all the chairs out of the room. Believe me, nobody will be willing to listen to someone go on for hours when everyone is standing up.

So step number one is **Stand up**.

Step 2. Ask OATS

Now that you are standing and have a piece of paper in your hand, where do you put it? There are only four places that a piece of paper or anything else in your In Box can go: OATS.

Step two is to **Ask yourself OATS**. Does it go to the Out Box? Is it an Action? Is it Trash? Or is it a Support?

Step 3. Decide the Category and the File

Have you ever filed away something and then a few hours later tried to find it but couldn't? I'd guess that was because you haven't set up a system for finding items, or if you did, it doesn't work. I'll bet it was because you didn't even give the paper or file a name when you first put it away. You just kind of mumbled as you shuffled it onto your credenza or dropped it into your drawer.

Imagine having a baby and not giving the poor child a name. As time goes on, you have a little boy or a little girl running around the house. When you want your child you say, "Hey you." Not real good parenting skills. Now if you had a bunch of little kids running around the house all nameless, you'd have a very interesting experience trying to get their attention. Of course, if you named them all the same name you'd be in for a time too. George Foreman did exactly that. He had five boys whose names are all George. I love it. George, George, George, George, George. You know George Sr. had to have a special name for each George or there would have been complete chaos.

Back to the system. This time imagine you're standing up with the item in your hand. You've decided where it will go according to the OATS system. If it's an Out Box you write directions on a yellow sticky note or on the upper right hand corner of the paper itself. If it's Trash, you throw it away. Good riddance. They both leave the office. However, if it's an Action or a Support, you need a system of how to keep track of it since it will be filed away in a drawer. You do this by deciding the Category and the File for each piece of paper.

A Category is a grouping of similar or like things and a File is one of its components. The benefit to categorizing items is that they become easier to find. We will describe Categories in an upcoming chapter.

If the item is an Action, it goes into one of the four Action Categories: To Do, Projects, Routine To Do, or Tickler. We'll be discussing the four Action Categories in Part 3.

> **Example**
>
> If you wanted to read something, where would it go? Step one would be Stand. Step two would be to ask yourself OATS. In this case it would be an Action. Next you'd decide into which Category and File it would go. In this case, Routine to Do would be the Category, i.e., things that you repetitively and routinely do, such as read. The File would be Read.

"Stand, Action, Routine to Do, Read."

If an item is a Support, it goes into one of the Support Categories. A few possible examples of Support Categories would be Clients, Personnel, Customers, Forms, and Training. If it was a form you used to reorder light sabers, then your first step would be Stand. Step two would be to ask yourself OATS. In this case it would be a Support. Next you would decide into which Category and File it would go: Forms would be the Category and the File would be Light sabers.

"Stand, Support, Forms, Light sabers."

So you have now decided what the Category and File is. Under Action and Support, you have Categories and Files to direct you where to file and find things.

Say you have some personal photos from the Christmas party. Uh-oh maybe not a good example. Instead, let's say they're personal photos that you want to keep in your office. Where do you put them? Hopefully in a Category called Personal. Going through your In Box you would say: Stand, Support, Personal. And what File would it be? Photos. What you are doing is creating a hierarchical system so you can find everything in your Action and Support Categories. Stand, Support, Personal, Photos.

So step number three is **Decide the Category and File.**

Step 4. Use all of your senses

Step number four is to use all of your senses. Say it, hear it, see it, touch it, and, if you're weird, smell it.

Think back to high school. Most teachers used to teach didactically, meaning they taught by talking and you learned by listening. Unfortunately, only a quarter of the population learns this way. I wasn't one of them. Instead, I learned very quickly when the subject involved a hands-on activity. Think back to your high school biology class. Most people remember cutting up a frog and the smell of formaldehyde but nothing of what the teacher said about the poor frog. The more senses that are involved, the more details you will remember.

The same is true when filing away documents. Another reason you may not remember things you have filed away might be that you don't have a system for relearning the name every time you touch the item.

What you'll be doing every time you go through your In Box and filing something away is relearning the name. The same is true when you look for something. This way you are learning coming and going. Think how easy it will be to remember the names when you go through your In Box and you:

- Say it out loud
- Hear yourself say what it is
- See and identify what it is that you have picked up
- Feel the texture or notice the weight of it
- And, if you are weird, smell it

Speaking of smelling it, I fondly remember getting perfumed letters from girls in college during summer break. Gosh, those were the days! Bonnie Lou O'Brien used to send the sweetest-smelling letters. They made a tremendous impression on me. I could hardly wait for those perfumed letters to get to my mailbox. They made the rest of the mail smell good too—even the bills. Whenever you can utilize your sense of smell, do so, as it profoundly increases your awareness and sense of learning. Many studies today show that certain smells can cause people to be more productive, among other things.

Say you were thinking about attending a workshop. There were various types you could attend. The first one allowed you to sit and listen for eight hours. The second allowed you to listen and watch movies. The third allowed you to listen, watch movies, and discuss what you learned. The final one allowed you to listen, watch movies, discuss what you learned, and work on what you learned. Which would you learn the most from and which workshop would you want to attend? I know, the one with free popcorn. Obviously, the last one, for both learning and interest.

Using your senses when you process your In Box is very important. The more you can use, the better. On the next page are statistics on retaining information.

In step four you say it out loud, hear yourself say it, look at it, touch it, and smell it. In other words, use as many senses as possible.

Let's say you are going through your In Box and you pick up a form. The very first thing you say out loud is "Stand." Why should you say "Stand?" Because after initially doing this standing up, you probably will start to sit back down when you go through your In Box. Saying "Stand" immediately will also get

We retain:
- 10% of what we read
- 20% of what we hear
- 30% of what we see
- 50% of what we see and hear
- 70% of what we say
- 90% of what we say and do

you started in the decision-making process and the five-step process.

A One and A Two

Exercise

Below are four examples of how it would sound going through your In Box. Say them out loud.

1. Stand
   Action
   Routine To Do
   Sign

2. Stand
   Trash

3. Stand
   Action
   To Do
   A (a File in the To Do Category)

4. Stand
   Out Box

Notice you still need to say Stand even if it's an Out Box or Trash. You want to stay in the habit of saying it. When you process your In Box, you can put the words into a four beat:

1. Stand (Beat) 2. Action (Beat) 3. To Do (Beat) 4. A (Beat)
Or a two beat:

1. Stand (Beat) 2. Trash (Beat)
1. Stand (Beat) 2. Out Box (Beat)

It sounds musical. We have a natural built in rhythm in our body. When we learn to use our rhythm, our retention and learning can be much greater.

So step number four is **Use all of your senses**.

Step 5. File it away

Step 5 is to simply file the paper or item away. That means drop it into the Out Box. Trash it. File it into one of your Action Categories to work on or file it into one of your Support Categories.

So step number five is **File it away**.

Doing Versus Deciding

Instead of calling it an In Box, start calling it a Decision Box, because you'll be using it to make decisions. When you go through your In Box, you will be deciding, categorizing, sorting, and prioritizing. You will not be "doing" it but rather "deciding" on it.

There are two exceptions to "not doing" your In Box. If you have a sheet of paper, such as a memo, read it first rather than file it away. Many times you'll receive single sheets of paper that you can read or scan in seconds. If you can do this, do it. If that same sheet of paper has two or three pages, don't read it then. Just file it into Stand, Action, Routine To Do, Read.

There's a fine line between deciding and doing. You want to be done processing the contents of your In Box in five minutes or less. If it takes you longer than this, be aware that you might be "doing" your In Box. This is what we have unconsciously been taught to do.

The second exception is when you sign your name. If you can sign your name and send it on its way, then sign it and move it out, partner. The goal is to get everything out of your office as fast as you can. Do a quick read-through and sign it.

> *There's a fine line between deciding and doing when going through your In Box.*

Now what would happen if you had 25 papers to sign? Would you sign them right then? No. Because you'd be crossing over the line from deciding to doing. The goal is to have everything filed away so you have complete knowledge of what to work on and where it is.

Look at your In Box as just a bunch of information. This is a whole new concept for a lot of people. You need to process it three times a day so you can stay in control. If you don't know what's out there for you to do, you'll feel out of control. So, three times a day, go through and prioritize and categorize the contents of your In Box.

Stand, Support, Forms, Duhhh

As soon as you stop using the five-step system, you may start forgetting where things are. The five-step system for processing information is a very, very powerful tool. Most people don't understand how powerful it really is.

Step 1. Stand up

When you stand up you create energy and limit the time it takes to process your In Box to a few minutes.

Step 2. Ask OATS

This is your first decision. There are only four places it can go. Either out of your office, to work on, to throw away, or to refer to. Nowhere else.

Step 3. Decide the Category and the File

Once you've decided to work on it (Action) or refer to it (Support), which means keeping it in your office, you need to identify the Category and name of the File where it goes so you can find it quickly and easily.

Step 4. Use all of your senses

By using as many senses as you can, you're causing yourself to relearn where it is every time you look for it and every time you put it away.

Step 5. File it away

Filing it away keeps your desk, floor, and credenza clean. You're getting it off your desk to a known location with a system that puts you in control. The only time to file is during this step of your In Box. Otherwise, throw it into your In Box.

> **The Five Steps Of The In Box**
> Step 1. Stand up
> Step 2. Ask OATS
> Step 3. Decide the Category and the File
> Step 4. Use all your senses
> Step 5. File it away

Now that your desk is clean and everything is filed away, you can work on what you want. You're in control because you're aware of where all your information is and what you need to do.

First In Then Out

Go through your In Box three times a day and distribute the contents of your Out Box when you have finished going through your In Box. That means drop off the entire contents to other employees, send it to the mailroom, file it in the Central Files or wherever it goes. Go through your In Box first thing in the morning, right after lunch, and late in the afternoon. You do this for a couple of reasons: If some of the things are urgent, you need to get to them within a few hours; you also keep the pile in the In Box manageable. Would you rather go through an In Box piled high or one with just a few items in it? Obviously, the one with as little stuff as possible.

> *The key to going through your In Box is in your ability to make decisions.*

Example

Say the times you have set up are at 9 a.m., 1 p.m., and 4 p.m. If you came in at 7 p.m. at night loaded to the hilt with a bunch of papers from a meeting, do you go through your In Box then or do you simply dump it in your In Box for the next morning? You get to dump it. Why go through it? You have a 9 a.m. In Box time tomorrow morning. Why do it late at night when you're tired? Instead of throwing it in a pile on your desk, drop it into your In Box, so tomorrow morning at nine you can go through it.

Out To Lunch

If you're out of the office most of the day, you won't be able to go through your In Box three times. If you start off the day in the office and will be out for the rest of the day, go through your In Box. Then, the next day get back on your regular schedule. If you don't come in until 11 a.m., you probably missed your first In Box time and will only have two times left. If you are out of the office, you can still check your voice mail and e-mail at the regular times.

Habits Create Needs

Why do you want to go through your In Box the same time every day? So you create a habit. Habits just come naturally to us, especially bad ones. We like habits. We're comfortable with them. We mindlessly follow them. Take smoking after a meal. Now I am not a smoker and am not qualified to make this statement, but what the heck, I will anyway. Why do people smoke after they eat? I always hear it tastes so much better right after eating. I have a different theory and I may be totally wrong. I believe they saw somebody else doing it and so they started to do it after they ate. In essence, they created a habit.

> *Habits create needs.*

Habits create needs. If you have the habit of going to the gym every morning, stop going to the gym for a week and see how your body feels. Your body will miss the action and you'll probably feel tired and sluggish. In essence, you have created the need for exercise. You can do the same in your office. Once you get into the habit of doing this, you'll never want to get back out of it.

Remember These Concepts

- Process your In Box. Don't "do" it.
- You spend more energy avoiding doing something than just doing it.
- Action creates energy.
- There's a fine line between deciding and doing when going through your In Box.
- The key to going through your In Box is in your ability to make decisions.
- Habits create needs.

Things To Avoid

- Stuffing paper back into an envelope after you just pulled it out to look at it.
- Working from or out of your In Box.
- Not making decisions.

2.6

The Category Model

What Is A Category?

- I Can Never Seem To Find Anything
- The Early Bird Gets The Bookworm
- Using Support Categories Is Like Going To The Library
- What's A Category?
- The Model Is Out There
- I Wanna Go Shopping
- Can Of Peas
- Computer
- I've Created A Monster! (Category)
- "Today's Categories Are: State Capitals, Opera, The Bible..."
- Paper Or Non-Paper
- Mozart
- Seeing Is Believing
- You Call It Corn, We Call It An A"Maize"Ing Mess
- Big To Little

What You Will Learn In This Chapter

- What a Category is
- How to group items into Categories
- How to find all your files within five seconds
- How to name your Categories
- Why it is important to use your words

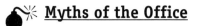 **Myths of the Office**

If I can't see it, I'll forget to do it.

What Is A Category?

I Can Never Seem To Find Anything

Have you ever been talking on the phone and needed to find something quickly but you couldn't locate it? As you stalled the caller, you frantically looked everywhere. Embarrassed and frustrated, you had to make some excuse and ask if you could call them back.

Are you able to find everything in your office in five seconds or less? Do you have a system set up that allows you to locate the files in your computer instantly? Do you have to number and index each sheet on the bottom of each file in your computer so you can find it? Do you use one system for all information storage or do you use different ones?

Think about the incredible number of hours that you waste looking for papers and information. If that's not bad enough, think how many hours you waste looking for files in your computer. My experience is that most people's computers and e-mail are even more disorganized than their paper files.

How much do all those lost hours cost you annually? If you bill hourly, multiply your hourly rate times .75, then multiply that number times the average number of work days in a year, 235.

For instance, if you bill $100 an hour or your time is worth that, multiply 100 by .75 which equals $75. Multiply $75 times 235 and you get $17,625.00. That's the amount of money a normal executive who bills $100 an hour loses in a year. Imagine how much you'd lose if you were really disorganized!

You may think that paper is disappearing and with modern technology we'll soon have the paperless office. Not in your lifetime. Our president, in an effort to create a new health care system, is taking aim at the paperwork jungle. He recently visited a Washington hospital's records room where he found that paperwork grew at 6 $1/2$ feet a week. If this is what the paperless office is going to look like, I would hate to see one with paper.

If you feel out of control and in overwhelm, imagine what it will be like in a few years when information is pounding at you at an even more rapid rate. Guess what that will do to your paperwork? You think your office looks bad now...

Don't despair. The solution to the problem is creating and using your own personalized information access system. It sounds complicated but it isn't. All it means is you get to create one system which allows you to store and access information in seconds. Make it as simple or as complex as you choose, just so it works easily for you.

The Early Bird Gets The Bookworm

I had my den remodeled and beautiful bookshelves built by brother, John. When I was ready to put away the books, I was puzzled. I sat there trying to figure out how I could possibly organize all the books. One way would be for me to separate the hard cover from the soft cover. Another method was to go by size. I could also break them down by subject matter such as History, Science Fiction, Business, and Self-Help. Then, if I chose, I could break them down even further. My history books could be broken down by time period, subject, or by country. A system was a definite necessity.

Using Support Categories Is Like Going To The Library

How would you go about finding a particular book at the library? Of course, if you wanted to be real productive you'd ask the librarian where to find it. But let's say you were doing this on your own. First you'd ask yourself what type of book it was and go to that section: Fiction, Nonfiction, Biography, etc. Next you'd look for the title or author.

You could use the card catalogue system the library has set up. The names of the books are listed alphabetically, as are the authors. On the cards are the sections where they are located. Why not use a similar system in your office that is sorted by subject, is personalized, and uses a terminology that is familiar to you.

What's A Category?

A Category is a grouping of similar or like things. A Category is broken down by a subject. Why break it down by a subject? Because that's the way the brain clusters information.

> *A Category is a grouping of similar or like things.*

The Model Is Out There

The Category model can be used for both Action and Support Categories. In this chapter we will deal with Support Categories. In Part 3 we will learn about Action Categories. The following are various models you will be using to create your system. They start with a basic model:

Basic Model
- Category
- File

Then if you want to expand it:
- Category
- File
- Subfile

Or:
- Category
- Subcategory
- File

Or that expanded:
- Category
- Subcategory
- File
- Subfile

You already know how the Category model works. It's constantly being used around you although you may have never made the connection. Here are a few examples of the models that are in place in your life right now.

> *You already know how the Category model works.*

- Retail stores
- Your home
- Your computer

I Wanna Go Shopping

Retail stores are already categorized. You go to a grocery store for food; a bookstore for books; a shoe store for shoes; and a liquor store to get snockered. Generally, you go to a specific store for the specific product or products they are selling. Clothes. Sporting goods. Auto parts. Lingerie. Hardware. Toys. You don't go to a hardware store to buy a cantaloupe or a watermelon. You go to a grocery store for that.

Many retail stores are also Subcategorized, such as department and grocery stores. In a department store, what do you always find right in front of the escalator? That little, white sign on a chrome stand. The sign is broken down by floors with departments alphabetically listed on the first, second, and third floors. You're already using the model since each section on each floor is categorized: Women's clothes, makeup, perfume, appliances, etc.

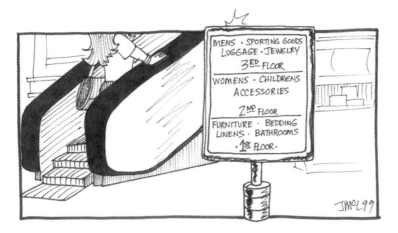

6-1
Department
Store Sign

The same is true in a grocery store. It's sectioned off by meats, fruits, and vegetables, etc.

Can of Peas

The model exists even in your home. How do you break down your home? (By having your mother-in-law stay too long?) By rooms. Some of the rooms are living room, dining room, kitchen, den, bedroom and bathroom. How is your kitchen broken down? Appliances, pots and pans, refrigerated foods, pantry, etc. Under pantry, you would have canned goods and packaged goods. Under canned goods you'd have a can of peas, a can of beans, and so on.

What you are doing is going from general to specific. The Category "Rooms" is general. The Subfile "Can of peas" is specific.

How do you break it down? One way is by subdividing the Category into two or more parts. They then become Subcategories. Under that are the Files. Then Subfiles.

Category / Subcategory / File / Subfile

Big to little. Left to right. General to specific.

When you subdivide a Category into big parts, it becomes a Subcategory.

Example

Category	*Subcategory*	*File*	*Subfile*
Rooms	Bathroom		
	Bedroom		
	Den		
	Kitchen	Appliances	
		Glasses	
		Pantry	Can of beans
			Can of peas

Where do you store a pair of shoes? In the Bedroom; more specifically in the closet.

- Room   (Category)
- Bedroom   (Subcategory)
- Closet   (File)
- Shoes   (Subfile)

Big to little. General to specific.

The model is out there. It's just a matter of you realizing it and using it in your office too.

Computer

A third way the model is present is in your computer. You can set up your system so that your computer files and paper files are aligned. The same is true to a certain degree for your e-mail.

Exercise

Look at Windows Explorer. Pick whichever drive you store files in. Generally it will be the C: drive. Under C: you'll have directories or folders. Under the directories or folders, you will have subdirectories or subfolders. Then files, and subfiles, and on and on. Top to bottom. Left to right. Big to little. This is the same configuration, the same model. We will be going into detail with computers and e-mail in Part 2, Chapter 10.

The above are three examples of how the Category model is already present in your everyday life.

Now let's use the basic model and create a Category. Say you want one called "Countries of the World." The goal is to have a Category with all the 200+ countries of the world in it. Most likely you'll choose a big drawer, put in files of all the countries, and arrange them alphabetically.

> ### Example
>
> | *Category* | *Files* |
> |---|---|
> | Countries of the World | Australia |
> | | Brazil |
> | | China |
> | | Germany |
> | | United States |
> | | Plus all the rest of the countries |

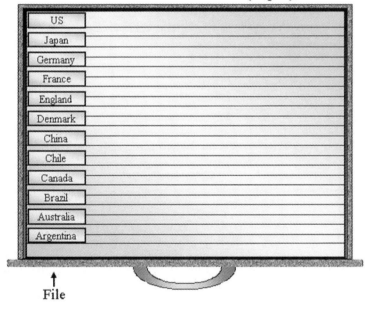

Countries Of The World (Aqua)

6-2
Countries
Category

Could you find every country in that file drawer? Sure. Let's just say that you really like geography and you often access that information. Can the Files be broken down even more so that you can find them more quickly? Absolutely.

You'd break them down by continents using Subcategories: Africa, Antarctica, Asia, Australia, Europe, North America, and South America. So it would be:

- Countries of the World (Category)
- North America (Subcategory)
- United States (File)

Example

Category	*Subcategory*	*File*
Countries of the World	North America	Canada
		Mexico
		United States

Countries Of The World (Aqua)

6-3
Countries
With
Subcat-
egory

When you think of how a Subcategory is used, think of a submarine—"sub" meaning under, "marine" meaning water. Thus submarine means under the water. When you use sub with a Category, sub is a part of and under a Category.

Can you break all of the countries in the world down so you can find them even quicker? Sure. Let's break it down another level to the Subfile. Subfiles in this case would be states. In Canada they would be provinces.

- Countries of the World (Category)
- North America (Subcategory)
- United States (File)
- Alabama (Subfile)

> **Example**
>
> | _Category_ | _Subcategory_ | _File_ | _Subfile_ |
> | Countries | North America | United States | Alabama |
> | of the World | | | |

Say you wanted to break it down another level. What would be below state? It could be counties, then cities, or cities or counties alone. Which would be the right way? The way you naturally think about it.

Countries Of The World (Aqua)

6-4
Countries
With Sub-
category
And Subfiles

- Countries of the World   (Category)
- North America   (Subcategory)
- United States   (File)
- Georgia   (Subfile)
- Fulton County   (Type)
- Sandy Springs   (Subtype)

Who decides how far you break it down or how simple or complex your system will be? You do. If you want to use the simplest and easiest level, use a Category and Files. Don't make it any more complicated than you need to. Most of the time, you will just have a Category and Files.

I've Created A Monster! (Category)

The following are other examples of Categories. The Category could be Clients, with all your clients' names.

Example

Category
Clients

Files
Equitable
Georgia Power
IBM
Mississippi Power
NationsBank

The Category could be Forms, with the names of all the forms you use. Make it as simple as possible.

Example

Category
Forms

Files
Applications
Faxes
Itinerary
Preprogram
Project management

"Today's Categories Are: State Capitals, Opera, The Bible..."

I've always enjoyed watching the quiz show *Jeopardy*. "Today's categories are: State Capitals, Opera, The Bible, Words That Begin With X." What they've done is broken down the answers by a similar subject. This is exactly what you get to do when you create your Categories—break everything down by a subject.

Again, let's return to high school biology where we studied a hierarchical system of classification for the animal and plant kingdoms. There were a bunch of Latin names that I never did remember. The system started out with Phylum and worked its way down.

Science
• Phylum
• Class
• Genus
• Species

You can use that same type of system for categorizing similar or like subjects.

Science
• Phylum
• Class
• Genus
• Species

Filing
• Category
• Subcategory
• File
• Subfile

Paper Or Non-Paper

Support Categories are broken down into two types: Paper and Non-paper.

Support Categories	
Paper Categories	Non-paper Categories

Paper is simply a sheet or sheets of paper or anything that fits into a hanging folder. Everything else, including objects, non-paper items, and books, goes into the Non-paper Categories.

Through the years, one of the major complaints I have heard is that items can be filed into more than one location, i.e., more than one Category. This is true, and it can be confusing. You'll continue to be confused until you use the five steps of the In Box. Naming an item (Step 3), especially when you use the first word that comes to your mind, and then relearning it (Step 4) every time you access it or store it will cause you to remember the name of the Category you put it into the last time. After a while you will have trained yourself to think of it with a particular Category name and File.

Another way to become confused as to which Category an item belongs is by not differentiating between Paper and Non-paper Categories. The way many people want to break down or organize their Support Categories is by putting similar types of things into the same Category. This works with the exception of physical objects or Non-paper Category items.

Example

Say you have the following Categories already set up: Reference (general or miscellaneous files that do not easily fit into any of the other existing Categories) and Financial (anything pertaining to money). You have the following:
- A thick book on financial information
- A three-ring binder on financial matters
- Profit and Loss pieces of paper
- A cassette tape about IRAs

Which Categories do they go into? Most people would say Financial because their content is all about financial matters. You want to put similar things together in a subject-based system. However, in most cases above, Financial is the incorrect answer.

Mozart

One of the biggest mistakes people make in the office is to put similar items of a subject together such as all computer items together. Manuals, software, binders, books, tools, mouses (mice?), tapes. Wrong.

If the books are computer books, they go into the Category called Books. You can Subcategorize the Category Books into Computer Books, Training Books, etc. Create as many Subcategories as you wish. But books go into the Books Category.

Another way is to Subcategorize the books alphabetically. Last, and probably least effective, is to throw them up on the shelf in any order that you want. This works only if you have a few books or if you don't look at them a lot. Manuals go with manuals, binders with Binders. This is a very important concept to understand. Many people have the tendency to say if it's financial, regardless of the shape or form it comes in, put it all with Financial. Paper and non-paper do not store or fit well together.

Think about how you store your music collection at home. You have a book on Mozart, two CDs on Mozart, some loose papers about Mozart, cassettes, and long-playing records on Mozart. Do you store all of the items together or do you store the CDs with the CDs, the books on the bookshelf, the cassettes with cassettes and the records with the records? You store them by putting like objects together. If you do it that way at home and it works, why not use the same concept at your office?

> **Question**: When deciding into which Category a book goes, when is a book not a book?
> **Answer**: Never. A book is a book is a book.

6-5
Mozart
Collection

There are Paper and Non-paper items. Paper items are simply pieces of paper. Non-paper items are things such as books, binders, telephones, disks, awards, coffee mugs, and so on—generally items that won't fit in a hanging folder.

Example

Let's go back to our first example with Reference (general files that do not easily fit into any of the other existing Categories) and Financial (anything pertaining to money). You'd put the papers into the Financial Category, all of the financial books into a Category called Books, all of the three-ring binders on financial matters into Binders, and any of the cassettes into the Category called Tapes.

Similar or like types of objects go into their simplest and most basic form. A book is a book is a book.

Example

In Support, you have a Category called Financial, a Category called Reference, and a Category called Forms. Say you have always kept a particular form with your financial stuff. Which Category do you keep the form with in your new system? Reference, Financial, or Forms? You keep it in the Forms Category. It doesn't matter where you previously kept the form, even if it was with financial stuff and it feels most comfortable there. If you start making exceptions, how can you tell which are the exceptions and which aren't? Generally you can't, so there are no exceptions. A form is a form is a form.

Could you have a form in the Reference Category and a form in the Form Category? No. This is how duplication and triplication occurs. A form is a form is a form. The system

> *A form is a form is a form.*

is set up to go as basic as possible. A lot of people make it too complex instead of making it very simple and easy to use.

Say you want to keep that dad-blasted form where you have always kept it, with the Financial stuff. Can you? Absolutely, but only if you don't have a Category called Forms. Any forms that you have can be kept in the Category to which they belong, such as Financial or Training. The File name of the form in Financial would be called Forms. This way no duplication would occur.

> ## Example
>
> You have Categories called Financial, Forms, and Reference. You have ten books. Three of the books are on financial matters. Which Category do the three financial books go into? Reference? Could a big book fit into a hanging folder? Not very well. Financial? Possibly but again a big book would have a hard time fitting into a hanging folder. A book goes where? With other books into a Category called Books on, of all places, the bookshelf. Isn't it nice that they've already named it for you!

Seeing Is Believing

> *The first way you organize anything is visually.*

The first sense we use when we assess anything is sight. Think about meeting someone for the first time. Your first assessment of them, if you've never met them or spoken with them, comes from looking at them. "That guy's goofy-looking." " Nice dresser." "She must have money." The same is true of the initial way in which you assess items in your office, which is by sight.

> ### Exercise
>
> Look at a piece of paper, a book, a VCR tape, a binder, a computer disk, and a knickknack. What do you notice about them? If you tried to store them together would they easily fit? Notice their different sizes and shapes. Now imagine storing all the tapes with the tapes in one area and the binders with the binders. Nice fit.

You Call It Corn, We Call It An A"maize"Ing Mess

Remember the commercial on TV years ago when a beautiful Indian princess was holding a corn on the cob and said, "You call it corn, we call it maize." Thus was created Mazola margarine, normally found in your neighborhood grocery store in the dairy section.

Now, if you went into her teepee and looked into her file cabinet for a file called Corn, would you be able to find it? Probably not. What you would probably find is a file called Maize. What she calls maize, you call corn.

6-6
Teepee

Now you can see why the potential for an a"maize"ing mess is there. When you see an object, a word forms in your brain without even thinking about it. Unfortunately for organizational purposes, everybody sees different words for the same things. Thus differently named files for the same thing can be created. "Where do we file away these articles?" one of my clients asked trying to determine a Category name to use for articles. Many times if we just listen to our thoughts or what comes out of our mouths, the correct name will magically appear.

The fact that everyone names the same thing differently became apparent when I was waiting tables in my restaurant in Atlanta years ago. I had just asked a customer if they would like something to drink. The woman said she would like a Coke, then she said a root beer. I was confused. Did she want a Coke or a root beer?

Growing up on eastern Long Island, we called soft drinks "soda," pronounced "so'der."

Going to college in Iowa, I learned they called the same thing pop. I remember the first time my Uncle Tom, in Michigan, asked me if I wanted

> *Less effort creates more results.*

a "pop." I thought, who does he think he is. I outweigh him by at least 50 pounds. Who is going to "pop" whom around here?

Back to the woman in the restaurant. In the South, I learned that all soft drinks are called "Coke" no matter what is ordered, except for New Orleans, where they say "cold drink." In New Hampshire, they call a soft drink a tonic. I'd be afraid to guess what you got for a gin and tonic up there.

Who's right? Everyone. There is a different voice and a different vocabulary in everyone's head. So unless you know how to use the Vulcan mind meld, the only way this system can work is for everyone to come up with and agree on the same Category and File names and their definitions. If you don't do that, when an emergency occurs and you can't find a file, somebody is going to get an undeserved pop, and I don't mean like in soda.

Many times, getting people to agree is a tough battle. We all think very differently. People often ask me to give them the names of the Categories they should use in their office. If you let go, the names will come. I tell them they need to allow the names to flow from within themselves naturally. Like in the movie *Caddyshack*: "Nah, nah, nah, nah, nah. Be the ball Danny. See the ball." That's why the harder you try, the better sounding you want the names to sound, the more correct you want the words to be, the less chance you'll have of being able to remember them and find what you're looking for. Less effort creates more results.

The best part is you already know the models and are using them every day in your life.

Remember These Concepts

- A Category is a grouping of similar or like things.
- You already know how the Category model works.
- A form is a form is a form.
- The first way you organize anything is visually.
- Less effort creates more results.

Things To Avoid

- Trying too hard to come up with the right word or name.
- Not allowing the first thought that comes into your head to be the name you use.

2.7

Creating Support Categories

Starting Out

- Your First Day At Your New Job
- It Can't Last Forever
- How Do You Create Categories? Let Me Count The Ways
- Congratulations! It's A Category

What You Will Learn In This Chapter

- How to create new Support Categories

💣☀ <u>Myths of the Office</u>

I can instantly find any items in files that are called general, miscellaneous, and other.

Starting Out

Your First Day At Your New Job

It's a new beginning for you. That lunatic you used to call your boss is finally far away from you and harassing other employees. You have a chance to start all over. A new job is about to change your life.

You're dreaming. Pinch yourself and come back to reality. Take a moment and think about what it was like when you first started the job you're in now. Try this exercise.

Exercise

Close your eyes and visualize your office. Imagine looking at it from behind your desk. On one side are your Action Categories (things to do). On the other are your Support Categories (things to refer to). On your Support side, create a basic Category to begin with and work from. All of the other Support Categories that you will create will originate from this one, basic Category. Since it contains items you refer to, call it your Reference Category.

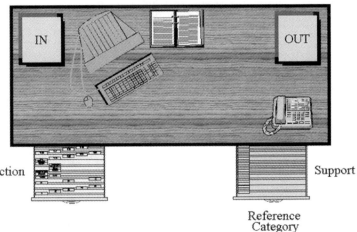

Action

Support

7-1
Starting
Out

Reference
Category

A Reference Category is like a belly button. Everyone has one (except Adam). Reference is the base from which all Support Categories originate. It starts the show. It's the first Support Category.

When you start out, the only Support Category you'll have is the one called Reference. Originally, the Reference Category will have every file that you have in it that is not an Action.

The following are a list of general file names that I started

All Support Categories originate from the Reference Category.

out with when I created my Reference Category. These will give you an idea of what you might want to put into your Reference Category. These worked for me; you get to come up with your own list.

Example

Category	Files
Reference	Accounting
	Advertising
	Car
	Clients
	Computer
	Financial
	Forms
	Legal
	Marketing
	Organizations
	Personal
	P/L
	PR
	Sales
	Stationery
	Telephone
	Travel
	Training
	Vendors

Anything that doesn't easily fit into an existing Category always goes into the Reference Category. That means any miscellaneous or general papers that you don't have a Category for always go into your Reference Category.

When I needed to store any information that I'd refer to, I'd put it into one of the above files. If I had other information to store and it didn't fit into one of the

All Support Files that don't easily fit into an existing Category always go into the Reference Category.

existing files, I'd simply create a new file and add it to my already existing Reference Files, such as the following new files:

- Business license
- Business plan
- Humor
- Printing

You can go on indefinitely and have as many files in your Reference Category as you choose. In fact, your Reference Category can be as many file drawers as you want and as large as you want. A lot of people already follow this method without knowing that they are. They usually use the standard drab olive green hanging folders for all their files.

It Can't Last Forever

After a while, many people find their files get too big as they save endless information they might need in the future. And the longer they are in a job, the more items they will have had access to.

See if any of the following describe the files in your Reference Category:

🖈 They are wider than your Aunt Zelda is after her seventh helping of pumpkin pie. It is way too fat and overflowing with too much clutter in it.

🖈 You can't find everything in five seconds or less in them. In fact, you just broke the all-time company record for not being able to find something in an office. You did give it a valiant try, though. Four hours, 26 minutes is very commendable.

🖈 You have more information in that one file than the Museum of Natural History has on dinosaurs.

🖈 You have an irresistible urge to jam as many manila folders into a hanging folder as possible in order to restore some order to it.

🖈 You can create five or more files from the information that you have in your existing file.

How Do You Create Categories? Let Me Count The Ways

Besides the Reference Category, where do any of the other Categories come from? Say you have a file in your Reference Category called Forms.

When you first started out in your office, you may have had only one form with five copies of the form in your Form file.

If you needed to get a form, you would say:

"Stand, Support, Reference (you only had one Category then called Reference), Forms."

You could find it pretty quickly and easily. All of your Support files would be in your Reference Category.

Now, as time went on, the number of forms grew. The Forms file got enormous! So now instead of having one form and five copies of it in it, you have 15 forms with five copies of each form in there. That's 75 pieces of paper. Will you be able to find a form easily and quickly now? Probably not. What can you do so you find the forms quicker? Create another Support Category. It will be your first offspring.

Congratulations! It's A Category!

How do you come up with your very own, first Support Category other than Reference?

By giving birth to a new Category. Here's how to do it.

1. Decide to have one
2. Be willing to care for it through the work years
3. Be committed to it even during stressful and trying times (there will be many)
4. Make sure you are healthy and of sound mind (there go half of you)
5. Go to the privacy of your office
6. Wear comfortable and loose-fitting clothing
7. Close your door
8. Set the atmosphere with soft light and soft music
9. It is just you and your office...alone
10. Notice the many items in it
11. Notice which are similar and can be put into a group
12. Now a very important step—make a commitment (That's right, guys...and gals!)
13. Come up with a name for the similar items, one that easily comes to your mind, is natural, you really like, makes you feel good all over
14. That name will be your very own first Category
15. Ready?
16. It may hurt
17. Ahhh!
18. You did it
19. Congratulations! You are now the proud parent of a ten-file Category!
20. How does it feel?
21. Hand out your cigars that say, "Congratulations! It's a Category!"
22. Smoking lamp is lit. Light 'em if you got them

Ready for another Category? What will you call this one? Your office really won't be complete until you have a few more!

I know it's a painful process. (Those people who have never given birth to a Category will never really know what real pain is, will they?) It will be easier this time since it will be your second. Deep long breaths. Ready to get started? Here you go.

1. Look at another item
2. Does it fit into your first-born Category? If not, you know what that means
3. Yup. You get to come up with another Category name.
4. You'll now have two Categories. Won't you be proud!
5. Most offices are not really complete unless every single item is in a Category
6. Believe it or not, many offices have over 15 Categories, even today
7. Good luck!

Pull the Form file out of your Reference Category. It's time for it to venture out on its own. What you're going to do is create a new Category called Forms, or whatever name you decide to call it. Choose a color for Forms, say blue. When I fill out forms I feel depressed and blue, so my Forms Category is blue.

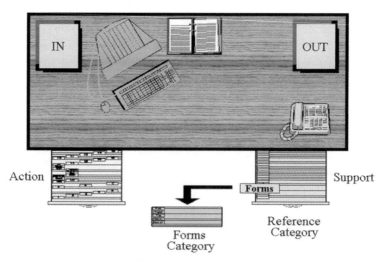

**7-2
Creating
A New
Category**

Color is an easy way to remember the name of a Category. Separate the 15 forms and make a file for each one in your new Forms Category. Simply call the files whatever the form names are or any name that works for you. You now have two Support Categories, Reference and Forms. Every piece of paper that is a Support will go into one of these two Categories.

Now say the number of forms has grown to 30 and you've found that you hand out ten of the forms. You see an advantage by separating them so you pull those ten forms out of the Forms Category and create a new Category. Give it a color, say purple, and give it a Category name. What will you call it? How about Handouts or Handout Forms? Forms that are handed out. It doesn't matter what you call it as long as it is the first word that comes to mind, is easy, and works for you. If you try too hard or want it to sound just too good, it won't work. You'll have a hard time trying to find the file. If the word "stuff" comes to mind, label it "Stuff." People laugh at that, but if it works why fight it? I say stuff a lot. I happen to like the word. I actually saw someone use the word stuff the other day for a file. I was very happy. After many years of doing this, I was glad to finally meet somebody who had the guts to write "stuff."

> *A Category has five or more files in it.*

In order to create more Support Categories, you need to consider a few things.

🗁 **You want to have them.**
Remember, if you choose, you could just have one big gigantic Reference Category. The idea is, when you pick something up from your In Box, a word or name naturally comes to you.

🗁 **You need to have at least five files.**
A new Support Paper Category needs to have five or more files in it. You must be able to create five files from the existing information or foresee having five files. Why five files or more? Hey, it's just a five-fingered rule of thumb. If you just had one file for every Category, you'd have

> *Unlike Paper Categories, you don't need five or more items to create a Non-paper Category.*

hundreds of Categories in your office. If you're going to do that, you might just want to use your Reference Category with hundreds of files. A Category is a grouping together of similar or like items so you can locate them quickly.

Five files are needed for Paper Categories, not Non-paper Categories, which can have any number of files.

📁 **You can not find information in five seconds or less**
If you can't find it in five seconds or less and you want to be able to do so, then break down the Category into a new Support Category.

📁 **The information you have has grown through time**
When you start going through your In Box and find you're receiving more and more information about a subject, then you know it's time to create a new Category.

When you start out in your office, your Action Categories need to be in yellow hanging folders and your Support Categories in various colors. Remember that everything in your office is either an Action or a Support. Otherwise it leaves your office.

It's crucial to understand that everything in your office needs to go into a Category. This means you get to make a decision on everything in your office including the picture on your wall. Many times it's difficult to do this since it requires a decision on items that you have never thought about,

> *Everything in your office needs to be in a Category.*

were just shoved into a drawer, or you have ignored for a very long time. That's all irrelevant. Decide or drown in a sea of information.

After you start creating Categories, any general or miscellaneous files that don't easily fit into any of your other Categories will always go into your Reference Category. The worst thing you can do is to try to force a file into a Category. You'll have as much chance of finding the file as Jacques Cousteau had of finding Atlantis.

Remember These Concepts

- All Support Categories originate from the Reference Category.
- All Support Files that don't easily fit into an existing Category always go into the Reference Category.
- A Category has five or more files in it.
- Unlike Paper Categories, you don't need five or more items to create a Non-paper Category.
- Everything in your office needs to be in a Category.

Things To Avoid

- The urge to create too many Categories. Remember that more is not always better.
- Not putting everything in your office into a Category.

2.8

The File Drawer

How To Set Up Your File Drawers

- What Color Is Your File Drawer?
- Green Is One Of My Favorite Colors
- Left To Right
- Information Mapping
- Road Hogs
- The Simple Way Is Usually The Best Way
- To The Right, Ever To The Right
- And The Band Played On And On And On
- A Short Cut
- Money, Money, Money
- A, B, C, Easy As 1, 2, 3
- One Of The Most Pressing Concerns Today: Tabs On The Front Or The Back?

What You Will Learn In This Chapter

- How to set up your file drawers
- Specific diagrams to show you how to file

☀ <u>Myths of the Office</u>

The tabs go on the back of hanging folders.

How To Set Up Your File Drawers

What Color Is Your File Drawer?

If you have to file, why not make it fun and easy? Each Support Category will have its own color. Colors work for both right- and left-brain people, they are nice to look at, and are easier to initially identify than letters and tabs. Most people don't enjoy looking at that drab, olive color hanging folders usually wear. No wonder no one likes to file! They don't even want to open up the drawer.

Colors are important to your mood and productivity. Imagine how you would feel if the walls in a room in your home were that drab, olive color. You definitely wouldn't want to spend a lot of time in that room. It's no different in your office.

How do you choose a color for your Support Categories? Simply pick a color that reminds you of the Category.

> ## Example
>
> Remember the Category "Countries of the World"? Brown reminds me of land but I personally hate the color (Sorry, President Reagan), so I wouldn't use it. I would pick the color aqua because oceans surround the countries of the world. You have the green Atlantic and the blue Pacific. Blue and green give you aqua. Whenever I saw the color aqua, I'd automatically know the Category is Countries of the World.

Green Is One Of My Favorite Colors

Colors are an easy way to remember Categories.

When I think of money I think about the color green; thus green becomes my Financial Category. As I mentioned earlier, when I get to fill out forms, I get very depressed and blue. So Forms get to be blue. When I think about

Countries Of The World (Aqua)

US
Japan
Germany
France
England
Denmark
China
Chile
Canada
Brazil
Australia
Argentina

8-1
No
Category
Tab

clients, I think about my biggest one, who sells a very popular soda pop, thus red. I used to live in Florida and the orange juice industry did a tremendous amount of public relations. So PR is orange. Reference is gray because gray is kind of bland and a combination of more than one color.

Utilizing colors allows you to eliminate the tab in the front of each Category. No tab is needed to denote Countries of the World, just the color aqua. When you see aqua, you know it is a specific Category, the same way you will know with any of the other colors you use. See Diagram 8-1.

Countries Of The World (Aqua)

US
Japan
Germany
France
England
Denmark
China
Chile
Canada
Brazil
Australia
Argentina

File

8-2
File Tabs

Left To Right

As I mentioned earlier, our culture dictates that we transmit information left to right and top to bottom. We read from the left and from the top. Everyone knows the system.

The same left-to-right concept is true with your filing system. Always start your tab on the far left. Other tabs are lined up directly behind it, all the way to the back of the

Left to right.

Category. Everything but the Category will have a tab—Subcategories, Files, Subfiles, Types, and Subtypes.

When you have too much information in a file and you want to break it down so you can find it quicker, create a Subfile.

That means creating a new tab in the next "lane" to the right and behind the existing file.

Countries Of The World (Aqua)

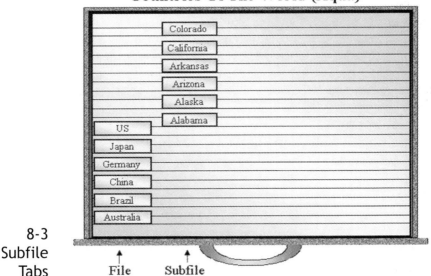

8-3
Subfile
Tabs

On a computer screen we read from left to right and from top to bottom. In a file drawer, we read from left to right and from the front of the drawer to the back. Remember every time you break the file down you create a new tab and move it to the right.

Countries Of The World (Aqua)

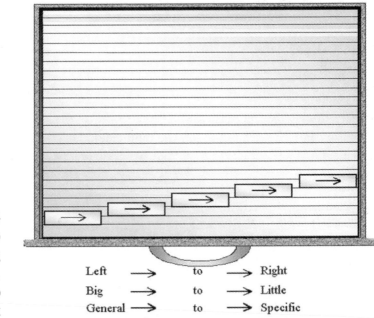

8-4
Left To
Right, Big
To Little,
General To
Specific

Information Mapping

Information mapping is a natural and easy way to understand information. A word or words are written on the left side of a sheet. Everything to the right of it and below it is a description or explanation of the word or words. We scan from the left, see the word and if we want more of an explanation, look to the right and read it.

- Classes →
  - "Raising Responsible Ruffians"
  - "Veg Out In Your Garden"
  - "Underwater Kelp Weaving"

- When →
  - Mondays & Wednesdays at 7:00 PM
  - Tuesdays & Thursdays at 7:30 PM
  - Saturdays at 9:00 AM

- Cost →
  - One Class - $25.00
  - Two Classes - $45.00
  - Three Classes - $65.00

If you look <u>here</u> → Your eye naturally goes here

8-5
Information
Mapping

The same principle works for a filing system. The main tab is all the way on the left. All of the tabs to the right of it and behind it are simply broken down for ease in locating the Subfiles.

Big to little, general to specific.

The way to read information in a drawer is from the left side to the right side, from the big (on the left side) to the little (on the right side), from the general (on the left side) to the specific (on the right side).

You also read a file drawer from the front to the back. The A's start in the front, the Z's (or the last used letter of

Front to back, A to Z.

the alphabet) bring up the rear. In other words, front to back, A to Z. Pretty tough, huh?

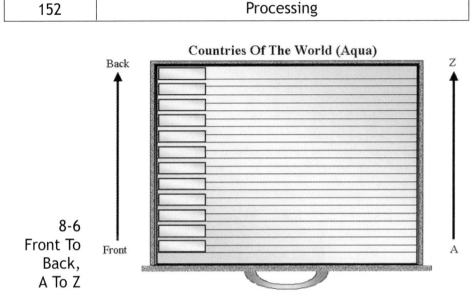

Countries Of The World (Aqua)

**8-6
Front To
Back,
A To Z**

Road Hogs

You're late. You're in the far left passing lane, high-tailing it down the highway. The car in front of you is putting along at ten miles below the speed limit. Now you know why your high beams and horn were invented.

**8-7
Tab Lanes**

Think about the "lanes" in a file drawer being set up the same way lanes are on a major interstate highway. Take I-285, the perimeter surrounding Atlanta. In most places, it's a five-lane highway. A hanging folder is also broken down into five "tab lanes" when you use one-fifth tabs (five of them end to end constitute the width of a hanging folder) which you need to do with this system.

The lane farthest to the left on a highway is the passing lane. If a car is driving along at a leisurely pace in that lane and a car going at a much faster speed comes up behind

Whenever you want to break down a file, create a tab to the right of and behind the existing tab.

it, the front car is supposed to move over to a lane to the right. The idea is that fast moving cars pass on the left and the slow ones drive on the right. Only in a perfect world, though.

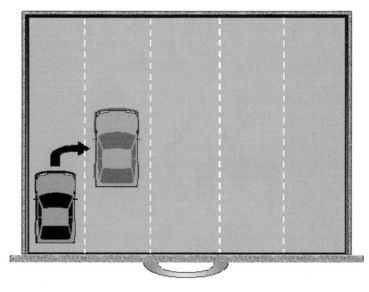

8-8
A Slow Car

The same principle can be used in your filing system. Any time you want to break something down into a smaller part, to explain it or be able to find it quicker, you kind of slow it down and move it from that fast passing lane on the far left over to the slower right lane. The more specific you want it, the more it moves to the right.

Now imagine each type of vehicle being limited to a lane. The cars could only drive in one lane, the buses in one, the trucks in one (preferably on the shoulder or another road), the vans in one, and the motorcycles in one. They would not be allowed to drive in any other lane.

When you are setting up a filing system, it's vitally important to look from the front of the drawer to the back and realize that whenever you Subfile anything, i.e., move it one complete tab to the right, similar types or Subfiles must be in that same "tab lane" of traffic. In a typical hanging folder, there are potentially five "tab lanes" going across from left to right.

The Simple Way Is Usually The Best Way

In Diagram 8-9, all the tabs are lined up to the left. This is the simplest and easiest way to file things. Your drawer will look like this 80 percent of the time when you start out with Categories and Files. Keep it as simple as you can.

Remember the earlier example of Countries of the World? Let's look at that again.

Countries Of The World (Aqua)

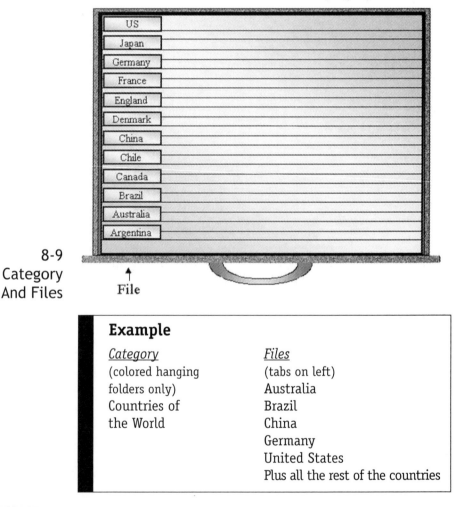

8-9
Category
And Files

↑
File

Example

Category	Files
(colored hanging folders only)	(tabs on left)
Countries of the World	Australia
	Brazil
	China
	Germany
	United States
	Plus all the rest of the countries

To The Right, Ever To The Right

Yes, even liberals must move to the right in this system. Whenever you want to break something down, you always shift it over to the right with a Subfile.

If you want to break the Category down into equally large parts, say, for example, continents, break the Category into Subcategories.

> *To the right, ever to the right.*

Say you constantly looked in your Countries of the World Category and you wanted to be able to find the files even quicker than you can now. The way to do this is to break them down into Subcategories. The Category would be Countries of the World, the Subcategories would be the continents, and the Files would be countries. Every time you break down a Category, the tab always moves one "tab lane" to the right. Left to right. Big to little. General to specific.

What would it look like if you Subcategorized the Category? Notice what happens—the tabs all shift over to the right. North America is on the left. Behind it and one lane over comes the File, United States. Behind the Subcategory South America, the Files would be: Argentina, Brazil, Chile, etc. (See Diagram 8-10.)

Example

Category	*Subcategory*	*File*
Countries of the World	North America	Canada
		Mexico
		United States
	South America	Argentina
		Brazil
		Chile

Countries Of The World (Aqua)

And The Band Played On And On And On

If you wanted to go one step further and break countries down by states, you'd move the tabs over to the right again. Countries of the World (Category), North America (Subcategory), United States (File), Georgia (Subfile).

Category	Subcategory	File	Subfile
Countries	North America	Canada	
of the World		Mexico	
		United States	Alabama
			Alaska
			Arizona

Example

Countries Of The World (Aqua)

8-11 Category, Subcategory, Files, And Subfiles

Could you also do that with Canada? Absolutely. Instead of states it would be provinces.

Category	*Subcategory*	*File*	*Subfile*
Countries	North America	Canada	Ontario
			Nova Scotia

A Short Cut

You will rarely use Subcategories. The first step to breaking a File down will typically be with a Subfile. (See Diagram 8-12.)

Example

Category	*File*	*Subfile*
Countries of the World	United States	Alabama
		Alaska
		Arizona
		Plus all others

Countries Of The World (Aqua)

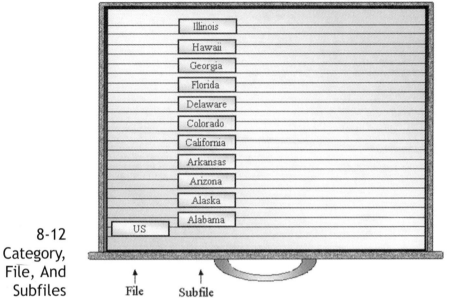

File   Subfile

Money, Money, Money

Anything to do with money, budgets, investments, etc., would go into your Financial Category. Some of the File names might be:

Example

Category	*File*
Financial	Accounting codes
	Bank
	Budget
	Investments
	IRA
	Loans
	P/L
	Savings
	Taxes

Financial (Green)

8-13
Financial
Category
And Files

Say you're at work and you have both business and personal financial information. You can keep it simple and use the Category/File model above or, if you want to split the two areas up, simply Subcategorize them into Business and Personal. Alphabetically, Business would come first.

Category	Subcategory	File
Financial	Business	Accounting codes
		Budget
		P/L
	Personal	Bank
		Investments
		IRA
		Loans
		Savings
		Taxes

Financial (Green)

8-14
Financial
Category,
Subcatego-
ries And
Files

Subcategory   File

Under Business you might have files like accounting codes, budget, and P&L. Notice you don't have to have five files when you use a Subcategory. Only when you're creating a Category do you need five or more files. Staple the Subcategory hanging folders shut. They're now simply dividers. When using Subcategories, you'll generally staple the hanging folder together since everything in them will be broken down and in a hanging folder behind and to the right of the Subcategory tab.

> *You don't have to have five files when you use a Subcategory.*

Expand the Loans File into the two types of Loans that you have: a car loan and a mortgage loan.

Example

Category	Subcategory	File	Subfile
Financial	Personal	Loans	Car
			Mortgage

Financial (Green)

8-15
Financial
Category,
Subcat-
egory,
Files And
Subfiles

Break down mortgage into the two mortgage companies that you might have: one with BancBoston and the other with Countrywide.

Example

Category	Subcategory	File	Subfile	Type
Financial	Personal	Loans	Mortgage	BancBoston
				Countrywide

Financial (Green)

8-16
Financial
Category,
Subcat-
egory,
File,
Subfiles
And Types

If you look at a file only once a year, would you want it broken way down to a Type or simply remain just a File? Probably just a File. The nice thing about the system is you can set it up whichever way you want and change it whenever you want. You can make your system very simple and leave everything in Files or break it into a Subtype, five levels to the right. Since the hanging folder will only handle five one-fifth tabs, you're limited to breaking down information to a Subtype. Five tabs across are very detailed and rare.

A, B, C, Easy As 1, 2, 3

If you use both letters (A-Z) and numbers (1999) in a Category, you need to decide which will come first in the drawer. It doesn't matter as long as you file them consistently. What happens to many people is they aren't sure where to locate files that start with numbers. A simple way is to locate all files starting with numbers in the back.

Financial (Green)

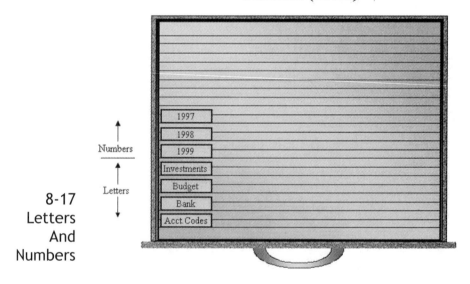

8-17
Letters
And
Numbers

A better way than using numbers is to change the way you say it and list it. If you have something that says 1996 Budget, consider saying it as Budget, 1996. Do it this way with the subject first if it is easy to do. If not, list it the other way.

One Of The Most Pressing Concerns Today: Tabs On The Front Or The Back?

This reminds me of the book, *Gulliver's Travels,* where two countries were at war because of differing opinions on where to crack an egg open, the little end or the big end. With all the important issues that face the world today, where to put tabs— on the front of the hanging folder or the back—is definitely not one of them. However, we still are going to talk about it because it will save you time.

The tabs always go on the front of the hanging folder, not on the back. I used to place them on the back, as many people do, but I found it took an extra step doing it that way. When you want to drop a piece of paper into a file and the tab is on the back, you have to push it back, pull it forward, then push it back to open it. With the tab on the front you simply pull the tab forward with your index finger, opening up the file, and then grab the paper you need or drop in the one you have.

Now, I can just hear some of you saying "Doesn't this guy have anything better to do than worry about where the tab goes?" Let me remind you we only have 24 hours in a day and the game is to do what we enjoy most. Every little bit of time you save while working is that much more time you can spend doing what you enjoy.

Remember These Concepts

- Colors are an easy way to remember Categories.
- Left to right, big to little, general to specific, front to back, A to Z.
- Whenever you want to break down a file, create a tab to the right of and behind the existing tab.
- To the right, ever to the right.
- You don't have to have five files when you use a Subcategory.

Things To Avoid
- Having dissimilar tab types in the same lane when you look down the tab lane row.

2.9

Support Category Examples

Examples Of Categories

- Avoid Them Like The Plague
- Home Sweet Cluttered Home
- Paper Support Category Examples
- Non-paper Support Category Examples

What You Will Learn In This Chapter
- What and how to name your Support Categories

☀ Myths of the Office

I can organize my home but I can't organize my office.

Examples Of Categories

Avoid Them Like The Plague

The first two sections of this chapter discuss Category names that you should never use and names that you can use at home. The latter two sections are specific examples of actual Category names, both Paper and Non-paper, to refer to if you need examples. You may want to skip this latter part and move on to the final chapter in Part 2: Computers and E-mail.

Avoid using the following Category names at all costs.

- MEMOS
- LETTERS
- CORRESPONDENCE

What's wrong with Memos, Letters or Correspondence? As Categories, they are too general and don't define what's in them. They say what they are but not exactly what they are about.

Start with Memos first. What's wrong with filing a memo from your boss under the Category named Memos in a File labeled

Boss (Memos/Boss)? The problem is that the subject of the memos could be about anything. The only thing you know is that it was from your boss. You want your Categories to reflect that they have information about a particular subject. Be very aware of creating terms that are too broad and are not specifically about a grouping of things or a subject.

> ## *This is a subject-based system.*

The same applies to Correspondence or Letters. They're too broadly based. Correspondence or Letters could be any type of correspondence with anybody. The solution is to put them under a specific subject in a file. If you had a letter from a client you would file it under Clients.

> ## Example
> Say a memo came in about a safety procedure from your boss. Rather than filing it under Memos/Boss, you'd put it into the Safety file in the Reference Category (Reference/Safety). If you found you had five or more files about safety, you could create a Category called Safety.

Home Sweet Cluttered Home

This system can be used anywhere. It especially works well at home. Below is a listing of a few possible Home Support Categories you may want to use:

- Reference: General miscellaneous items that don't easily fit into any other Category. At home, this is usually the largest Category

- Financial: Anything to do with money

- House: Information pertaining to your home

- Children: Anything about your kids. Records, report cards, medical visits, etc.

- Yard: Information on landscaping, your lawn, anything outside of your house

- Accounts Paid: All money that you pay out through the year can be broken down into files. This is especially helpful for your taxes at the end of the year with files such as Medical, Childcare, and Mortgage (interest).

At the end of the year, simply take out all the receipts in each file, bind them together or place them in an envelope. Put them into a storage box with the year printed on the top and side of the box and store them away.

Remember the concepts are the same for your house as they are for your office. You get to come up with your own Home Category names.

Paper Support Category Examples

Here are some of my Paper Support Categories with a definition and examples of file names.

◆ Computer: Information about computers in paper form

File examples: Equipment   Software
Internet   Warranties
Mindspring

◆ Public Relations: Ways to promote my company

File examples: Articles   Radio
Photos   TV
Press releases

◆ Marketing: Promotional literature

File examples: Articles   Client list
Biography   Interviews
Brochures

◆ Forms: Sheets with blanks on them not yet filled out—filled-out forms go into another Category.

File examples: Action plan   Preparation
Application   Project Manage-
Itinerary   ment

◆ Testimonial Letters: Letters from satisfied clients that I use to sell my services. They're filed alphabetically with the last name first. Originally, the File Testimonials was in the Category called Marketing. It grew and became its own Category.

File examples:

Bucherati, Steve	Hill, Jackson
Collins, Steve	Landry, Mike
Courtet, Robert	Smith, Betty

◆ Clients: All my current clients. They are filed alphabetically by company name.

File examples:

Equitable	Mississippi Power
Georgia Power	NationsBank
IBM	

◆ Stationery: All paper products

File examples:

Address Labels	Labels
Cards	Letterhead
Envelopes	

◆ Speaking: Anything pertaining to giving speeches

File examples: Closings
Georgia Speakers Association
Introductions
Openings
National Speakers Association

◆ Old Projects: Projects that have been completed or which are not currently active. There are several possibilities on what to do with old projects.

File examples:

Budget	Organizing sales
E.I.S.	Vetter Institute
Goals	of Productivity

◆ Productivity Issues: Information to which I refer relating to topics in my business

File examples:

ADD	Ergonomics
Desks	Right-brain people
Delegation	

Other possible Paper Support Category examples:

- Administration
- Advertising
- Agents
- Brochures
- Classes
- Corporate
- Customers
- Directories
- Education
- Home Office
- Financial
- Insurance
- Investments
- Leases
- Legal
- Literature
- Management
- Managers
- Media
- Organizations
- Partnerships
- Personal
- Policies And Procedures
- P/L
- Presentations
- Promotional
- Publications
- Real Estate
- Regions
- Research
- Seminars
- Software
- Special Events
- Speeches
- Training
- Travel

Or any name that works for you.

Non-paper Support Category Examples

Along with Paper Categories that are composed of pieces of paper that fit into a hanging folder, there are also Non-paper Categories in your office. If you can put information in a hanging folder, do so. The more similar the areas are in which you store information, the easier it will be to find that information.

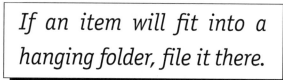

If an item will fit into a hanging folder, file it there.

Non-paper Categories also have files. Each book or binder itself is a file in the Category. Just because it isn't paper or doesn't fit into a hanging folder doesn't mean it's not a file. Most people think about a file being a manila folder or hanging folder. In this system, it's any component or piece in a Category.

Some Non-paper Categories are:

◆ Books: Books are pieces of bound paper—bound for your bookshelf. Once they are on the bookshelf (never on your desk or credenza), you can put similar types of books together by Subcategorizing them. You can do this by keeping them all on one shelf or by using bookends to separate them. You can also just throw them up in no particular order if you don't have that many.

File examples:	Computer books	Insurance books
	Training books	Self-help books
	Financial books	Benefit books

Hint

If you choose, keep your Tool drawer slightly open when you are working so your tools will always be accessible. This allows you to keep them off your desk.

◆ Manuals: Notebooks, binders, instruction booklets, how-to-do books

◆ Binders: Three-ring binders or, as they are sometimes called, three-ring circuses when you try to update them with all the current information they continually throw at you. Binders allow you to take perfectly good pages out and inconveniently replace them with new, revised, more current pages. When adding new pieces of paper, don't forget to three-hole-punch the sheets or with some of the fancier ones, four-, five-, six-, or seven-hole them, which of course, means you need to buy the special hole punch too. Changing paper in binders is one of my favorite ways to watch people waste time. I don't have a single three-ring binder in my office. In case you haven't guessed, I hate them—but please feel free to have as many as you wish.

Question: What's the difference between a manual, book, binder, and notebook?

Answer: What you decide to call them or how you see them.

◆ Notebook: Some people call three-ring binders notebooks.

◆ Drawing: Blueprints

◆ Catalogues: Bound books with soft covers

◆ Tapes: Cassette tapes or VCR tapes

◆ Tools: Items that you use over and over again that allow you to finish the job more quickly. Think of a carpenter using his tools: a level, hammer, saw, plane, nail punch, and a cat's paw. These items are used over and over to make the job easier.

File examples:	Stapler
	Ruler
	Letter opener
	Business card box holder
	Stamp and a pad
	Scotch-tape dispenser

Hand-held recorder
Hole punch
Letter opener
Staple remover
Paper knife

Tools can even be paper items as long as you use them often, such as a phone number list. Even a book that you refer to constantly can be kept in your Tool drawer.

What about a Rolodex? Into your Tool drawer if it will fit or next to your phone if it won't. Put your Tool drawer on the same side as your phone so you can easily look at phone numbers by simply opening your Tool drawer.

Another variation of Tools is:

◆ Maintenance Tools: Tools that you use to repair things

File examples: Screwdriver
Pliers
Channel locks
A hammer

◆ Office: Items that you use up in the office or buy at an office supply store. Duhhh!

File examples:
3 x 5 cards	Markers
Paper	Highlighters
Yellow sticky notes	Paper clips
Business cards	Rubber bands
Pens	Erasers
Pencils	

What's the difference between office supplies and tools? Office supplies go into one drawer and are expendable. Tools go into another drawer and are used over and over.

A carpenter also uses building materials or building supplies. Lumber, shingles, drywall, nails, and Band-Aids when he hits his finger. Building materials or building supplies are items that get used up. So, on one side of your desk, you'll have a drawer called Tools; and on the other side or right below your Tool drawer, you'll have a drawer called Supplies.

In your Supply drawer, keep just one of everything. What you don't want is 30 pens in your drawer. Unless you have the special skill that allows you to use more than one pen at a time, keep only one of each kind or color in the drawer.

Store all excess supplies in a back-up cabinet, area or drawer, and call the Category Back-up Supplies. Or have your assistant

Hint

If you constantly refer to sheets of paper, such as phone numbers, here is a way to take four sheets and make two out of them. Take two sheets of paper and reduce them down so both of them will fit on an 8 1/2" by 11" sheet of paper, long side butting to long side. Do the same with two other sheets. Then put them back-to-back in a plastic sheet protector (a distant relative of the pocket protector) and you will have a one-piece tool for your Tool drawer with information on both sides.

keep them. No need to hoard ten packages of sticky notes. How many can you use at one time? Keep only one small pad and one large pad in your Office Supply drawer. The rest go into Back-up Supplies.

◆ Stationery: Paper items used for writing

File examples: Cards   Thank-you notes
                 Envelope   Writing paper
                 Letterhead

I personally include this Category in the Paper Categories since it's paper and can easily fit into a hanging folder. Storing them in a drawer gets messy, especially when you mix the sheets in with office supplies.

◆ Personal Drawer: Another Category you might want to have would be a Personal drawer. Any Non-paper items that are personal in nature go into it.

File examples: Food (Including crackers and
                   microwaveable popcorn)
                 A plastic silverware packet
                 Salt and pepper
                 Lip gloss and makeup
                 Purse
                 Contact lenses and solution
                 Hair net
                 A comb
                 Gum
                 Photos
                 Your keys
                 Small knickknacks
                 Change
                 Some people put their toothbrush (with
                   out a holder or container, yuck!) and
                   toothpaste in it.

◆ Food Drawer: In all my travels, I have only encountered three of these. If you have that much food, by all means make it a Category. I was very sure what their favorite pastime was after seeing how much food they had in their drawer.

File examples: Crackers
                 Artificial sweeteners
                 Microwaveable popcorn

Coffee cup
Plastic silverware packet
Salt and pepper
Gum
Napkins
Anything edible

Do some of these look familiar from another Category? Remember, anytime you have a bunch of similar items you can create a new Category with them.

◆ Memorabilia: Items of no real value except to the owner. Sometimes called mementos, knickknacks, toys, and junk. Whatever word you want to use to describe them is fine. These are kept out on a shelf or on a credenza. (Never on the desk!)

File examples: Awards   Pictures
                 Trinkets   Trophies
                 Knickknacks   Coffee cups

◆ Diskettes: Can be stored in a cabinet, container, or drawer

◆ Software: Any programs that are used with your computer

◆ Equipment: A large piece of technology

File examples: Computer   Printer
                 Phone   Facsimile
                                   machine

◆ Furniture: Any real big piece in your office

File examples: Credenza   End table
                 Chairs   Tables
                 Desk

◆ Decorations: Things that make your office pretty

File examples: Art work   Flower arrange-
                 Vases   ments
                 Pictures   Plants

By now you are thinking "Who the heck cares about these Categories? Why do I have to have stupid Categories such as Furniture or Decorations?" The answer is that it is vitally important that everything in your office be decided on and assigned to a Category. If one item remains unassigned, with no decision made, it creates the opportunity for you to stop deciding on everything. It's like those potato chips—you won't stop with just one. Before you know it, you'll have an unruly gang of rebel papers terrorizing your office. Then a pile of undecided, shuffled paper begins to develop. And it's all down hill from there.

Remember These Concepts

- This is a subject-based system.
- If an item will fit into a hanging folder, file it there.

Things To Avoid
- Not putting everything into a Category.

2.10

Computer/E-Mail

Your Computer Files

- Mine Eyes Have Seen The Clutter And The Coming Of The Computer
- Compute This
- Will You Be Driving Alone Or With Someone Else?
- An Explorering We Will Go: Windows 95, 98, and NT
- The Models
- Scanners
- Tag, You're It
- E-Mailed Me
- How To Save An E-Mail
- Setting Up Your System

What You Will Learn In This Chapter
- How to align your computer files with your paper files
- How to instantly access your computer files
- How to create one system that totally aligns your computer files with your paper files, Central Files, e-mail, and your long-term storage

---

Myths of the Office

My computer files could never match my paper files.

Your Computer Files

Mine Eyes Have Seen The Clutter And The Coming Of The Computer

After working with clients for a number of years, I discovered a shocking secret. Many of their computers were in worse shape than their offices and that was saying a lot, considering the offices I've seen.

I was once featured on the five o'clock news for a local TV station. The station was to film me as I toured and commented on the condition of their station. As I walked through the station, I noticed one of the beat reporters actually had paper stacked over six feet high on his desk against the wall. They did the story on me, shot the guy's desk, and then on the news, actually admitted they didn't doctor his desk in any way. Finally, truth from the media. I'm not sure I would have been man enough to look at his computer files after seeing the condition of his office.

Another time I had an appointment with a mortgage banker from Chicago in his one-room office. I had to carefully walk on paths to get to his desk. Other than on the paths and behind his desk, there was paper literally covering his entire floor, in some places over two feet high. He also had about seven or eight four-drawer file cabinets randomly situated around the room, stuffed to the gills. I left stating the training would take more than the usual day that I had mentioned on the phone (more like a month!). I didn't even consider organizing his computer. I am, after all, only a mortal.

Many people's computers are more cluttered than their offices. When people talk about being disorganized, they generally mean the paper in their office. They wouldn't even consider mentioning their computer. It's a deep, dark secret they never want anyone to find out. Yet, if they don't have a system for paper, why expect one for their computer? Some people can actually find items in those giant stacks of paper on their desks faster than they can in their computers. Considering how long it takes to find anything on their desk, they'd be lucky to find it in their computer in less than an hour.

10-1
Your
Secret
Fear

Compute This

I once explained to a computer consultant that I could show him how to align his computer files with his paper files. He said it would be worth a million dollars if I could. I showed him but somehow he never managed to send the million. He learned an extremely valuable system of how to align computer files with paper files. So instead of having to use two separate systems, the same system could be used for both.

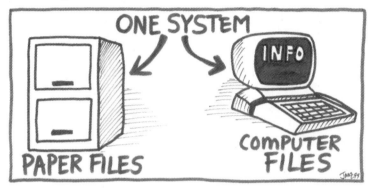

10-2
One
System

Surprisingly, many people think the system in their computer should be totally different than the one they use for their paper. Or worse yet, no thought is given to how the computer should be set up. It just happens. A totally different system or possibly no system at all is used to find documents. Unfortunately, "Find" is used all too often and takes way too much time.

I'm always amazed when I see file numbers on the bottom of computer documents signifying how to locate the document. Instead of using the same simple system you use with your paper, numbers and indexes are used. This forces you to refer to a document list to look up the location of the folder or to reference the old sheet with the folder number on it.

10-3
Computer-
Indexed
System

Your goal is to create a system that aligns your computer files with your paper files so you can process, store, and access information utilizing the same system in both your computer and paper file systems.

Will You Be Driving Alone Or With Someone Else?

The first question you need to ask yourself is whether you're on a network. A network simply means that your computer is hooked up with one or more other computers. If you are, you need to decide on which drive you will be storing your files: a shared drive or your own C: drive. Matt Huet, a well-known computer consultant, advises storing your personal files on the network in the personal space provided for you, since many networks back up their files nightly.

Many people store their personal files on their C: drive. This is great, except C: drives are not usually backed up like networks are. Whether you're on your own or on a network, it's extremely wise to use a backup program. Remember, whatever you don't back up you are in danger of losing.

An Explorering We Will Go: Windows 95, 98, And NT

Through my travels, I've discovered that many people have never heard of Windows Explorer. I figured out how to store information in the computer in a nontraditional way using Windows Explorer since I had never had any computer courses. Many computer people teach a different way. I like Windows Explorer since it works well with the Category/File model.

What follows is a way to align your paper files with your computer files.

Windows 95, Windows 98, and Windows NT are very similar. In all three you will be using Windows Explorer. Windows Explorer is nothing more than a big listing of all the places you can store files or documents. It's like a directory or an index in a book; it will tell you where

> *Using Windows Explorer is the quickest way to find anything.*

to find your files. Think of each yellow file folder on the left as a separate drawer with files contained in each folder. It works exactly like a file drawer. Select the folder and all of the files in it will appear. To open a file, double-click it, and you will be able to find your files in seconds. In Windows 3.1 or Windows for Workgroups version 3.11, Windows Explorer was called File Manager, a perfect name since it was a way to manage all your files.

Picture how Windows 95, Windows 98, and Windows NT work. Typically, on the bottom left of your screen, you have a Start button on your Task bar. Select the Start button. A drop-down menu will appear, except this one goes up. Select Programs. Click it or hold your mouse there for a second. A second set of dialogue boxes will appear to the right listing more of your programs. If you can't find Windows Explorer in those boxes, select the arrows on the right in those boxes and a third listing of boxes will appear. Find and double-click Windows Explorer.

Scroll to the top of the split bar, which is the main vertical bar. Look to the left. The first item at the top left of it will be an icon with Desktop printed to the right of it. Under that and to the right will be an icon of a computer accompanied by the words My Computer. Under that your drives will be listed as: A:, B:, and C:. Generally you will store documents on the C: drive or a specified drive on your network.

Under and to the right of the C: drive will be a vertical row of yellow folders. Each of the folders will consist of the various programs or software applications you have in your computer, such as Lotus Notes, Mavis, Microsoft Office, or Quicken. Under these folders to the right will be more folders, and then even more to their right. The folders go from the left to the right, the general to the specific, and the big to the little. Haven't we heard this before?

Your computer and paper use the same model. Left to right. General to specific. Big to little. The only difference is you read a computer screen from the top to the bottom like you do a book. In a file drawer, you read from the front of the drawer to the back of the drawer.

Your goal is to be able to store all your files in one main yellow folder or directory. This is very helpful when backing up the files in

> *Left to right, big to little, general to specific.*
>
> *Front to back (file drawer), top to bottom (computer).*

your computer. You need to create a folder under your C: drive called _Support. The goal is to list all your Paper Support Categories under that one yellow folder called _Support. For example: Articles, Clients, Financial, Training, Workshops will all have their own yellow file folders and will go under and to the right of the _Support yellow file folder. Under the folder Workshop, you'll have all the documents or file names of your workshops on which you have information.

Exercise

Now is a great time to create your new yellow folder or directory called _Support.

1. First select your Start button.
2. Scroll up to Programs.
3. Find Windows Explorer and select it. (Another way to do this is to right-click your Start button. Windows Explorer will appear. Select it.
4. Select the drive you will be storing your files on, which normally will be C:.
5. Once you've selected the drive, go to the Menu bar and select File. A pull-down menu will appear.
6. Select New or rest your mouse on it for a second. A pull-down menu to the right of it will appear.
7. Select Folder. Click it.
8. At the bottom of all the file folders to the right of your split bar, a selected folder will appear with a blinking cursor, asking for a name. Since it's already selected, simply type in _Support. (That is an underscore preceding Support. Use your Shift key when typing it.)
9. Press Enter.
10. Select the drive you're working in.
11. Click the box to the left of of the icon of the drive you're in so the + symbol appears.
12. Next select View on the Tool bar. The pull-down menu will appear.
13. Select Refresh. Or you can press F5, which will also alphabetize the listing of folders. The underscore symbol allows _Support to appear at the beginning of the alphabet or at the top of the list of folders. It's easier to see there.

You now have a brand-spanking-new folder called _Support which appears at the top of all the directories or yellow folders. Your new folder will appear in your Windows Explorer under the C: drive. Take a look to make sure it's there. All the documents you store in your computer from now on will be in that one folder or directory—a very easy and convenient place to look as well as back up.

Exercise

Next type in all your Category names under your new directory or folder called _Support.

1. Select your new folder _Support. Follow the same procedure you used above for creating a new directory or folder.
2. Go to the top and select File on your Tool bar. A pull-down menu will appear.
3. Select New or rest your mouse on it for a second. A pull-down menu to the right of it will appear.
4. Select Folder. Click it.
5. At the bottom of all the file folders, a selected folder will appear waiting for a name. Since it's already selected, simply type your first Category name, Reference.
6. Press Enter.
7. Select the drive you are working in.
8. Next select View on the Tool bar. The pull-down menu will appear.
9. Select Refresh. The new directory will appear in its proper place. You might want to wait until you type in all your Category names and alphabetize them only once.

Your new folder, Reference, will appear in Windows Explorer under the _Support folder. Take a look to make sure it's there. All the documents you store under Reference will go into that one folder (Category).

After you've typed in all your Category names and created directories or folders with them, you get to move all your documents from all of the different software programs. The file folders (Categories) will be listed alphabetically under the _Support folder, which now will be on the top of the list of all other folders.

You'll need to go through any directories or folders under the C: drive in which you've been storing files. Some people store some of them under My Documents, some under the specific program, such as Word, WordPerfect, Excel, or Corel Draw. Your mission is to gather all documents that are not part of that software or program and relocate them under the appropriate Category folder. That means any files that were created by man, woman, or robot need to be moved from where they are currently stored.

Note

Each application has its own file icons or file extensions. What that means is the icon or specific ending is used by the computer to identify it from other files. Do not go on a mindless moving spree and clean out every document in the application. If you try to move any of the application's documents from it, you may disable your application.

Example

For instance, if you are in the Word for Windows application, there will be an icon with a W on it signifying a Word document. Or the endings you'll want to move or drag and drop will end in .doc. Each application has its own icon or file extension. Move only those files or documents that have a W or a .doc on them. Files that end in .exe or those you don't understand shouldn't be touched or moved. If you feel the need to move a file and you're not sure, check your software manual.

Simply select the folder you want moved by dragging it and dropping it into the appropriate folder (Category).

The Models

Let's take a look at the comparison between the model used for paper and the one used for your computer. The concept is the same. The farther to the right you go, the more the file will be broken down into specifics. First, let's examine the paper model.

There are five models for paper, from basic to more detailed. This should look familiar because it was covered in Part 2, Chapters 6 and 7.

Paper Model #1

The simplest form is a Category with Files.

- Category
- File

Example

An example of a Category would be Financial; its Files would contain anything pertaining to finance. The Financial Category will be used for all the following models.

Category: Financial
     Files: 🗀Accounting codes
                🗀Bank
                🗀Budget
                🗀IRA
                🗀Loans
                🗀P/L
                🗀Savings
                🗀Taxes

▤ Paper Model #2

The next model would be a Category, Subcategories, and Files.

- Category
- Subcategory
- File

Example

Category: Financial
Subcategory: 🗀Business
     Files: 🗀Accounting codes
             🗀Budget
             🗀P/L
Subcategory: 🗀Personal
     Files: 🗀Bank
             🗀IRA
             🗀Loans
             🗀Savings
             🗀Taxes

▤ Paper Model #3

The next model would be a Category, Subcategories, Files, and Subfiles.

- Category
- Subcategory
- File
- Subfile

Example

Category: <u>Financial</u>
Subcategory: ⌂Business
Files: ⌂Accounting Codes
⌂Budget
⌂P/L
Subcategory: ⌂Personal
Files: ⌂Bank
⌂IRA
⌂Loans
Subfiles: ⌂Car
⌂Mortgage

▤ Paper Model #4
The next model would be a Category, Subcategories, Files, Subfiles, and Types.
- Category
- Subcategory
- File
- Subfile
- Type

Example

Category: <u>Financial</u>
Subcategory: ⌂Business
Files: ⌂Accounting Codes
⌂Budget
⌂P/L
Subcategory: ⌂Personal
Files: ⌂Bank
⌂Ira
⌂Loans
Subfiles: ⌂Car
⌂Mortgage
Types: ⌂BancBoston
⌂Countrywide

▤ Paper Model #5

The last model would be a Category, Subcategories, Files, Subfiles, Types, and Subtypes.

- Category
- Subcategory
- File
- Subfile
- Type
- Subtype

You can use five tabs across if you're using one-fifth tabs. A Subtype would be in the farthest position on the right. I've never gone that far to the right although a president and a CEO of a convenience store chain once went to four tabs. I was surprised; I expected them to be less detailed than that since they were the bigwigs. By the way, I just learned where "bigwig" came from. In revolutionary times, the bigger your wig, the more powerful and rich you were. And where do you think they powered their wigs? In the powder room. And who goes to the powder room now? We lost another one guys.

Example

Category:	<u>Financial</u>
Subcategory:	⬛Business
Files:	⬛Accounting Codes
	⬛Budget
	⬛P/L
Subcategory:	⬛Personal
Files:	⬛Bank
	⬛Ira
	⬛Loans
Subfiles:	⬛Car
	⬛Mortgage
Types:	⬛BancBoston
	⬛Countrywide
Subtypes:	⬛Payment
	Schedules
Files:	⬛Savings
	⬛Taxes

Now let's look at the structure in the computer. The model you used for paper is the same model you'll use with the computer. The 🖳 symbol will represent the computer model. The model for the computer starts the same way as the paper one does, simple and basic, and then gets larger and more complicated.

🖳 Computer Model #1

Go to Windows Explorer and notice how Windows Explorer is set up. Notice the similarities with the previous paper models. It starts off with a drive where you store your documents. Under the drive are the directories.

- Drive
- Directory

Say the directories in the C: drive here are: Chessmaster 3000, Mavis, MS Office, and Quicken.

> ## Example
>
> Drive: ▢ C:
> Directory: __ ▢ Chessmaster 3000
>   __ ▢ Mavis
>   __ ▢ MS Office
>   __ ▢ Quicken

Now let's add a new directory or folder called _Support. This will be the one location where all your documents and files will be stored.

I'm always amazed that people store their documents in multiple directories and then try to guess where they're stored. Documents they created in Corel Draw are stored in Corel Draw; anything created in Word is stored in Word; and so on. Doing it this way can be compared to going through an additional layer of middle management. (And you know what eventually happens to middle management.)

The most common way many people locate a document using this method is by first going into an application. They select Open on the Menu bar or the Open icon on the Tool bar. When a dialogue box appears, they select a drive, scroll through all the directories, finally find the directory or folder the document was created in, then work their way down to locate the document. This is like going to four bookstores to buy a book rather than calling ahead and checking to see who currently has the book in stock.

Instead of trying to find the document under the application where it was created, do it the easy way. Locate the file under the folder (Category) pertaining to that subject. Go into Windows Explorer. Then go to the drive in which you store all your documents, say the C: drive. Select _Support, which is the only directory or folder where you will be storing documents in. Select the folder (Category) and under it will be your document.

Imagine creating a document in Excel. Say it's a document that relates to a specific subject that's stored in another application. How will you know where to look in Excel to find that particular document? If it's in the folder (Category) relating to what it's about, you'll be able to find it in seconds.

Getting back to our model, here's what it will look like with the directory _Support added.

Example

Drive: ☐ C:
Directory: __ ☐ _Support
__ ☐ Chessmaster 3000
__ ☐ Mavis
__ ☐ MS Office
__ ☐ Quicken

🖥 Computer Model #2

Now let's add another level of folders to the model. This next row of folders are called Categories. Keep your computer folders alphabetically listed the same way you position your paper files in the drawer.

- Drive
- Directory
- Category

Example

Drive: ☐ C:
Directory: __ ☐ _Support
Category: __ ☐ Financial
__ ☐ Chessmaster 3000
__ ☐ Mavis
__ ☐ MS Office
__ ☐ Quicken

🖳 **Computer Model #3**

Next add Subcategories.
- Drive
- Directory
- Category
- Subcategory

> ## Example
>
> | | |
> |---|---|
> | Drive: | 📁 C: |
> | Directory: | __ 📁 _Support |
> | Category: | __ 📁 Financial |
> | Subcategory: | __ 📁 Business |
> | | __ 📁 Personal |
> | | __ 📁 Chessmaster 3000 |
> | | __ 📁 Mavis |
> | | __ 📁 MS Office |
> | | __ 📁 Quicken |

🖳 **Computer Model #4**

Now add Files.
- Drive
- Directory
- Category
- Subcategory
- File

> ## Example
>
> | | |
> |---|---|
> | Drive: | 📁 C: |
> | Directory: | __ 📁 _Support |
> | Category: | __ 📁 Financial |
> | Subcategory: | __ 📁 Business |
> | File: | __ 📁 Accounting codes |
> | | __ 📁 Budget |
> | | __ 📁 P/L |
> | | __ 📁 Personal |
> | | __ 📁 Bank |
> | | __ 📁 IRA |
> | | __ 📁 Loans |
> | | __ 📁 Chessmaster 3000 |
> | | __ 📁 Mavis |
> | | __ 📁 MS Office |
> | | __ 📁 Quicken |

You can extend the folders to the right as far as you'd like. They just keep shifting to the right the same way your paper files do.

🖥 Computer Model #5
Now add Subfiles.
- Drive
- Directory
- Category
- Subcategory
- File
- Subfile

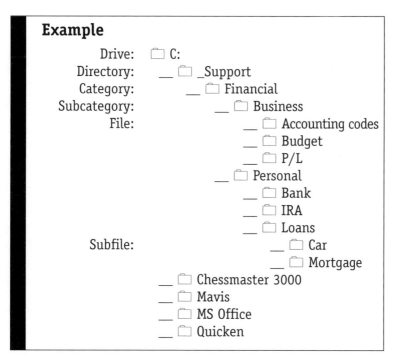

> ## Example
>
> | | |
> |---:|:---|
> | Drive: | 🗀 C: |
> | Directory: | __ 🗀 _Support |
> | Category: | __ 🗀 Financial |
> | Subcategory: | __ 🗀 Business |
> | File: | __ 🗀 Accounting codes |
> | | __ 🗀 Budget |
> | | __ 🗀 P/L |
> | | __ 🗀 Personal |
> | | __ 🗀 Bank |
> | | __ 🗀 IRA |
> | | __ 🗀 Loans |
> | Subfile: | __ 🗀 Car |
> | | __ 🗀 Mortgage |
> | | __ 🗀 Chessmaster 3000 |
> | | __ 🗀 Mavis |
> | | __ 🗀 MS Office |
> | | __ 🗀 Quicken |

🖥 Computer Model #6
Now add Types.
- Drive
- Directory
- Category
- Subcategory
- File
- Subfile
- Types

Example

Drive:	📁 C:
Directory:	__ 📁 _Support
Category:	__ 📁 Financial
Subcategory:	__ 📁 Business
File:	__ 📁 Accounting codes
	__ 📁 Budget
	__ 📁 P/L
	__ 📁 Personal
	__ 📁 Bank
	__ 📁 IRA
	__ 📁 Loans
Subfile:	__ 📁 Car
	__ 📁 Mortgage
Type:	__ 📁 BancBoston
	__ 📁 Countrywide
	__ 📁 Chessmaster 3000
	__ 📁 Mavis
	__ 📁 MS Office
	__ 📁 Quicken

Scanners

The paperless office probably won't occur in your lifetime, but you can save on paper cuts and reduce a majority of clutter in your office by using a scanner. A scanner digitally captures a picture of the printing or graphic on a piece of paper and reproduces it in your computer. Once it's in there, you can make edits or change any of the information, depending on the scanner. Having the information in one source, i.e., the computer, will eliminate a tremendous amount of clutter and paper in your office.

Tag, You're It

It used to be that if you needed to talk with someone, you'd be the one who was responsible for getting a hold of him or her. The ball would be in your court, since you initiated the action, to keep the initiative and be responsible for reaching that person. Today, you can transfer that responsibility by leaving a voice mail or e-mail. It's as if I said, "The ball is in your court. I contacted you last. It's up to you to get a hold of me." Yikes! Today, due to the technology, the responsibility is forced on the other person.

From an April 4, 1997, edition of *PC Week*: A survey of a cross-section of Fortune 500 manufacturing and services companies by Ed Wel & Co. Inc., a Chicago-based consulting and training firm, found high levels of inefficiency in the e-mail messages being sent in corporate America today.

According to a recent study, the average e-mail user receives about 30 messages a day and spends an average of over an hour just reading those messages. When you consider that half of those messages require a response—and often an in-depth response—it's not uncommon for an e-mail user to spend a quarter of the day reading and responding to internal communication. The study also reports that 65 percent of all e-mail messages fail—that is, leave the receiver unable to act without first getting more information.

Some people press the Button of Doom—the Forward All button—any time they wish, which can create hours of wasted time forcing everyone to read or, minimally, delete all those unnecessary messages. It's vitally important that your people are trained as to when or when not to use e-mails. Voice mail can be used in many cases rather than e-mail. It's easier for me to hear brief information than to read an e-mail. It's also a lot quicker for me to talk than to type. Boundaries, once again, are the issue with some people regarding e-mails.

E-Mailed Me

Okay, you're now using the same system for both your paper and computer files. Can you, by any chance, use it for your e-mail too? Absolutely. The problem is that many people use yet another system for their e-mail that does not even remotely resemble their other systems.

First and foremost, though, your goal is not to save e-mails, but rather to clean them out the same way you clean out your In Box.

Most of the e-mail programs allow you to add folders. You can add names to categorize the temporary Action e-mails you keep. Some programs have a Send, Wastebasket, In Box—names that hopefully look familiar. If you find you need to temporarily save a few of the messages, use the same system you've been using to process, store, and access your computer and paper files with OATS.

The idea is to direct e-mails to one of four places using the OATS system.

Your e-mail	The Concept
Out or Sent	Out Box
Action (Create folders for temporary file storage.)	Action
Trash or Wastebasket	Trash
Support (Don't keep them here. Save them to your hard drive.)	Support

✔ Out Box

The first place e-mails can go is to someone else. The goal is still to get everything out of your In Box and office, and that includes e-mails too. They can be forwarded to someone else.

✔ Trash

Trash your e-mails by deleting them. Every application has a Wastebasket or Trash where you can drag and drop the e-mails when you want them to vamoose.

✔ Action

In your e-mail, on the list of folders on the left, you can create more folders. If you're in the process of using certain e-mails as a part of a project, or something you're working on requires a lot of sending and receiving, you can create a folder called Action. If you have several projects, break them down by the name of the Action Categories.

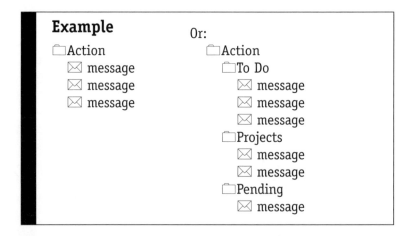

Example

Or:

◻Action
   ⊠ message
   ⊠ message
   ⊠ message

◻Action
   ◻To Do
     ⊠ message
     ⊠ message
     ⊠ message
   ◻Projects
     ⊠ message
     ⊠ message
   ◻Pending
     ⊠ message

Remember, the fewer e-mails you store, the better. Your goal is to empty your e-mail In Box the same way you empty your paper In Box.

✔ Support

You don't want to store files in your e-mail that are Support. If you do, all you'd be doing is creating yet another place to look for Support information besides your paper and computer systems. You'll definitely want to save some of your e-mails and/ or their attachments for referencing later. You can do that by getting them out of your e-mail program and moving them to your Support directory on your hard drive.

How To Save An E-mail

You just received an e-mail that you want to save for future reference. Where, oh, where can you store it? You'll save your e-mail on your hard drive in your computer under _Support under the appropriate Category folder, the same way you'd save it in your paper system.

To save an e-mail:

1. Open the e-mail or attachment.
2. Go to your Menu Bar.
3. Depending upon the e-mail program you're using, you'll need to select different choices from Menu bars. In some you need to select File, then Save As. When a dialogue box appears, you need to locate the C: drive, _Support, and the directory or folder (Category) you wish to save it in. Then type the file name and add .doc in the blank space if you use Word. In Lotus Notes, select Export. You'll need to experiment with how to save it with your particular application.

By the way, when you send an e-mail, use the same format that you'd use for sending a memo. (Part 2, Chapter 1.)

Setting Up Your System

You now have everything you need to align your computer documents with your paper files.

Exercise

Your goal is to align your computer documents with your paper files. Here's how to set up your system in your computer:

1. If you haven't made a list of your Categories, do so now.
2. Type in _Support or any other name as the directory or folder where you'll be storing your files or documents.
3. Type all your Categories into your computer under the _Support folder. Remember, Reference is where you store miscellaneous documents that don't easily fit into the other Categories.
4. Type in any new document names under the appropriate Category in your computer.
5. Look through all of your applications and move or drag and drop all the files you have created, making sure they aren't part of an application. This way, all documents that were created by you or someone else will be under one folder. To select one, simply decide which Category it goes into and drag and drop it. Many times you'll need to open the folder on the left side of the split bar so you'll have the folder you want available when dragging and dropping it.

Depending upon the e-mail program you're using, there are different ways to add folders on the left side if you will be temporarily storing e-mails under Action.

You're now using the same system for your paper, computer, and e-mail. Your Paper Categories and Files should be aligned with your computer folders. Will your computer documents match your paper documents exactly? I hope not, unless you like to duplicate everything. You'll have some paper files that aren't in your computer, some computer documents that you won't have in paper, and some in both.

Example

You may have paper files that you don't want on your computer. Why?

- You may decide not to type the paper files into your computer and leave them as paper files.

- If you don't have a scanner and can't scan the paper in, you'll keep them as a paper file.

- If you use a paper file frequently, such as a form, you may want to print a few out and keep them handy in a paper file rather than having to print them out each time.

You definitely won't have a paper file for every computer document. When you need a hard copy of a computer document, simply print one out.

Finally, if you want to speed up the process of saving files (using Save or Save As), go through the following exercises, which show you how to make changes in various programs.

Exercise

Word

Go to your Menu bar or, by now, any bar you can find. Select Tools, select Options. A dialogue box will appear. Select the File Locations tab. Under File types:, select Documents. This is where your computer is saving documents for you now. Select the Modify button. A Modify Location dialogue box will appear. In the blank area to the right of Look in:, type the drive, such as C:_Support. All of your Support Categories will now be listed under C:_Support. The folder name at the bottom should say C:_Support.

When you make these changes, the document is automatically saved to _Support with a listing of your Categories under it. Simply select the Category in which you wish to store your files, and type the file name you want to name it. Then select the Save button.

Excel

Go to your Menu bar, select Tools, select Options. An Options dialogue box will appear. Select the General tab. Go to Default file location: and in the blank area to the right, type in C:_Support. Select the Okay button.

Power Point

Go to your Menu bar; select Tools, select Options. An Options dialogue box will appear. Select the Advanced tab. Go to Default file location: and type in C:_Support. Select the Okay button.

The more you can do this with all of your programs, the easier it will be to Save files to C:_ Support and your Categories.

Remember These Concepts

- Using Windows Explorer is the quickest way to find anything.
- Left to right, big to little, general to specific.
- Front to back (file drawer), top to bottom (computer).

Things To Avoid

- Using different names for the same file in your paper and computer files.

3.1

Action Categories

Action Categories

- Lights! Office! Action!
- Who Cut The Cheese...Out?
- Days Of Future Past

What You Will Learn In This Chapter

- A new approach on getting work done in the office
- Four new ways to work

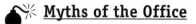 **Myths of the Office**

Hey, I'm a salesperson. I'm not supposed to be organized.

Action Categories

Lights! Office! Action!

Part 2 covered a system of how to Process information. Part 3 will cover a system of how to work in the office—in other words, how to Produce. This chapter shows you how to break out of the old, self-defeating, time-based way of working and learn a fresh, new method for working in the Information Age.

During the War Between the States, along with getting the most troops to the scene of the battle fastest, communication and troop-positioning was key. Being aware of the enemy position and its numbers were vital in achieving victory. The cavalry acted as the eyes and ears for the army. If they didn't accurately report the enemy troop numbers and positions, the army would be at a great disadvantage. Imagine going into battle and not knowing who your enemy was, how many of them there were, and how they were forming to attack you. Your chance of victory would be greatly diminished.

When you approach your work from a time-based, urgency, today, tickler mentality, you are not positioning yourself to be completely aware of your enemy, which is all the work you have to do. If, however, you break your work down into various approaches or ways to work, it will be much more manageable and less stressful.

When I talk about this new approach in my workshops, I often feel like Columbus did as he tried to prove the earth was round. The sheer terror of sailing off the edge of the world was too much for most people of his time; they decided to avoid long trips and were content to leave things as they were. The same could be said today of many people's reluctance to change how they work. Unfortunately, most of us won't have a choice, due to the tidal wave of information that will soon flood into our lives.

I believe there is a whole New World of how to work to explore. Your ship may be rocked to the point of capsizing with this new approach, but, rest assured, there is a life preserver out there for you if you decide to embark on the voyage. In fact, there will be calm waters and smooth sailing beyond the initial turbulence—smoother than you ever realized was possible.

Who Cut The Cheese...Out?

Years ago, the ADA (American Dietician Association) came up with a chart illustrating the four basic food groups: dairy, meat and poultry, whole grains, and fruits and vegetables. (Five

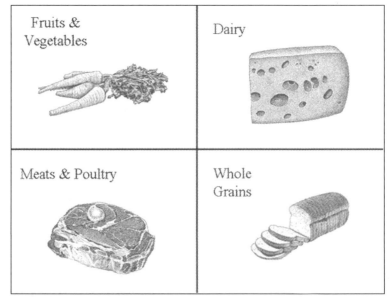

1-1
Four
Quadrants
Of Food

servings a day of vegetables. Yeah, right.) Now they insist there are five food groups with the fifth one being fats. I love the discipline and exactness of science.

Imagine creating a new diet. The dairy diet! Just what we need, another diet. Say you got up in the morning and for breakfast you had a bowl of cottage cheese and a big glass of whole milk. For lunch you had some yogurt and a glass of chocolate milk. Dinner came and you ate three types of cheese: Swiss, cheddar, and Muenster (like in Herman) and a glass of eggnog (no, it doesn't have to be Christmas). That night, when it was snack time, you had a large bowl of ice cream with whipped cream piled high on it and a glass of skim milk, since you thought you just might be taking in a little too much dairy.

How long do you think you would live on a diet like this? Now this pains me to say this as my mom is from Wisconsin, the Dairy State, but the truth must be told. Dairy basically isn't very healthy for you (this coming from a boy who drank a gallon of milk in two and a half days). Any nutritional items you get in dairy can be obtained from other food groups that are much healthier for you. (I guess I can kiss any future business in Wisconsin goodbye.)

If you consumed only dairy products, you would eventually die and, if you didn't, you probably would want to due to the gas pains you'd be experiencing. This would happen even if you weren't lactose intolerant, believe me. In other words, you wouldn't live a long and happy life, nor a quiet one! However, after you died, I'm sure the dairy farmers would erect a statue in your honor in Wisconsin.

Instead of just eating exclusively from the dairy group, let's say you ate a small portion of food from all three of the other groups. From the whole grains you ate some brown rice and a piece of whole grain bread. From the meat and poultry you had a piece of red meat once a week, getting the three amino acids you can't get from fruits and vegetables. From the fruits and vegetables you had a carrot and an apple. (See Diagram 1-2.)

You could still eat a majority of dairy as long as you also ate from the other food groups. Would you live longer eating a little something from all the food groups? Probably. In fact, the more you ate from the other groups, the more balanced your eating was, the greater the chance of your living longer would be.

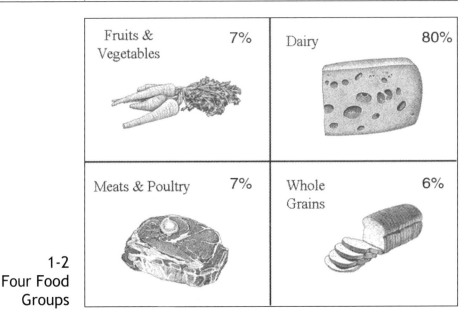

1-2
Four Food
Groups

Days Of Future Past

Approaching your work from this time-based, urgency, deadline, when-is-it-due tickler mentality is similar to limiting your food intake to only the dairy group. Yet many people continue to work on tasks based on their deadline (time-based) rather than their importance (value-based).

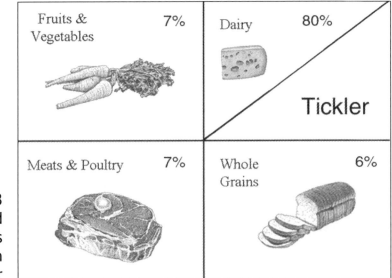

1-3
Four Food
Groups
With
Tickler

Instead of attacking all your work from this time-based, reactive, deadline mentality, start approaching it differently.

When you need to take action on something, ask yourself:
- Is it important? Can it be done ahead of time?
- Can similar tasks be batched together to be done at the same time?
- Will it take a while to do because of how large it is? Can it be broken into steps?
- Does it have to be done today? Can it only be done on a certain date?

The key is to work in all four quadrants rather than just the one. Think of the right side in Diagram 1-6 as red, hot, and fiery. The left side is cool, blue, and calm. The goal is to spend at least

> *The key is to work in all four quadrants rather than just the time-based one.*

20 percent of your day on the left side. Many people's methodology for accomplishing tasks is to jam them into a date or assign them a deadline. I believe deadlines are often given to employees as artificial boundaries because they really don't understand what their real priorities are. For example, a deadline can be used by a boss to create an artificial boundary to get something important done quickly. When I used to manage, I used deadlines because I didn't do a good job of teaching my employees what their real priority was. I gave them a deadline that forced them to complete a task by a specific time, thus artificially making it important. Or so I thought.

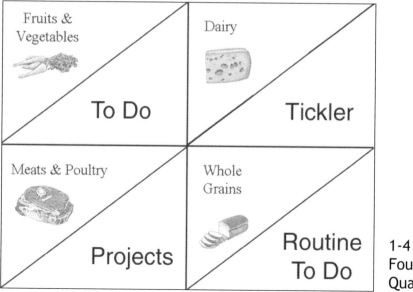

1-4
Four
Quadrants

Why do dates or deadlines work so well? When you say a task needs to be accomplished by the 23rd, there can be no getting around it. Dates are specific. When you say it's important or a priority, the degree of importance is open to interpretation.

Instead of using this typical tickler, time-based approach, your new system has four ways to work, broken down into Action Categories. They are:

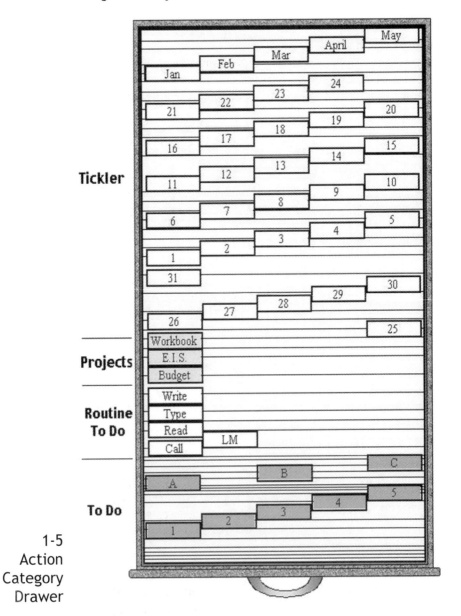

Tickler

Projects

Routine
To Do

To Do

1-5
Action
Category
Drawer

1. Tickler (Reactive)

- Now
- Must be done today
- Can only be done on a certain date
- Urgent
- Materials to take with you on an appointment or for a meeting
- A reminder
- Follow-ups
- Tickets (for a specific date)
- Reactive (such as having to do something that you didn't anticipate right away)
- Materials to take with you on a trip on a specific date

2. Routine To Do (Reactive)

- Similar tasks that can be done at the same time or batched together
- Routine tasks
- Tasks that are repetitive, that you do over and over daily, every couple of days, weekly, monthly, or quarterly
- Habitually mindless activities
- Maintenance items (you know, the ones you live to do, like making copies, doing mindless reports, reading exciting memos, and filling out expense reports)

3. To Do (Proactive)

- Important
- Proactive
- Value-driven
- Big payoff
- Impactful
- Can be done before the task is due
- Tasks that are not necessary or mandatory; may be a one-time activity that nets a big result and gets you from point A to point B much more quickly than normal (such as taking a computer class that will increase your efficiency on the computer)

4. Projects (Proactive)

- A large task that is too big to do at one time
- A large task that can be broken down into a series of tasks over a period of time (such as doing your taxes)

The following is the breakdown of the four Action Categories:

Reactive Time-Based

1. Tickler

Today. A specific date. Must be done today or on a specific date.

✔ **Files in the Tickler**
- 1-31
- Jan. - Dec.
- Pending

✔ **Uses of a Tickler**
- Urgent. Something that has to be done today.
- Follow-up. Something you delegated and want to follow up on.
- Tickets. Tickets to a game on a specific date.
- Call. Someone to call on a specific date. Calls to return from that day.
- Must do. A task that can be done on that date only.
- Reminder. It reminds you to do something on a certain date or in a specific month in the future.
- Sales call. Materials to take on your appointment.
- Take with. Something you want to take to a meeting or on a trip out of town.
- Pending. Anything you are waiting for without a specific date.

✔ **Explanation of the Tickler Files**
- 1-31: Thirty-one folders that correspond to the days of the month
- Jan.–Dec.: Twelve folders that correspond to the months of the year
- Pending: A folder that you drop items into when you are waiting for something from someone else. Pending is passive. If you had a date or a month, it would go into one of the date or month folders.

✔ **Action needed:**
- Go through and do everything in today's Tickler (a date) folder. Do your Tickler after every Processing (voice mail, e-mail, and In Box) time.

2. Routine To Do

Tasks that you can batch together and do at the same time. Maintenance tasks. Tasks you do over and over—daily, every couple of days, weekly, or monthly.)

✔ Possible Files in the Routine To Do

- Call
- Copy
- Expense report
- Left message
- Newsletter
- Order
- Pay
- Read
- Reports
  - Monthly
  - Weekly
- Send
- Staff meeting
- Talk with
  - Moe
  - Larry
  - Curly
- Type
- Write

✔ Uses of a Routine To Do

- Any similar tasks that you do over and over, either daily, every couple of days, weekly, or monthly. The goal is to batch your similar tasks together and do them at the same time rather than do one now and then do one later. When you work on only one type of task at a time, you will get more work done in less time.

✔ Explanation of a few of the Routine To Do Files

- Call: Calls to make that aren't dated
- Read: Items to read or review
- Type: Anything that you can enter or type into your computer

The above are examples. You will create your own file names and definitions.

✔ Action needed:

- Every day, go through and look at every folder in your Routine To Do Category. Choose any folders that you think have enough "batched" tasks in them and then do them. Make sure you go through and empty each folder at least once a week.

Proactive Importance-Based

3. To Do

Important tasks to do. A one-time task to do. A step from a Project.

✔ **Files in the To Do**
- A
- B
- C
- 1-5

✔ **Uses of the To Do**
- Any tasks that are important or impactful. Tasks that have a deadline or are due in the future that can be done now. Tasks that increase your effectiveness that you normally wouldn't do, such as planning or improving one of your skills. A step from one of your Projects.

✔ **Explanation of the To Do Files**
- A: Very important tasks
- B: Important tasks
- C: Somewhat important tasks
- 1-5: These are your top five To Do A's, which you pick out from all of your To Do A's. You go through all of your A's right before you start your QT. You work on your 1-5's in your QT.

✔ **Action needed:**
- Take a Quiet Time (QT) every day at the same time. Your QT is a block of time, approximately 20 percent of your workday, when you are uninterrupted, with your phone off the hook, your beeper turned off, and your door closed. Before your QT, look at all of your To Do A's and pick out the top five most important tasks from them. Prioritize your top five A's and place them into your 1-5 folders. Work on your 1-5's during your QT. If you complete all five, go back to your A's and pick out the next five most important tasks and place them into your 1-5 folders and then work on them. Your 1-5's are the only things that you work on in your QT.

4. Projects
A series of steps to do. A big task that takes time to do that can be broken into smaller steps.

✔ Files in Projects
- The names of each Project are the File names.

✔ Uses of Projects
- Any big, long, difficult task that takes a while to do and has more than one step. A Project is a hybrid consisting of both Action (guide and steps) and Support (reference and completed) materials.

✔ A Project consists of:
- A guide

- Steps to do

- Support material

✔ Explanation of Project Files
A sheet that gives you an over-all view with a list of steps and due dates.
Each separate step on the guide that will be used to activate that step.
Completed work and materials that you refer to regarding the Project.

✔ Action needed:
- Projects are unlike the other three Action Categories in that Projects are more like a holding area. The Project is activated and accomplished by moving each step into one of the other three Action Categories. Generally, the steps will go into To Do A. If you have a meeting to attend or a call to make on a specific date, the step goes into the Tickler. Occasionally, a step will go into the Routine To Do. When you have completed the step, go back to your Project folder, check off the step you just completed, and activate another step. Usually, only one step will be activated at a time per Project. One of the exceptions would be something you are waiting for in Pending.

Take a look at diagram 1-6. The Tickler and the Routine To Do are on the Reactive side while the To Do and Projects are on the Proactive side.

Action Categories

Proactive (Importance)	**Reactive** (Time)

• **To Do** (Important tasks)
  • 1-5 My top five To Do
  A's which I do in my
  Quiet Time (QT)
  • A Very Important
  • B Important
  • C Some Importance
	• **Routine To Do** (Items to batch)
	  • Call
	    • Left message
	  • Expense report
	  • Pay
	  • Read
	  • Send

• **Projects** (A series of
steps to do over time)
  A Project consists of:
  • A Guide
  • Steps To Do
  • Reference material
    and work completed
	• **Tickler** (Must do on a
	  specific date)
	  • 1-31
	  • Jan. - Dec.
	  • Pending

1-6
The Four
Action
Categories

Each Action Category will be broken down in great detail in its own chapter.

Remember These Concepts

• The key is to work in all four quadrants rather than just the time-based one.

Things To Avoid
• Continuing to work from a time-based mentality.

3.2

To Do Lists

Deadly To Do Lists

- Throw That To Do List Away
- The Straw That Broke The Camel's Back
- 3 x 5 Cards
- Yellow Sticky Notes
- Other Interesting Types Of To Do Lists
- This Is A Test

What You Will Learn In This Chapter

- Why not to use to do lists
- Why a 3 x 5 card is one of the most valuable tools in your office

---

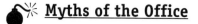 ## <u>Myths of the Office</u>

When you make to do lists, you prioritize the list.

Deadly To Do Lists

Throw That To Do List Away

Let me make this perfectly clear. I like to do lists. In fact, I love to do lists. Some of my best friends use to do lists. I've spent most of my life using them. Some of my happiest moments occurred when I had finally completed marathon to do lists. Using the lists gave me a tremendous sense of control and, when I finished one, a feeling of accomplishment. "Get rid of my to do lists? Are you crazy? They're the only things that stand between me and insanity. Get rid of them? I'd just as soon get rid of my..." is what I commonly hear when I broach the idea to one of my clients.

I've learned never to advise my workshop participants to get rid of their to do lists for fear the workshop mob would tar and paper me. Making to do lists and prioritizing them is fine—if that's what is really being done. Unfortunately, prioritizing rarely occurs, which is one of the reasons a to do list shouldn't be used. Uh, oh. Here comes that mob.

The Straw That Broke The Camel's Back

The following is a short history on the various stages of to do lists.

> 🗒 Stage 1. You don't know what a to do list is.
> Everyone starts here. You don't know what a to do list is. You try to remember things, using your infallible memory, which you find as you get older, is not very infallible.

> 🗒 Stage 2. You use to do lists.
> Somewhere along the way, you find out there's a better way to keep track of tasks than the way you've been doing it. Perhaps a friend awakens you to the benefits of the to do list or you see a to do list pad in a hotel room.
> You use the list a few times. You love it, you're hooked. You can't live without it. No more having to rely on that fallible memory. Finally, a system to do the remembering for you. Now if you can only find all the lists.

> 🗒 Stage 3. You no longer use a to do list except occasionally at home or on rare occasions.
> One day it dawns on you. You're spending way too much time rewriting the lists. There has to be a better way. Make that A Vetter Way™.
> Graduation day occurs. No more to do lists at work. Before you avid to do list supporters out there have a conniption fit (remember, I used to be one of you), please hear what I have to say.

Back in my to do lists days, I found various aspects were not working as well as I thought they should be, such as:
1. Finding the list
2. Doing the list
3. Having different types of tasks on the list together
4. Recopying the list

1. Finding the list

The first thing I had to do was find the list. This was difficult because of the numerous lists I had made. As a business owner, I had a million ideas popping into my head. I wanted to remember to work on all of them. As a result, I needed about ten different to do lists. Things to do, people to call, items to buy, people to follow up with, books to read, places to go, people to meet, babies to kiss, nations to conquer, universes to explore...all different types of activities with lots of to do's on each list.

2-1
Find the
List

As a result of having so many lists, I found I spent a lot of time just trying to keep track of them all.

2. Doing the list

This is the one that really kills you. Remember when I said earlier that making to do lists and prioritizing them is great, except most of the time you don't prioritize them? What most people do is "urgentize" them.

They look at their to do list and figure out what the most urgent task is—the one that screams the loudest. "Take me, do me! Now." They take it and they do it—the squeaky-wheel syndrome. Today, the squeaky wheel gets almost all the oil. And, in this case, "urgentitis" comes into play. Urgentitis is what I call the condition that people have who feel as if they have to do everything immediately. All tasks are urgent.

While some people go for the squeaky wheel, others work on the quickest and easiest task. The payoff is a false sense of accomplishment, a quick fix, a high from getting something done, no matter how small or inconsequential it is. It feels great in the short run, like the sugar high from a big bowl of ice cream. But, in the long run, like the extra pounds you put on from the ice cream, you have a sense of doing the wrong thing.

2-2
Do The
List

These individuals always seem to be behind, never able to catch up with their work. The way they approach work is actually the reason they're always behind. When people work from to do lists, they rarely pick the important tasks. Instead, they do the urgent or easy ones.

You can tell whether you're working this way simply by taking a look at your to do list. Do you work on the high-impact tasks? The hardest tasks? Are these tasks even on the to do list or are they on a wish list somewhere in your head? Someday you will have time to do them. Someday your prince will come too. If, at the end of the day, you feel as if you really didn't get anything important done, then you were probably working on the reactive, easy, or urgent tasks rather than the important ones.

3. Having different types of tasks on the list together

The actions necessary to make a phone call are totally different than the ones needed to write a sales letter. By having tasks with different actions grouped together on a list, you easily fall prey to the squeaky-wheel and easy-task syndrome. You do yourself a great injustice as you will see when how to work is covered in the next couple of chapters.

4. Recopying the list

The straw that broke the camel's back for me was having to recopy that ridiculous list, day in and day out. I figured I was wasting about 20 minutes a day recopying it.

When I was using an appointment book, every day I'd have to rewrite the tasks I hadn't finished on the next page. After getting tired of that, I figured I could write a "refer to" on the page. A refer to sends you back to something you need to do on a particular date. The problem is, you have to carry the refer to's forward every day in your book which can lead to quite a list. As a result, I was spending a tremendous amount of time referring back to all the pages with to do's on them. When I found I had to spend 25 minutes a day just copying my to do list, I decided enough was enough.

2-3
Recopy
The List

3 x 5 Cards

Instead of making a to do list or recopying a task, use the actual document or file that you need to work on as a reminder. This way, you'll never have to make a list or recopy it. Simply place the paper or file into your In Box. Later, when you go through your In Box, put it into one of your Action Category folders.

> A device with no bulky keyboard, no mouse, and no user-unfriendly software is on the market. It can accept handwritten input at incredible rates of speed, easily fit in your pocket or appointment book, store all vital information, especially Action items, and provide at-a-glance recall. It is called a 3 x 5 card.

Think about the zillions of thoughts you have during the day— hundreds for some people, thousands for others, and, of course, none for others. It's exhausting trying

When the thought hits you, write it down.

to remember all those thoughts. What you don't want to do is simply keep them in your head and try to remember them all.

Many people rely on their memory for things that they need to do. Why not reduce your stress, give yourself room to be more creative, and be more productive by clearing all those thoughts out of your head?

> *Use the actual file or paper to remind you of a task rather than writing it on a to do list.*

How? By writing them on a 3 x 5 card. If it's a new thought, or you don't have the file or piece of paper, write the action down on a 3 x 5 card. Think of all the thoughts that come into your head during the day (and night) that you don't want to forget. From now on, simply write each thought on its own 3 x 5 card. When you get back to your office, dump the 3 x 5 cards into your In Box. It feels great to dump things.

Write only one thought or task per card. If you start to list them, you will have created a to do list and will be back where you began. The reason to list only one thought or task on a card is that, when you go through your In Box, you'll be separating the cards by the type of action needed. Each

> *Write only one Action per card.*

action will be categorized and prioritized in a totally different manner than the way you are doing it now. As I stated earlier, many of us approach our tasks only from a time-based, deadline, urgent approach. In the next chapters, you'll learn the other ways to work; in the meantime, it is crucial to know that each action needs to be a separate piece of paper.

> *Let the 3 x 5 card do the remembering for you.*

Think about being in a meeting and taking notes. A thought hits you. A great thought. You don't want to forget it. What do you do? How do you keep track of it?

Many times what happens is you write the things you need to do (Actions) on the same sheet, such as a legal pad, that you are writing your notes to refer to (Support) later on. When you need to work on those tasks and store those notes, where do you put them, in Action or Support? That's why separating Actions from Supports is so important.

The next time you have a thought in a meeting, simply pull out a 3 x 5 card from your appointment book and write your idea or task on it. Stick it back into your appointment book, and when you get back to your office, drop it into your In Box.

Another problem with to do lists is how and where to store the papers or files from the tasks on the to do lists on which you need to work. That problem is eliminated since the paper or files are what you will use to remind you of what needs to be done.

Another way you can use 3 x 5 cards is to leave your paper and files in your Support Category files and use the cards to remind you as to what needs to be done and where they can be found.

Example

When I work with divorce lawyers, much of their clients' lives are contained in a large number of boxes. Rather than grappling with the boxes to find what they need to do, they use 3 x 5 cards to trigger the actions needed to take regarding the boxes. Their files or boxes stay in the Support area and the 3 x 5 cards go into one of the Action Categories.

What if you have a drawing or a blueprint or a giant piece of paper that is too big to fit into a hanging folder in your desk drawer? Where do you keep it so you can be reminded that you need to work on it? In a section called the Bulk area.

Example

Say you need to check over a set of blueprints. Take a 3 x 5 card and write "Check out Hick's blueprints" on it. On the bottom of the card write (BULK). This will alert you to the fact that it's in the bulk area. After dropping the card into your In Box and then into an Action Category file folder, put the blueprints into a cabinet or big drawer where you'll be storing all your bulk items. The 3 x 5 card with (BULK) on it in one of your Action Categories will alert you what you need to do with an item and where to find it.

2-4
Blueprints

Yellow Sticky Notes

Imagine having a desk with a hundred yellow sticky notes all over it. (I know, some of you don't have to imagine. It's a reality.) Your head would be constantly turning to the left and to the right, up and then down. Each and every yellow sticky would constantly be interrupting you, screaming for attention and action.

I love people who use yellow sticky notes. They rip them off left and right, scribbling madly and announcing, "I have to do this" (plaster on the desk), "I have to do that" (plaster on the wall), covering every square inch of open space in their office. Helloooo. Every sticky note is a guaranteed way of visually interrupting yourself every time you look up.

A short background on the little critters. The glue on the back of them was invented accidentally. Some enterprising individual figured out that it had a temporary sticky quality and could take the place of a 3 x 5 card and paper clip. Thus was born one of the most misused "productivity" tools of our time. I'm sure, however, they are a big moneymaker due to their rampant use. (There goes any potential business with that company).

For the record, your honor, before I'm sued, there are legitimate uses of the yellow sticky notes.

▤ Communicating directions or information on an existing piece of paper.

If you're going to put something into the Out Box and need to convey directions or information to someone else, use a yellow sticky note. I always suggest the top right corner of the page for it. This is an ideal use for them.

▤ Reminding yourself of the action you need to do.

Barbara Hannah, a business coach, suggests the

following. If you need to remind yourself of a specific action regarding a piece of paper, write the action you need to take on a yellow sticky note and stick it on the piece of paper. That way, the yellow sticky will remind you of the specific action you need to take.

🗐 A piece of paper that you want filed away by your assistant.

Say you want your administrative assistant to file a piece of paper away in his or her area. Simply write the Category name/File name on a sticky note stuck in the upper right-hand corner and place in your Out Box.

The following are examples:

On the yellow sticky note, write:

Client/Hansen Flooring	(Category/File)
PR/Radio	(Category/File)
Forms/Workshops/Exercise	(Category/File/Subfile)

2-5
A Sticky
Note

By writing the Category/File or Category/File/Subfile, you are letting your administrative assistant know exactly where you want the paper to be filed.

If you are sending a file to Patti and you want Patti to file it away, don't waste time and write a long message. "Dear Patti, Would you please file this outside in the file drawer with the client files in the State Farm file? Thank you very much, Greg." Write the Category and the File on the upper right-hand corner and let Patti take it from there. Period. No more meetings, conversations, or interruptions to explain it—just a sticky note.

If you're the boss and you're sending something to your administrative assistant or secretary, don't waste time writing their name or your name on it. If there's no name on it, they'll know it's from you and for them, since it came from your Out Box.

The following are uses of yellow sticky notes that are Bozo no-nos:
- For phone numbers
- For things to do (I always enjoy seeing my new clients stick their yellow stickies on a 3 x 5 card. So do the office supply companies!)
- For reminder notes on:
  - the desk
  - the wall
  - the phone
  - the computer monitor

Have you ever walked into an office that looked like it was attacked by a hoard of yellow stickies? Not a pretty sight. I've seen offices that looked as if they were trying a new yellow wallpaper scheme. Remember, the more yellow stickies you have plastered around your office, the more distractions and interruptions you have and more scattered you will be. Send a 3 x 5 card or original piece of paper to the rescue!

Other Interesting Types Of To Do Lists

Here are some items I've actually seen that have been used as a to do list. Batten down the hatches, nothing is safe.
- Assorted commercially produced, multicolored, multithemed, multiethnic, to do list pads
- Hotel to do list pads
- Matchbook covers
- Sugar packets

- Napkins
- The backs of old notebooks
- Pages in books
- Pages in brand new, good books
- Pages with no books
- Pages that have never even seen a book
- Newspapers (Never the sports section, please!)
- Legal pads
- Letter-size pads
- Pizza boxes
- The backs of business cards
- Index cards
- A piece of cardboard
- Assorted scraps of different sizes of paper
- The backs of checks
- Deposit slips
- Hands

Do you see a pattern here? In other words, anything that can be written on or torn off that is handy can be used. Perish the thought that one would be organized enough to have the same thing to write on each time. How about a simple, light, easy-to-carry, fits-into-a-pocket, mobile 3 x 5 card?

The reason for always using one type of visual aid is your brain sees that one thing, the same thing, a familiar thing, a 3 x 5 card and it says, "Ah ha! There's information here. I need to do something with it." I don't care if it's a 4 x 6 card. Just use the same type of thing every time.

This Is A Test

Think about what you do while attending a meeting (Z-Z-Z-Z). During the meeting, you write down information, probably on something like a legal pad, that you will refer to later. The more information you write, the more pages you use and the more pages you flip over. As the meeting progresses, you start to come up with ideas that you want to work on. Since the legal pad is handy, you simply jot down those ideas on the pad. When the wonderful and inspiring meeting is over, you return to

> *Separate Actions from Supports.*

the safety of your office. You drop off your now folded-over legal pad onto your desk. The next day, you flip over to a clean new page on your legal pad. What boo-boos did you just commit?

1. The pad always goes into your In Box, never on your desk.
2. Never keep a legal pad with folded-over pages. Always tear the pages off and place them into your In Box.
3. Never write Action items with Support items on the same piece of paper. When you go through your In Box later and you come to those sheets, where do you put them, in Action or Support? Instead, use 3 x 5 cards for your Actions tasks.
4. Going to the meeting.

Remember These Concepts

- When the thought hits you, write it down.
- Use the actual file or paper to remind you of a task rather than writing it on a to do list.
- Write only one Action per card.
- Let the 3 x 5 card do the remembering for you.
- Separate Actions from Supports.

Things To Avoid
- A case of urgentitis.
- Keeping folded-over written pages on a legal pad.
- To do lists.
- To do lists.
- To do lists.
- To do lists.
- To do lists.

3.3

Tickler

Tickle Me

- The Revenge Of The Nuns
- It Has As Much Chance As A Snowball In Hades
- It No Longer Tickles My Fancy
- Whatever Do You Put Into Your Tickler Then?
- The Set Up
- Remind Me To
- Pending
- Appointments

What You Will Learn In This Chapter
- The less you put into your Tickler, the more you will get done
- How to diferentiate between important and urgent tasks
- What really should go into your Tickler

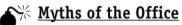 **Myths of the Office**

Put things to do in your Tickler file a few days before they are due.

Tickle Me

The Revenge Of The Nuns

The nuns could hardly wait for the first day of school. After their having had to endure countless pranks, endless smart remarks, and thumbtacks on their chairs the year before, revenge was almost within their grasp.

What would their instrument of torture be this school year? The story about the communists invading America, the one that gave students the choice between having to stamp on a crucifix and burn in hell, or refuse to do so and be shot by the commies? Nah. They used that one last year. What could provide the necessary day-in, day-out guilt for months to come? The ill-timed book report. Of course!

To completely demoralize any troublemakers from the get-go and to insure instilling maximum guilt, the assignment had to be given out on the first day of school. Getting it the first day was painful, but dishing out pain was their forte. No, this was more devious. The book report would be due on the Monday following Thanksgiving vacation, which gave them three long months to torture us. Subtle remarks about how dependent our grade was on the book report were strategically and conveniently dropped whenever needed. Worst of all, the final reckoning came on Thanksgiving weekend. They knew we could never really enjoy Turkey Day if we still had the book report to do.

3-1
Nuns

Being industrious, intelligent, and proactive students, we would, of course, complete the book report that same first week we received the assignment. Right. And there was no such thing as Original Sin, either.

Getting it the first day was a bummer, but there was plenty of time for us to do it—three whole months. Plenty of time. Besides, we had other things we needed to do. Important things. No book reports yet, thank you.

The days, weeks, and then, suddenly, months passed. Thanksgiving came and went. It was Sunday night, 7 p.m., the night before the book report was due. On NBC was *The Wonderful World of Disney*, on ABC was *Lassie*, and on our bed upstairs was that stupid book report which still wasn't done. The dilemma was no longer which show to watch or when to do the report, but rather how to get it done before school started the following morning. Why did we leave it until the last minute?

The sad truth is most of us have never had the correct model to learn from. Our parents certainly didn't teach it to us because they were never taught it either.

How often does your company reward you for working on tasks ahead of time? In corporate life, you are rewarded for managing an effect of rather than preventing the cause of a problem. In real life, firefighters are the heroes and the fire marshals are complete unknowns. The same is true for corporate life.

> *In corporate life, you are rewarded for managing the effects of a problem rather than preventing its cause.*

It Has As Much Chance As A Snowball In Hades

When you need to work on a task, where do you put it? Into a Tickler file a couple of days before it is due. Everybody knows that. That way, you have a couple days to spare before it's due. Doing it that way leaves you extra time to do it, just in case something pops up the day before—not that it ever does, though.

The problem with putting things to do into your Tickler a couple of days ahead is that it doesn't always work. In theory it should; in reality, it doesn't. When it doesn't work, you have to work late, take work home, work on the weekend or work at a frenzied pace. Worst of all, all of the tasks you didn't have time to do have to be moved to the next day when you again won't have enough time to do them. When it does work, it makes you feel as if someone is holding a gun to your head, since you are constantly trying to meet so many deadlines.

Look at Diagram 3-2. Say you have decided to put things to work on two days ahead of the date they are due to ensure their completion on time, a system many people use today.

3-2
Two Days
Ahead

Say you have something due on Wednesday. You put it into the Tickler to do on Monday giving you two full days to accomplish it. A report is due on Friday so you put it into Wednesday to do. Say, for example, you have five tasks to do every day in your Tickler, with all tasks being due in two days. Five things to do every day that must get done because in two days they will be due.

- **Day 1**

  You get them all done. Life is good. What's this nonsense about the Tickler being an inefficient practice?

- **Day 2**

  You have a bad day. You are constantly interrupted and don't get any of your five tasks done. Where do you put them? In the next day, of course.

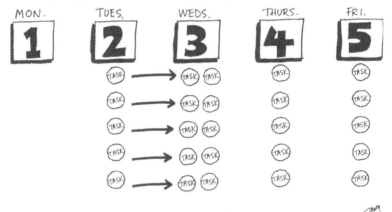

3-3
Day 2

- **Day 3**

  And you thought you had a bad day yesterday. You now have ten things to do today instead of only five and your day is even worse than the day before. Even so, you stay until 11 o'clock and get two of the to do's done which means you still have eight to do for the day plus the five waiting to be done tomorrow. Tomorrow might be a good day to take one of your sick days. Perhaps a few vacation days too.

- **Day 4**

  You now have your five tasks to do plus the eight from yesterday that you didn't get done. Thirteen items in all plus your normal work, including meetings and interruptions. What do you do? Stay late. Real late. Work like a fool. You're angry because, once again, you have ended up staying late. By the way, what's a home life?

3-4
Snowball
From
Hades

I see secretaries using the Tickler this way all the time. Many people do. They have been instructed to use it as a tool to get organized. Instead, it creates this giant, overflowing, ever-expanding mass of tasks that continually grows in size. Ticklers are like snowballs rolling down a hill after a recent snowfall. They pick up everything in their path, growing to an unbelievable size as they barrel down the hill.

The Tickler won't work if you use it this way. Why? Because the Tickler is based on a theoretical system, not a realistic one. If this were an ideal world and there were no unforeseen emergencies or last-minute unreasonable requests by bosses or crazy demands by customers, then the Tickler would work. But, in the real world, using the Tickler this way has as much chance of working as a snowball does in Hades.

What inevitably happens is another crisis occurs, another emergency erupts, one more frantic phone call gets you off track. "Could you pleeeease do this for me?" "By the way, I need it today." It just won't work. You'll never get caught up unless you decide to make a giant shift in how you work.

It No Longer Tickles My Fancy

Where do you put things to do when they are due in two weeks if you don't use the Tickler? Where do you put items that are repetitious, that you do daily, weekly, monthly or a couple of times a day? The answer is other Action Categories, such as your To Do or Routine To Do.

Take as many of the tasks as you can from your Tickler and put them into one of the other Action Categories.

> *The less you put into your Tickler, the more you will get done.*

Render unto Caesar those things that are Caesar's, and render unto the Tickler those few well-defined things that go into the Tickler. The less the better, as you will soon learn.

Whatever Do You Put Into Your Tickler Then?

The Tickler Category should be for urgencies, follow-ups, reminders, and tasks that can only be done on a certain date. If you return phone calls the same day or within 24 hours, they go into your Tickler. If the boss says, "Get this out immediately" or "Get it out today," that's an urgency and goes into your Tickler. If your top customer calls and emphatically states that if you don't get it fixed today, you can say Sayonara to their account, put it in the Tickler.

Ticklers can be used for reminders, for follow-ups, for hockey tickets for a particular game, or for papers you need for a meeting on a specific date. There are specific types of tasks that go into the Tickler. The following are a sampling:

✔ **Phone calls for a particular date**
    You told someone you would call them on a particular date, say on the 7th. Stand, Action, Tickler, 7. Remembering birthday calls and cards are easy when you use your Tickler.

✔ **Urgencies**
    Your boss just told you to prepare a report for a 4 p.m. meeting today and it is 11 a.m.

✔ **Something that must be done on that date**
    A sales report can only be done on the last day of the month from 1 p.m. on, after all the statistics have been gathered.

    If you've ever been on a snipe hunt, you know there are only specific days to hunt snipe. Snipe is a particular type of bird that can only be hunted on particular days with good friends. A perfect example would be going on a snipe hunt on a particular date. If you've never been on a snipe hunt, ask a friend who has to take you on one. You'll be amazed when it is all over at what you have caught. And what your friend has caught.

✔ **A follow-up with one of your direct reports**

You've delegated an important task to one of your people and you want to make sure it is done by a specific date.

✔ **Materials for a meeting**

You have a 3 p.m. meeting today to which you need to take the report you wrote. It goes into today's date (File). However, doing the report, which would take some time, would be a To Do A. Stand, Action, To Do, A. When it was completed, you'd drop it into the date that you had the meeting (Tickler).

✔ **Sales information for an appointment**

You're meeting with Darrell to discuss a proposal you will be making to his Internet company.

✔ **A reminder**

You need to pay your quarterly taxes in September. (More money the IRS can give to the international bankers.)

✔ **Tickets for a specific date**

You have hockey tickets for the 30th to see the New York Rangers play.

✔ **A file to take with you on an out-of-town trip**

You have an appointment out of town on the 12th. The file goes into the date you are leaving. If you leave the night before, put it into the 11th.

What do you do with the time-sensitive tasks in your Tickler when you are out of town for a few days? On Fridays, or your last work day of the week, you'll be checking all of your Action Categories (Processing). You'll know what you have coming up and can handle it before you leave or can simply take your work with you on your trip and handle it on that date like you normally would.

Quiz

The following are specific examples of things to do that go into the Tickler Category. Which files do they go into? The answers are on page 1,091. Just kidding. The answers follow the test.

The File it goes into:

_____ 1. You need to make a phone call on a particular date, the 23rd.
_____ 2. You have tickets to a Spinners concert on the 10th.
_____ 3. You need to follow up with someone on the 11th.
_____ 4. You want to be reminded to pay your quarterly taxes in September.
_____ 5. You have a call to make on the 1st.
_____ 6. You were just given an emergency task to get done today, the 4th.
_____ 7. You have a meeting to go to today (the 14th) and need to take a file along to discuss in the meeting.
_____ 8. You are going out of town on the 16th and you want to remember to take something with you.

1. 23, 2. 10, 3. 11, 4. September 5. 1, 6. 4, 7. 14, 8. 16

The following are specific examples of things to do that do *not* go into the Tickler Category:

📌 **You have to prepare for a meeting on the 12th (today is the 4th).**

You have a week to prepare for it. Why wait until the end and have to fight it along with all the other emergencies that unexpectedly pop up? If you put it into your Tickler on a particular date just before it's due, you may clog up that day with all the other tasks in your Tickler. If you don't get it done that day, that snowball will begin to grow and it will roll from date to date in the Tickler eating up your time and resulting in a last-minute, late-night, emergency work session. Drop it into your To Do Category. Stand, Action, To Do, A.

📌 **You have a sales lead you want to call. You can call them anytime.**

Drop it into your Routine To Do. If you put it into your Tickler on a particular date, the chances of you calling on that day, especially if you have a lot of sales calls to make, are slim. If you don't get to make the call, you'll continually move the call from date to date in the Tickler. Snowball from Hades again. Stand, Action, Routine To Do, Call. (If it's a hot lead and you'll call it today, then by all means, drop it into the Tickler. Close that sale!)

📌 **You have a speech to prepare for on the 23rd of March (today is the 3rd of February).**

Same as the meeting on the 12th. Get it done ahead of time. You can always make slight changes as time goes on to it if you wish. Stand, Action, To Do, A.

📌 **You are a plant supervisor and one of your bottling lines go down.**

You need to call someone to handle it immediately. This is not an urgency. It is an emergency and you handle it immediately. Emergencies occasionally will occur. When they do, do not classify them—handle them immediately.

The Set Up

Your Tickler Category will have at least 44 hanging folder files in it. Thirty-one files for the dates in a month (1-31), plus 12 files for the months (January through December) and at least one for Pending. You'll probably add a few more Subfiles in Pending as you use and learn the system.

The first file in the front of the Tickler will always be today's date. At the end of each day you'll pull out the front file (today's date) and move it to the back behind yesterday's date.

Say today is April 8th (Diagram 3-5). The first file in the front will be 8. When the day is over, you simply move today's date, the 8th, behind the 7th in the back of the drawer and then the 9th will be the first file in the drawer. This rotating filing system keeps the current date right up front where it is easy to find. No hunting for the file, no wasted time.

Some people want the first file to be the current month they are in, say April. You certainly can do this, but I usually advise people not to because most people already know what month they're in. Instead, keep the current month all the way in the back behind the other months, a year from the current month. This works especially well when a potential customer asks you to call them in a year.

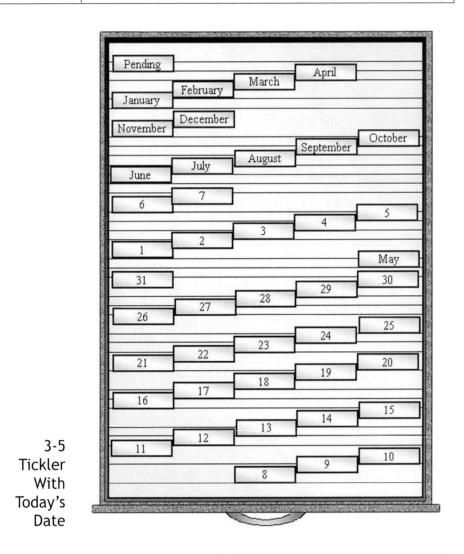

3-5
Tickler
With
Today's
Date

Exercise

Look at Diagram 3-6. What would today's date and month be?

3-6
Tickler
With May

It would be May 11. Why? Because the first file is 11 and the first file is always today's date. The first month following the last day of the current month is June. This gives you a visual sense of June following the last day in May. Or if you prefer to keep all the months together, locate June in the back with all the other months (Diagram 3-7).

3-7
Tickler
With June

Quiz

Today's date is May 11th. Where in the Tickler would you put the following Actions? Refer to Diagram 3-7.

1. You have a call to make on May 17th. Where would it go?
2. You have a call to make on June 4th. Where would it go?
3. You have a call to make on June 18th. Where would it go?

Answers:

1. In the File labeled 17
   You're in the month of May. Today's date is the 11th. Six days from now will be May 17th. Drop it in.

2. In the File labeled 4
   Why would you put it into the 4th instead of June? The 4 showing is actually June 4th. You'll save a step by dropping it directly into the 4th. If you put it into June, you'll just have to move it from the June file to the 4th file at the end of the month (May), when you distribute the contents of the June folder. If you can, put an item directly into the proper file and save yourself the step of having to move it later.

3. In the File labeled June
   This time, if you dropped it into the 18th, you would be dropping it into May 18th, so you drop it into the June file. On the last day of the month, May 31st, you go to the June file and pull out anything that's in the June file, and drop it into one of the dates in June (to do on that date) or into your To Do Category (something important you decided to work on in June).

If something stays in your Tickler overnight, it's not really a Tickler. If a task is not completed on its Tickler date and is moved from that date to the next date, it's not a legitimate Tickler and shouldn't go into your Tickler. It should go into one of the other Action Categories.

Example

You have your fall sales projection that's due September 15th. It's now summertime. Stand, Action, Tickler, September. You file it in September in your Tickler Category. So far so good. You go through your Tickler on the last day of the month, August 31st, to distribute next month's contents into the appropriate dates and locations. You look at it and say, "Ah, ha. That's something I need to do in September." It doesn't go into your Tickler on a date a few days before the 15th but rather into your To Do Action Category.

A client once asked, "How can it be important if it's not time-based?" He couldn't understand how anything could be important without a due date or without it being done on a particular date. This is how prevalent the time-based mentality is today.

Remind Me To

You can use your Tickler to remind you to do certain activities on specific dates or months by using different colored 3 x 5 cards for each activity. You can also write the activity in different colors such as PAY or BILLS in green letters. After a while the color will trigger which activity you need to do.

Many managers have a terrible time trying to delegate anything because they don't have a system to follow up on the tasks they delegated. Any time you delegate a task and give it a date, drop it into your Tickler on the date it's due. With no date, simply drop it into your Pending file.

Pending

Years ago I ordered a kitchen knife set for $10. "Order today and the bamboo steamer is yours," the announcer barked on TV. It was too good of a deal to pass up, so I ordered the knife. They told me I had a wait of who knows how long before I received it. I figured I could trust them but I still wanted to keep tabs on the knife. You can never tell with a TV offer and I needed a way to remind myself.

On a card I wrote "knives" as a reminder. I placed the card into the next day's date in the Tickler. Tomorrow arrived. The knife set didn't come. I moved it to the next day in the Tickler. It didn't come. I looked at it and moved it to the next day. It still didn't come. Every day I waited for it looking at the card in that particular date's Tickler file and it still didn't come. Finally, after I had handled the card 50 times, it arrived. Why did I have to handle the card so many times? I didn't, but I didn't know any better at the time.

Instead of doing it that way, I could have written "knife set" and the date of the order on a card or used the order sheet and simply dropped it into my Pending file. Stand, Action, Tickler, Pending. Why in the Tickler? Because it was time driven. Tickler = time. Why in the Pending file? Because I was waiting for something and didn't know the specific date it was coming in. Pending means waiting for something that doesn't have a specific due date. Pending = passive. If there were a specific date of arrival, I could put the card into that date. Stand, Action, Tickler, 2 (the date). Anyway after all that, I was so embarrassed about ordering the knives and the bamboo steamer that I

> ## *Pending = Passive.*

never did pick them up at the post office. They're probably still there. I sure hope an angry postal worker doesn't get their hands on the knives.

Could I have picked a random date six weeks down the line, dropped the card into the date and hoped they would arrive around that time? Sure. However, if I needed to find the card or get any information off of it, I would have had a hard time trying to find it in all those dates in my Tickler.

When you're waiting for something without a particular date, drop a reminder card, or better yet, the paper itself, into your Pending file.

Say you are a saleswoman and you have a couple of proposals out. You were specifically told that they would contact you. "We'll call you." Sound familiar? Scratch another sale. But, just in case you want to keep them somewhere close (you are feeling lucky) so you can find them and also be reminded that they are there, drop the proposals into your Pending file. Once a week on Friday, or your last work day of the week, check the contents of your Pending file. This provides a place to store items you must wait on and a regular time (once a week) to update their status.

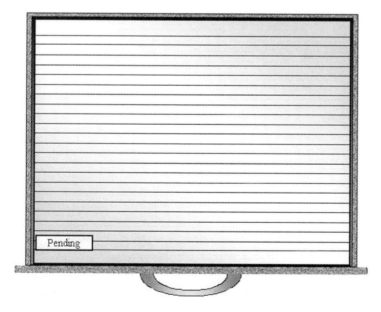

3-8
Pending

Say you're that same saleswoman and you have a lot of proposals out. Normally you wouldn't put them into your Pending file, but you have so many of them that it would clog up that file. You can set up a Subfile in Pending called Proposals. All the sales proposals you are waiting for would be in Proposals (Diagram 3-9).

3-9
Pending
Proposals

If you had a lot of proposals out, you could even break them down by major groups or by types or by names. Any way that you decided to set them up would work.

Another example of a use for Pending could be waiting for your credit card statement. When you use your card, you receive a receipt slip from the transaction. You could have a Subfile called Credit Card and wait for your monthly statement to arrive to check the slips with the statement. Stand, Action, Tickler, Pending, Credit cards.

3-10
Pending
Credit
Cards

You could be the boss and have a Subfile called Direct Reports. In it would be the items you were waiting for from your direct reports without having assigned a specific date to them. Any items with specific dates would go into a date in your Tickler.

3-11
Pending
Direct
Reports

If you wanted to list all the names of your direct reports, you would move over to the right and list all their names. (See Diagram 3-12.) You can go on and on and on—or at least five tabs over.

Remember, you're the one who determines how far to the right your tabs will go.

3-12
Pending
Direct
Reports/
Names

Remember, you're the one who determines how far to the right your tabs will go. The more specific you want to be, the more you access the information, the quicker you want to find it, the more tabs to the right you will have. The alternative is just to put all the items in the Pending. The file may be a little crowded but it's a simpler way to do it.

Anything that you're waiting for from someone else on a particular date is always dropped into that particular date, not into the Pending file. Once after a training I said to one of my clients, "Hal, would you send me a testimonial on the workshop?" "I would love to Greg." he said. "What date can I expect it?" I asked. He replied, "Don't press your luck, Greg." So I put it into my Pending since I didn't have a specific date. Stand, Action, Tickler, Pending.

Suppose he had said, "I will send it to you on the 12th." Stand, Action, Tickler, 12. His business card or a 3 x 5 card would go into the 12th.

Back to the testimonial. The reminder card is in my Pending file. One week passes and on Friday I check my Pending. No testimonial yet. Another week passes and I check my Pending. Still no testimonial. Two more weeks pass, no testimonial. I take the reminder card and move it to my Call file in the Routine To Do. I call Hal to find out how the letter is coming. "Don't press your luck, Greg." I either throw it away if I don't believe I am going to get it or I put it back into the Pending. Of course, I know I'll be getting a letter since the workshop went so well, so I put it back into the Pending.

When you think of Pending, think of passive, of waiting. The action is out of your control to a certain degree. Don't put those things to do about which you are undecided or unsure in the Pending. That's definitely a Bozo no-no. An item you haven't come to a decision about is not the same as an item you are waiting on. Items of little importance will go into your To Do Category, behind C.

> *Don't put those things to do about which you are undecided or unsure in the Pending.*

Example

Some items you could be waiting for:
- A testimonial letter
- Anything you have ordered through the mail
- Bids
- Things people are going to send to you
- Sales proposals
- Credit card financial statements
- Reports
- Assignments given to your direct reports without a date
- Assorted knife sets (and accompanying bamboo steamers)

Have you ever loaned out a book, forgotten to whom you loaned it, and never seen it again? Any time you loan something out and you're waiting for it to come back without a specified date, it goes into your Pending or in the Subfile Books if you loan out a lot of books (Diagram 3-13).

Every time you lend out a book, write the name of the book, the date, and to whom you lent it on a 3 x 5 card and simply drop it into your Pending file. You can even make a list on the 3 x 5 card and cross them out when the books come back. That's right folks, a list.

3-13
Pending
Books

Appointments

How does your appointment book fit into all of this? Your appointment book is, after all, a form of a Tickler. I always love to ask the question in my workshop "What is the only thing that goes into your appointment book?" Duhhhh. The only thing that goes into your appointment book should be appointments. That's why they call it an appointment book. If

> **Question**: What is the only thing that goes into an appointment book?
> **Answer**: An appointment.

you put things to do in your appointment book and things to do on piles on your desk and things to do in your briefcase and other things to do in your computer on your contact manager and even in your car, you'll waste a tremendous amount of time having to look in all the places, shifting from system to system rather than just using the one system. You'll have too many sources to check on and work from. The key is to look in only one spot, your Action Category drawers.

Do appointments go into your Tickler? No. Write the appointment in your appointment book or type it in your contact manager. Only papers that you need for that appointment go into the Tickler on the date you are meeting with them.

Another thing to write in your appointment book is your Quiet Time (QT). It is vital to write it down a month in advance so as to help you block out your daily time. Say your QT is usually from 3 p.m. to 5 p.m. In your book, write "QT" and draw an arrow from 3 p.m. to 5 p.m. In your appointment book all you're doing is listing appointments and blocking out some work times. We'll get into QT in the To Do chapter coming up.

By the way, you can keep phone numbers, addresses, and other items you refer to and which you want to have with you in your appointment book, along with, of course, a supply of white 3 x 5 cards. Don't list things to do in your appointment book. Also don't use your appointment book as a permanent catchall for loose papers. Use it as a temporary In Box so that when you get back to your office, you can empty out your appointment book and put the loose contents and used 3 x 5 cards into your In Box.

The goal is to take some of the tasks and activities from the time-based Tickler Category and place them in one of the other three Action categories: the To Do (important), Projects (tasks that have more than one step in them), and the Routine To Do (batched tasks you can do at the same time). You can continue to work from the time-based Tickler Category as long as you also work on Projects, Routine things To Do, and important things To Do. This is a whole new approach to work, your life raft in the swelling sea of information and technology in which you are about to drown.

The Tickler is just the first of four Action Categories. Next up—the Action Category called Routine To Do.

Remember These Concepts

- The less you put into your Tickler, the more you will get done.
- Pending = Passive.
- Remember, you're the one who determines how far to the right your tabs will go.
- Don't put those things to do about which you are undecided or unsure in the Pending.

Things To Avoid
- Putting things to do in your Tickler.
- Approaching work from a time-based mentality.
- Putting things to do on which you have made no decision in the Pending.

3.4

Routine To Do

Batch This

- Get Out Of Bed
- Pardon Me While I Interrupt Myself
- The Farmer In The Office
- Just Call Me
- A Little Help From My Friend

What You Will Learn In This Chapter
- How to batch similar tasks together

💣 <u>Myths of the Office</u>

I don't have time to return phone calls.

Batch This

Get Out Of Bed

Psychologists say that over 90 percent of everything we do is a habit. Sometimes we have all the spontaneity of a rock. For example, if you don't like men with mustaches who have salt and pepper hair, every time you meet one, without even being conscious of it, you'll react the same way—you won't like them.

We are so habitual in the way we do things—and unconscious of our habits—that it is almost frightening. Think of the hundreds or thousands of things that you do every day. Shaving is a good example. Each morning, as we men face the mirror, we start at the same side, at the same spot, with the same amount of pressure, with the same fingers pulling our face the same way.

Exercise

Try this exercise. Think of everything you do for the first hour each morning, beginning with the moment you awaken. Make a list of the first ten things you do after you are aware you are conscious, no matter how small or inconsequential they seem.

Most people don't list activities such as opening their eyes or pounding on the snooze alarm ten or more times. When I ask women what the last step in putting their makeup on in the morning is, very few say look in the mirror. Most of them say apply lip gloss. (All these years I thought it was lipstick.)

Go to bed. Wake up. Say your morning prayers. Hit the bathroom. Brush your teeth. Take a shower. Put your clothes on. Read the paper. Eat. Feed your family. Dress your kids. Bark at your dog. Drive to work. Your routines are so set that you forget many of them and can't describe them when asked. It's just one big blur. You go through the motions unconsciously because you've done them for so many years. If I asked you to walk on your hands for two weeks, do you think it would be a little different than walking on your feet? Of course it would. You'd go through a learning phase then adjustment period. What I want you to do is to start recognizing your work patterns so you can batch them together and work on them at the same time.

Pardon Me While I Interrupt Myself

Stop and think how many times during the day you interrupt yourself. That's right, it's accountability time, folks. You're working on a task (Produce), someone hands you a piece of paper and you stop what you are doing, look at the paper (Process), and then start working on it (Produce). You are working on a project (Produce), the phone rings, you stop what you're doing to answer the phone (Process). Then, to add insult to injury, you look at the item from the phone call (Process), start working on the task (Produce), and leave that important project until the night before it is due.

The Farmer In The Office

The farmer in the office, the farmer in the office, high-ho the derio, the farmer in the office. The farmer takes the call, the farmer takes the call, high-ho the derio, the farmer takes the call. The farmer's interrupted, the farmer's interrupted, high-ho the derio, the farmer's interrupted. The

> *Batch and block similar activities together.*

farmer gets upset, the farmer gets upset, high-ho the derio, the farmer gets upset. The farmer goes bankrupt, the farmer goes bankrupt, high-ho the derio, the farmer goes bankrupt. And so it goes, on and on.

If you analyze your behavior, you'll notice that, over and over during the course of the day, you're constantly shifting from Producing to Processing. The secret is to combine similar activities that you do repeatedly and block them together, working on one type of task at a time. When you do this, you'll be focusing on one type of behavior rather than performing your juggling act in the center ring.

Think about what you do over and over. Daily. Every couple of days. Weekly. Monthly. Quarterly. The Action Category, Routine To Do, is a place to store tasks instead of trying to remember them or make a lot of to do lists for them or keep little pieces of paper all over your desk so you don't forget to do them. Right now, you're either keeping them in your head, on to do lists, on scraps of paper, or in piles on your desk. Worse yet, you could be forgetting them.

Routine To Do applies to activities that are repetitive. You must continue to do them over and over. They might be considered maintenance items. They can be done daily, every couple of days, weekly, biweekly, monthly, or quarterly. As long as they are repetitive or similar activities, they are Routine To Do.

Example

Some possible Routine To Do files:

- Call
- Expense reports
- Left message
- Meetings:
  - Sales
  - Staff
- Pay
- Read
- Reports
  - Month end
  - Quarterly
- Sales

- Review
- Send
- Talk with
  - Elaine
  - Jack
  - Johnny
- Type
- Write

Some common files for administrative people:

- Call
- Computer
- Copy
- Fax
- Left message

- Order
- Proof invoices
- Time cards
- Type
- Write

4-1
Routine
To Do's

Whenever possible, use the kind of task or action you'll take for your file name in the Routine To Do Category. However, the first name that comes to you is always the best. The following is an explanation of some of the Routine To Do's.

✔ Accounts Receivable

Many people try to put accounts receivable and accounts payable into a Support Category called Financial. Bozo no-no. Remember, anything you intend to do goes into one of your Action Categories. Putting it into your Support will not remind you to do it and it will die a slow and painful death in that lonely place. (So will the bills you need to pay and the money that's due you since you won't have any money coming in.)

✔ Call

Call simply means you want to call someone on the phone. Think about the difference between a call in your Routine To Do and your Tickler. Calls that need to be made on a certain date go into that particular date in the date-driven Tickler. Other calls that can be made at any time can go into your Routine To Do. If you are in sales, think how many times you drop business cards into a specific date in your Tickler and then don't call them on that date. Where do the cards go? Into the next date, the Snowball from Hades again. And you wonder why you feel so overwhelmed with so much to do every day. They keep building and building.

To separate your calls even further, you could create a file called Prospects. That way, only people you wish to sell would be in that file and other people to call would go into Call.

✔ Expense Reports

All of the slips of paper, credit card copies, and receipts can be dropped into the file labeled Expense Reports. Then when you

4-2
Left
Message
Behind
Call

process them, either weekly or monthly, they'll all be in one spot for you to work on. Routines To Do's can act as temporary storage, keeping items off your desk until you can work them.

✔ Left Message

How do you keep track of people you call if you don't use a contact manager on your computer? By dropping their cards or files into the Left message file.

Left message can be its own file as it is in Diagram 4-1 or you can put it behind the Call file as a Subfile in Diagram 4-2.

You can use a Left message, a Left message 1 and a Left message 2 if you're in sales or make a lot of calls. This works well since many people don't return calls within the first 24 hours.

Being in sales, I give people three days to return my calls. I'll call them the first day and drop their card into the LM (Left Message) file. The next day, I'll move their card to the LM 1 file and the people that I call that day whom I don't reach, go into the LM file. The next day I'll move yesterday's calls into the LM 1 file and the calls from the day before will go into the LM 2 file; and any calls that I make that day go into LM. Finally, I'll move all the calls in LM 2 and put them back in the Call file and call them again or trash them.

When someone returns your call the same day you called, after celebrating, you can instantly refer back to the Left message file and pull out his or her card or paper.

4-3
Left
Messages

Just Call Me

Just a note about returning phone calls: Does anyone ever return phone calls anymore? Besides being highly unprofessional, not returning a phone call is very discourteous. I could write a book on the subject.

Of course, you can say that you don't have time to return phone calls, especially to those really aggressive salespeople. You can use that excuse for anything you don't want to deal with. Think about your company for a moment. What would happen to your company's sales if all of your salespeople were treated the way some of you treated salespeople who were trying to sell you? Your company would go bye-bye and you'd be out of a job pretty quickly. For those of you who are asleep, wake up! Return the calls.

If you are besieged with phone calls, accept them only at certain times of the day. Return them after 6 o'clock and leave a message thanking them but letting them know you're okay in that department. Or delegate the calls. Have your secretary call them for you. Either way, call them back. Give salespeople a couple of minutes to sell you as long as they are courteous enough to ask if it's a good time for you to talk. Remember, "Whatever ye shall sow, so shall ye reap."

Some salespeople do become presidents and CEO's later on and when your salespeople call on them, believe me, they'll have long memories. I did. I remember being thrown out of a prospect's office years ago when I was selling long distance programs. Five years later when I was running my first business, two of their salespeople called on me. Was that ever an enjoyable experience. I told them the story and they relayed it to their boss. I ended up buying from them anyway since two wrongs don't make a right. I wonder if three do.

✔ Meetings
This includes any information you want to discuss in a meeting such as your staff meeting.

✔ Order
This is a great file, especially if you're in an administrative job. Every time you need to order something, simply jot it on a card. When your people need you to order something for them, have them write it on a 3 x 5 card and drop it into your In Box. Then you drop the card into your Order file. Rather than having to call a bunch of times, call the order in once a week or so.

✔ Pay, Accounts Payable, Or Bills

I have a file in my Routine To Do called Pay. I pay my bills on the 8th and 23rd of the month. You can call it Pay or Bills or whatever word works for you. When I check my files in my Routine To Do, I will be reminded to pay them. If I want to double-remind myself to pay them on a particular date, I can use my Tickler.

Create a 3 x 5 card that says PAY on it. Drop it into Tickler, 8. It reminds you to pay your bills on the 8th. When a bill comes in, after it goes into your In Box, put the bill to be paid in: Stand, Action, Routine To Do, Pay. When you are done, simply move the PAY card to the 23rd, in your Tickler reminding you to pay them on the 23rd. It only takes a second to move the card. If you don't want to have to use that little voice in your head to remember to pay your bills on the 23rd, then check your Routine To Do every day as you are suppose to or use the Tickler to remind you of the date.

4-4
Pay 3 x 5
Card

Could you put the bills to pay in your Tickler on the 8th? Sure. However, having a file that says Pay will allow you to keep your bills separate and not clog up your Tickler.

You can do it any way you want as long as you have a consistent system. Remember, if you consistently use the entire system, you will not forget anything. Each of your Action Categories can be intertwined with the other Action Categories, creating a very sophisticated system or a simple one.

✔ Proof Invoices

Check to make sure invoices are correct or match them up with other sheets.

✔ Read

This file is for any materials you wish to read. They say you'll meet everyone that you've ever met in your lifetime a second time. The same is true of information that comes into your office—it will be back a second time. This is especially true with casual information and junk mail. Unfortunately, you'll meet it a lot more times than you care to. Many clients feel they need to be in the know about their industry and amass a huge collection of paper, articles, and books to read. I'm all for it if they actually read it all. But what generally happens is they think they don't have enough time to read it or it's not important enough to read, so they collect way too much stuff and feel guilty about it to boot. If it's not important enough to read, why keep it? If you were really going to read it, you would have already.

✔ Reports

Do you do them weekly, monthly, or quarterly? Any information that you need to use to compile the report goes into here.

✔ Review

What's the difference between Read and Review? Some people put light reading into the Read file and items on which they need to act or make a decision, such as memos or updates, go into the Review file. Very important items to read and think about go into the To Do Category.

✔ Send

This is information that someone wants from you or anything that you need to send to someone.

This is a common type of mistake that wastes an incredible amount of time. I received a call the other day while I was in the middle of working on something very important. I answered, "Good afternoon, Vetter Productivity. This is Greg."

"Hi, Greg. I heard about your workshop on how to be more productive. Would you send me some information on it?"

After qualifying the person, I said, "Of course. I would love to. May I have your name, address, and phone number?" I wrote it down on a card. "Thank you for calling. May I call you in a week to make sure you received the information? Thanks. Good-bye."

All right, potential business. I turned to my computer and I started typing a letter to them. Dear Brian... I turned to the right where my Support Categories were and gathered my articles, brochures, testimonials, and an envelope. I addressed the envelope, stamped it and put the packet together. Thirty minutes later I put it into my Out Box. Whew.

What did I do wrong? I interrupted myself. I stopped what I was working on which was very important and changed direction.

Hint

Create a boundary for yourself. Keep only a certain number of items to read in your Read file. I suggest seven. When you go through your In Box, if there is something else you want to read and you already have seven items in your file, make a decision and throw one of the seven items away, keeping the six that are most important.

Remember, everything that comes into your office will be coming back through at least one more time. Unless it happens to be a copy of the real Declaration of Independence, you can generally throw it away.

Instead of interrupting yourself, simply write the information on a 3 x 5 card and drop it into your In Box. Continue to work on what you were working on before the call. When you go through your In Box the next time, say: Stand, Action, Routine To Do, Send, and drop it into your Send file. Then later on in the day, when you check the files in your Routine To Do and you come to Send, determine whether you'll send the items or not. The secret is to accumulate enough "Sends" so you can save time in the process. I usually wait until I have three or more items in the file. Then when I am gathering my promotional materials, I put together my packets in assembly-line fashion.

If you think about your work patterns during the day, you are probably doing "onesies" all day long. You do it so frequently you wouldn't believe it. What you're doing is interrupting yourself over and over. If you feel like you can never finish anything you've started, performing similar tasks one at a time is probably the reason why.

One thing I guarantee you I'll never say to a caller when they ask me to send it is "When would you like it?" or "Would you like that immediately?" If I do, I am setting myself up to be reactive to their deadline. If they ask you to send something right away and you don't want to be reactive but still keep them happy, you may want to say, "I send out materials on Friday. Will that be okay?" Most of the time it will be.

You can get more done in less time when you are working on the same type of thing and performing the same motion. Think of a bottling plant and an assembly line. If they had to change the product every hour and clean out the machine, their output would be minimal. If there is any way you can put an action off and batch it with others, do so.

✔ Talk With

This is one of the most used files in Routine To Do. There's a group of people with whom you speak more frequently than others. If you were a boss, it would be your direct reports and your executive assistant and your boss. If you work on projects, then it would be the people who you're in contact with during the course of the project. Every time you have a thought or an idea that you want to talk over with someone, simply write it on a 3 x 5 card and drop it into your In Box. Then, when you go through your In Box, drop it into the Subfile under Talk with. In Diagram 4-5, notice there are two Subfiles called "Field" and "Office." Rather than listing all the names, you can split them up by those who are working in the field or in the office.

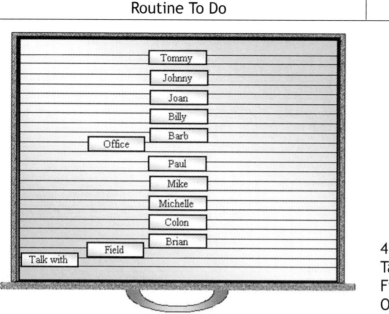

4-5
Talk With
Field And
Office

Think about all the people you talk with regularly. Who do you stay in touch with? How about regarding a particular project or a particular job on which you're working? What about fellow employees? If you talk with the same people all the time, create a file in your Routine To Do called Talk with.

Remember, you'll be checking every file in the Routine To Do Category every day. You're not necessarily working on each file, but definitely looking at all to stay in control.

✔ Type Or Enter

Anytime you need to type something or enter it into your computer, drop it into the Type file. What you don't want to do is stop what you are doing and type every piece of information into your computer the moment you get it unless someone is dictating it to you. Instead, if the information is on a piece of paper, just drop it into your In Box. Then, when you go through your In Box, say: Stand, Action, Routine To Do, Type.

Instead of entering information into your computer all day long, do so once or twice a day. Imagine having eight kids and all of them wanting breakfast at different times. Would you want to make eight different breakfasts for each of them or have one breakfast when they all ate at the same time? Administrative people face the same problem when they are asked, sometimes several times a day, to stop what they are doing and type something.

If you have several tasks of one type of activity, perform them all at the same time. Be focused on that one activity instead of trying to answer a phone, talk with somebody, write a letter, or file. Forget multitasking.

Carol C., a secretary at a major corporation I was working with, was just about ready to quit. She was administering to five extremely demanding managers who would constantly interrupt her during the day and ask her to type things—immediately. I intervened and asked her if it would be possible for her to type everything once in the morning and once in the afternoon? She loved the idea. She devised a schedule. The managers put what they needed typed into their Out Boxes, which she would come by and pick up. What she collected at 9 a.m., she put back in their In Box by 1 p.m. when she made her second pick-up, which she returned by 4 p.m. And they lived happily after.

✔ Write

Anytime you want to write a letter or drop a thank-you note to someone, simply drop their card into the Write file.

✔ Filing

Would filing be a file in your Routine To Do? Absolutely not! Get that thought out of your head forever. Be gone! The only time to file is when you go through your In Box. It's Step 5 in going through your In Box: File it away. I often catch administrative people doing whatever they can to avoid filing. They say they have too much to file. You would too if you never filed. The problem is they don't file three times a day and it builds up—kind of like waxy build-up on your floor. Another reason is that they don't have a good system that allows them to file items away in seconds. Many have created a file called Filing. It usually looks like a big pile of files that they don't want to file.

Look through all your Routine To Do's every day. You don't necessarily need to do every Routine To Do, but you must look at every file. Looking at all your files allows you to be aware of what is going on. The more aware you are, the more in control you are. The more in control you are, the less stressed you are. When you go through and look at your Routine To Do's, whatever you decide to do it that day, do it right then during your Routine To Do time. If not, check them all again tomorrow and decide if you have enough of them to do. You want to empty every file at least once a week. That means everything in your file will be new each week. Of course, there are exceptions. You may want to pay bills every two weeks or do a report on a monthly basis.

Remember, you can save an hour a day by changing this interruptive behavior. The purpose of the Routine To Do is to batch similar tasks together, do them at the same time, and stop interrupting yourself and shifting from Processing and Producing.

A Little Help From My Friend

A secretary can assist a manager by presorting some of his/her Routine To Do files, saving the boss some time. Typically, the administrative person can set up yellow-colored manila folders that have the same file names as his/her boss's Routine To Do files, such as: Sign, Read, and Review. One file that you don't want to use would be Urgent.

The boss can then take the contents of each of these files and drop them into his or her Routine To Do files. Better yet, the administrative assistant can drop them directly into his/her boss's Routine To Do files when bringing information in during their three visits.

Remember These Concepts

- Batch and block similar activities together.

Things To Avoid

- Working on similar tasks individually or separately.
- Having to have it now.
- Multitasking.

3.5

To Do

The Purpose Of The System

- The Proactive Side Of The Street
- In The Eye Of The Beholder
- Buzz Me Now
- A, B, C, Easy As 1, 2, 3
- Flying A's
- Do B's
- The C Section
- Firefighting
- A Taxing Time Fer Sure
- Go To Your Room And Be Quiet
- The Few, The Proud, The 1-5's
- Life In The To Do Category
- The Apple Of My A
- Administrative People

What You Will Learn In This Chapter

- Differentiating between important and urgent activities
- What a Quiet Time is and how to set one up
- Why your Quiet Time is the most important time you can spend

---

💣☀ <u>Myths of the Office</u>

Urgent items must be important.

The Purpose Of The System

The Proactive Side Of The Street

We have covered one side of the Action Categories containing the Tickler and Routine To Do Categories. Now we are going to look at the other side which contains the To Do Category. We'll cover the other half of this side, Projects, in the next chapter.

Unfortunately, few people ever venture into this proactive, impactful, importance-based left side. They are too busy reacting to the urgencies of the day, thus eliminating time that could be spent on their important tasks.

> *Create time from time you think you don't have.*

The way to work in this side is to create time from time you think you don't have but actually do have. In other words, if you spend your time reacting all day, you won't have any time to proact. The key is to create a time every day when you work on important issues and then fit in all your other tasks around it. This is Quiet Time. We'll talk about Quiet Time later in the chapter.

The rules are simple. You get 24 hours a day. Do with them as you wish. The way to win the game is to realize that you can't get everything done, no matter how hard you try. My guess is businesses will generally try to give their employees two and a half times the amount of today's work in the future. The way to accomplish more, especially your meaningful, important tasks, is to spend time working in each of the four Categories—not just in the reactive Tickler. Working in the To Do Category gives you a self-controlled, self-managed, proactive focus on your impactful and long-term goals—a tremendous benefit.

In The Eye Of The Beholder

Pick up a book. Now hold it out flat in front of you at eye level so that when you look at it, you can only see two dimensions—its height and its length. When you look at it from this angle, you'd swear it has only two dimensions. Now tip either corner of the book. You're now viewing it from a different perspective. Three dimensions are now evident—height, length, and depth. It looks totally different, yet it's the same book.

The same can be said of the way you view your work. You can view your tasks from a deadline, time-based perspective, such as the Tickler, or view them from an importance-based perspective, such as the To Do Category. The way you choose to view them will dictate how you work, your stress level, and how much work you accomplish.

Buzz Me Now

Years ago, Alec Mackenzie wrote a book called *The Time Trap*. He described a system of working by rating the importance of the tasks. A's were most important, B's were the next while C's were the least important. I liked the concept and used it.

However, after using it for a while, I discovered that what I wanted to work on were primarily C's. In doing so, I sorely neglected my A's. Why the C's? Because C's were easy to do. They were easily accomplished and gave me a quick buzz, kind of like the payoff the Tickler gives you—instant nirvana.

At the end of the day, though, I always seemed to have a sick feeling in my gut—a feeling that I hadn't gotten anything done. That wasn't quite true. I was getting a lot done but not what I needed to get done—the real important stuff. My rationale was that I had no desire to work on an A, which felt like kissing my sister, when I could work on a C, which felt like—oh well, never mind.

Getting that buzz is the payoff that most of us want. Remember, all our actions are dictated by a payoff. If it feels good, we'll do it. We love to live for the moment, the here and now.

Think how many people have more than two TV sets in their home. Many have one in every room. How about that new car they have to get every three years? What about that yearly three-week vacation to a new and exotic location? Yet when it comes to putting some money away for savings, there never seems to be any left.

You think I'm exaggerating? Credit card debt today is around a trillion dollars. An average cardholder balance is $6,000, with a third of all payments simply being minimum installment payments. Instant gratification, ladies and gentlemen. Never mind that cardholders are losing hundreds, thousands of dollars in interest payments each year. They have whatever they want, right now.

Some of us are nothing more than little kids in big bodies. The difference between a child and an adult is discipline, i.e., delaying gratification now for a greater benefit in the future. If you were to categorize payoffs, instant gratification would go on the Tickler side and delayed gratification would go on the To Do side. Now you can see why we have this urgent, get-buzzed mentality at work. We brought it to work in our lunch box without ever even knowing that we were doing it.

A, B, C, Easy As 1, 2, 3

What should go into the To Do Category? Tasks that are important or value-driven. Tasks that make an impact. An activity that nets a big result later on. Something that can be done before it's due. Something that you normally wouldn't have the time to do that you make time to do. Something that you do now with no immediate buzz or instant high that will bring big benefits down the road. In a way, To Do's are the opposite of Ticklers. To Do's are importance-based and Ticklers are time-based. If you don't do your To Do's, many of them will become urgencies which will eventually end up in the Tickler.

The To Do Category consists of the files A, B, C and 1-5.

- A   Is a Very Important task

- B   Is an Important task

- C   Is a Somewhat Important task

- 1 - 5 Are the top five most important tasks that you work on in your Quiet Time (QT) which occurs every day at the same time.

The definition of an A, B, and C is up to you. You may substitute words for Very Important (A), Important (B), and Somewhat Important (C) as long as you don't use words such as "urgent," "critical," or any others that specify time. They belong on the other side of the chart in the Tickler, the reactive and time-based side.

The following are some examples of tasks that are proactive and go into the To Do Category.

Proactive Action	Result
◆ Taking a computer class	Your typing speed zooms from 15 words per minute to 30 words per minute. You are productive!
◆ Planting bulbs in the fall	A beautiful yard with beautiful, blossoming flowers in the spring. You are happy!

◆ Taking a week at the beginning of the year to set goals and plan a chart of action for the upcoming year

More focus and direction all year long; increased revenues. You are in control!

◆ Saving $100 a month for your IRA

$100 a month in a fund that nets 10 percent will yield a million dollars in 20 years. You are rich! (Although I can do the math, I am not a financial planner. Please consult a professional.)

Flying A's

Let's talk about what a To Do A is. To Do A's are the most important and impactful actions you can take. A's are for activities that make you more efficient or effective. A good example is taking time to plan. The more time you spend planning, the more focused you'll be and the better results you'll experience. In order to get, you have to give.

Tasks that are very important will be the majority of your To Do A's. Writing a letter to a prospect that is interested in licensing your system. Working on a client's file. Making a change to your web page.

A's are tasks that are due in the future—anywhere from a few days away to months

> *In order to get, you have to give.*

away— that you can accomplish before they are due. Remember my book report that was due the Monday following Thanksgiving? I could have enjoyed three worry-free months if I had chosen to do that stupid book report earlier. Time is always a factor. If a deadline enters into a task that is important, always make it an A.

Anything that I feel is very important goes into my To Do A's, especially if time comes into play. I need to do a report for my boss, which is due in a week. Stand, Action, To Do, A. Rather than filing it into my Tickler the day before it is due, I put it into my To Do A's and do it way before it is due.

Think about a task that doesn't have a deadline or isn't due in the near future. Most people automatically assume that if something doesn't have a deadline, it can't be that important. When you have a long time to work on something, you tend to think of it as unimportant. Why? Because people believe that time, meaning when an item is due, is what dictates its importance.

Say I want to spend more time on devising ways to deliver more interactive workshops. What can I do? I write "Deliver workshops" and "20 minutes" on a 3 x 5 card. I drop it into my In Box. When I go through my In Box, I say: Stand, Action, To Do, A. What I'm doing is creating a 20-minute

> *When you have a long time to accomplish a task, you tend to think of it as unimportant.*

block of time in my QT to think about how to make my workshops more interactive. A To Do A can be something that isn't mandatory, a task you've chosen because you think it is important for you to do rather than something that you have to do.

A final example of a To Do A: On the golf course you have a brainstorm about something you want to do at work. You whip out a 3 x 5 card. (Yes, they're everywhere, even in your golf bag!) and jot down your thought. What you're doing is committing yourself to thinking about or working on this thought during your QT. Once you start to add these types of proactive activities to your arsenal, you are on your way to becoming a Jedi knight. May the Proaction be with you!

If you want to teach your children to be successful in the business world, there are three concepts you can teach them. Writing down goals, reviewing them regularly, and being proactive.

What prevents us from doing To Do activities is the mindset that we don't have the time and there's no immediate gratification. It's tough to change direction in midstream. We're so programmed for instant gratification that it may be one of the hardest habits you'll ever change.

Do B's

Understanding what constitutes an A is easy. It's the most impactful action you can do. What is a B? My first thought is to say B's are things that buzz around and sting you. Of course, there are also good B's like the Do Bee on the old Romper Room show or the musical group, The Doobie Brothers. So much for my definitions. You need to come up with your own.

To Do B tasks are important tasks; they don't have the same impact as A's, but they're more important than C's. The difference is in the degree of importance.

An example of a B could be filling out a new frequent-flier form. If you flew a lot, you wouldn't want to lose any miles so it would probably be an A. Again, it is how you view and rate the task and its importance to you or others.

The C Section

I had very little money when I first started my business. I was living and working in a $425 a month apartment, working on a old dining room table, using a file cabinet I had found next to the dumpster, and driving a '78 Monte Carlo. I was the picture of success.

I knew I needed to promote myself. I wanted to spend $1,500 on public relations but at the time, getting $1,500 meant winning the lottery. I wrote "$1,500 for PR" on a 3 x 5 card and dropped it into a folder in the To Do C section. I knew I didn't have the money then but would in the future. Once a week, on every Friday for a year, I looked at that card in the C section with "$1,500 for PR" written on it.

A year later I finally had saved enough money to do it. On Friday, I pulled it out of the C's and moved it up to the To Do A's. What's so nice about moving A's, B's, and C's around in your To Do Category is you simply pick up the hanging folder and move it behind any of the stapled A, B or C hanging guide folders. No fuss or muss. No more having to rewrite the task or fool around with to do lists.

Monday came. After dropping my most important task into the 1 File, I then dropped the card into the 2 File in the 1-5 section and worked on it in my QT. A year after I dropped it into my To Do C, I finally spent the $1,500 for public relations. As a result, I had a newspaper article that went in front of 400,000 people, a spot on the 5 o'clock news, and two magazine articles. So much exposure for such a small investment. A good return for a lowly To Do C that I wouldn't throw away.

Some things are going to be very important, some important, and some of little importance, depending on a lot of different factors. It's okay to put your tasks into the C section because, eventually, if they become important enough for you, or the conditions are right, you'll want to move them up and take action on them.

Putting tasks into the To Do C section allows you to empty your mind of all those thoughts that constantly buzz around in your head—small things that you want to do, but don't want to spend time on. On the other hand, many of the C's will bite the dust because, after while, you will throw them away due to lack of interest or changes in your condition.

Firefighting

People say to me there's no difference between putting a task into the Tickler Category or the To Do Category. It's still work you have to do, no matter where you put it. I agree, partially. However, breaking down your tasks into four approaches or Categories gives you that much more control over your work life. Don't forget that when you approach everything from the Tickler mentality, you'll encounter the Snowball from Hades. Would you rather perform a task on your terms or on someone else's hectic and rushed timetable?

Question: If you have to put out the same fires over and over, what does it tell you?
Answer: You are a firefighter, not a fire marshal. You are a reactor rather than a proactor. You may be in the habit of doing something, unaware that it's not working.

If you constantly firefight, then something is wrong with your thinking or your company's culture. Of course, you may just have picked a job that is totally reactive, though they are far and few. Ask yourself what fires you put out over and over. With whom? Why? The sooner you find a solution, the sooner your life will run more smoothly.

Finding a solution would be a To Do A. You could write it on a little card with a 20-minute time limit. You could spend 20 minutes in your QT thinking about what was happening and the patterns that you were repeating. Otherwise, if you don't change, you are probably going to go up in one big blaze. No individual or company can constantly continue to firefight 24 hours a day. People will eventually burn out. I see them all the time. Toast!

A Taxing Time Fer Sure

If you are scheduled for a speech a month from now, you certainly don't want to put it in your Tickler 28 days from today. That would leave you just three days to do it. You'd be rushing around trying to get it done in time. Why wait? Emergencies and urgencies will no doubt pop up; you'll be interrupted more times than ever before. Unforeseen dark forces from another planet will swoop down upon your perfectly normal days, ruining them and causing you to have to work late into the night just to finish your tasks.

Why not put that task into the To Do Category and get it done early? When you take time to work on things that are due in the future and you get them done now, your life changes in a way that is difficult to understand unless you actually experience it. It's the easiest and least stressful way to accomplish a task.

I used to wait until April to do my taxes. They'd hang over my head for months. I now do them in January, as quickly as possible, even with the deadline of April 15th still far off in the future. I take the first two weeks of the new year to organize my office, do my taxes, and plan my year. I spend a week in pure strategic planning so I know exactly where I am going and how I will get there during the course of the year. The old saying "If you don't know where you're going, you'll never get where you want to go" is true.

> *If you don't know where you're going, you'll never get where you want to go.*

When I tell people I take two whole weeks to do this, they give me a suspicious look and ask, "How can you afford to take two weeks off? Where do you get that kind of time?" I make that kind of time. I want to knock it out and get it done as quickly as possible. This gives me February, March, and April stress-free with my taxes already done. Even more important, I get to experience smooth, stress-free sailing from May through December due to the yearly plan I created.

I'll never forget a conversation I had with a president of a company. "How much time do you spend on planning?" I asked. "I don't have time to spend on planning," he actually responded. As I got back up into my chair after falling out of it, I inquired as to who did the planning for his company, his secretary? It's frightening. If a president doesn't plan or doesn't think he or she has the time to plan, who's going to do the planning? What kind of an example is he/she setting? If you're an officer or in a management position, you better darn well take time to plan. It's an essential, proactive activity of yours. Getting it done now is going to be a whole lot easier than trying to do it down the line when all heck is breaking loose. And rest assured, it will break loose.

Go To Your Room And Be Quiet

Our work environment today is hectic. Too much to do, too many distractions, too noisy, and not enough hours in the day to get it all done. The only way to get ahead is by getting behind. Life is one big irony. The more you give away the more you get. Give up the need to be popular and you will be. Your degree of success in life will be determined by how willing you are to fail.

What do I mean by getting behind? Losing in the beginning in order to gain later on. Taking time out of your already hectic day that you feel that you can't afford to take and working on high-impact work. The time to do this is in a Quiet Time.

A QT is a totally undisturbed time—that means your door is shut, your phone is off the hook, you don't allow any interruptions—that you take at the same time every day. It allows you to work on your most important tasks rather than your most urgent ones.

> *A way to get ahead is by getting a little behind.*

Ideally, your QT needs to be 20 percent of the total hours you work. Say you work ten hours a day. Your QT would be two hours. The benefit of keeping your QT at the same time every day is that people will recognize it as your time and eventually learn not to interrupt you.

The other benefit of taking it at the same time every day is that you will create a habit. Have you ever stood in front of the mirror in the morning with your toothbrush in one hand and your toothpaste in the other and asked yourself if you were going to brush your teeth? Of course not. You just merrily brushed away because you've been doing it that way for as long as you can remember. Habits are very beneficial since little or no thought is needed to accomplish those tasks that have become part of your routine. When your QT becomes a habit, you get to work undisturbed, completely focused on important tasks, for a specified time every day. And you thought you didn't have time!

It's vitally important to write down your Quiet Time in your appointment book or in your contact manager 30 days in advance and block out the time. This will greatly assist you with doing it.

If you really want to play in the big leagues and double your company's productivity, institute a company-wide QT every day at the same time. You won't believe how much more will get done or the change in your bottom line!

The Few, The Proud, The 1-5's

Every day, right before your QT, look at all of your To Do A's. You'll be picking out the top five most important and impactful tasks. Select the most important task. After you remove the task from the yellow folder, place it in the 1 File and place the empty yellow folder in the front of the drawer where the other empty yellow folders are stored—right in front of the 1 File. Repeat the procedure with the next four most important tasks. When you are finished, 1-5 will be filled with your top five most important tasks.

Another way to do this is, instead of removing the task from the yellow folder and placing it into one of the 1-5 folders, place both the folder and task into one of the 1-5 folders. Or you can staple the 1-5 folders shut and simply place the task and folder behind each 1-5 folder. It doesn't matter as long as you're working on your top five most important To Do A's every day in your QT.

Every day you are going to look at all your To Do A's. It's like a 3-D to do list, except instead of being on a list, your important tasks will be in hanging folders. Do not look at your B's and C's every day because they are not as important as the A's are. You have enough to do without worrying about the lesser important tasks. You'll be checking your B's and C's only on Friday.

You'll be working on your 1-5's, which are your top five A's. You'll start with 1 and then 2 and continue until number 5. If you finish all of your 1-5's, go back to your To Do A's, pick out the next top five tasks and place them in the 1-5 folders.

Once a week, you'll review all your A's, B's, and C's and reprioritize them. B's will move to A's, C's will move to A's, sometimes A's will move to B's and C's. When you set up your Action Categories in your file drawer, the first items will be empty file folders. Behind them will be your 1-5 Files followed by your A, B, and C Files. You'll never have an A-1. The only A-1 is a steak sauce and belongs in your kitchen, not your office.

Is it easy to do a QT every day? It can be a challenge. Why? Because business life happens. If a meeting comes up during your normal QT, you'll probably need to go to that wonderful meeting. Reschedule your

> *Take a QT every day at the same time, working on important rather than urgent tasks.*

QT for another time that day. Remember, everything should be scheduled around your QT. Do it the same time every day and before you know it, it will be a habit and you won't have to think about it as much.

The more you do it, the more of the big stuff you'll get done. One day, perhaps 30, 60, or 90 days in the future, you'll subtly be aware that all the work and time you have put in during your QT is starting to pay off.

Life In The To Do Category

Clear out all the thoughts of things to do in your head and write each one on a 3 x 5 card. Let the system do the thinking and worrying for you. This will allow you to keep your head clear and focused on what you are really supposed to be doing. It's time to let go (Diagram 5-1).

There are 1-5 and A, B, and C Files. The A hanging folder is stapled together, as is the B and C, so you can't put any of the tasks in them. Each A, B, or C task will go into their own separate hanging folder rather into just one big A, B, or C folder. I tried putting all the A's into one folder, the B's into one and the C's into one. What I found was they were too jumbled up and I wasn't disciplined enough to look through the tangled mess in each folder. So unlike the Tickler and the Routine To Do, each To Do A, B, and C go into a separate hanging folder behind the stapled A, B, and C hanging folder guide.

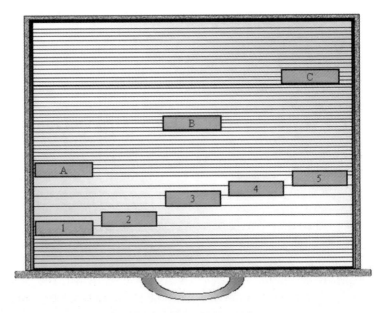

5-1
To Do's

Every time I go through my In Box, and I decide a task is a To Do A, I say: Stand, Action, To Do, A. I drop it into an empty hanging folder that is located in front of my 1- 5's. I then place the hanging folder behind the guide A hanging folder file. Why do I keep empty folders in front of the first file? Because it's the easiest place to grab them, it keeps them together, and by not having empty hanging folders scattered throughout my To Do Category, I'll have an accurate view of how much I actually have to do. Keeping empty hanging folders throughout the To Do section will bulk up the drawer, making it seem overwhelming with work to be done. When I have a To Do, I simply drop the To Do into the first empty folder in the front and then place the folder behind either the A, B, or C stapled folder guide.

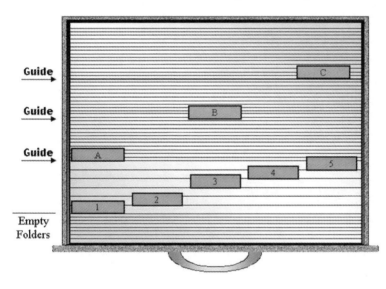

5-2
Empty
Folders
With Guide
A, B, and C

All the hanging folders with your A's, B's, and C's will be tabless. How will you know what's in each folder if there's no tab on it? The ones you'll be most concerned about are your A's. You'll look at all of your To Do A's every day right before your QT so you'll always know what they are. They won't be in the A section long since you'll be working on your top five To Do A's every day.

Don't put more than a dozen To Do A's behind the A guide folder. If you have too many A's, you will just overwhelm yourself. If you ever run out of all your A's, all you need to do is move up B's to the A section and make them A's. There's an extremely slim chance that you'll ever run out of A's, since you'll be feeding your To Do Category three times a day from your In Box. There will be plenty of B's and C's. You can have as many as you wish. The goal of the To Do's is to constantly move B's and C's up to become A's.

Remember, never do a B or C. What you will be working on are your top five A's which are made up of your most important To Do A's.

When you go through your In Box and process it, you will never say Stand, Action, To Do, 1. There are only A's, B's, and C's which go into their own separate hanging folders.

Finally, feel free to work on your 1-5's as much as you can during the day, even if it's not your QT.

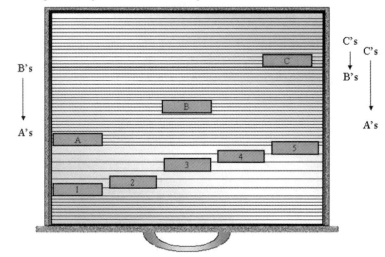

5-3
C's to B's
to A's

The Apple Of My A

What happens when you leave a bad apple in the barrel? They all go bad. What you don't want to do is leave an A in the A section for more than a couple of weeks. If you notice that you have, ask yourself if it really is an A. If not, move it to the B section.

Years ago I had a form to fill out to advertise my services in a magazine aimed at a certain profession which will remain nameless. It stayed in To Do A for three months. (This happened many years ago. Hey, I'm human too!) Finally, when I came to my senses on a Friday while I was doing my weekly review, I moved it to B. The next week it moved to C. Then the following Friday I trashed it. It finally occurred to me that the reason I wasn't doing it was because many of the people in this profession were not very scrupulous (now you know about whom I am speaking) and I really didn't want to work in that industry.

Another reason an A stays in the A section too long is that you are procrastinating. If you are, immediately move it to 1-5 and do it in your next QT. If you still won't do it, make it a Project and break it down into little steps. In the next chapter, you'll discover that Projects are nothing more than big tasks that are broken down into a lot of To Do A's.

Administrative People

If you are an administrative person and can work in a QT, so much the better. Take a Quiet Time by switching with another administrative person. In return, cover for him or her. Have one administrative person be in a Quiet Time and another one answer the phone for both of you. To get 30 minutes a day or an hour every two days or even an hour a week is a bonus.

If your boss is out of the office, go into your boss's office and close the door during your QT. Check to make sure it is okay with El Bosso first or you may be experiencing a lot more Quiet Time at your place of residence than you ever wanted.

If you're in a management job, give your administrative people some Quiet Time. They need it more than anybody else does, because they're under the gun and are interrupted often.

If you can't get a QT, work your 1-5's any time you can during the day. If that is still too much, use only the A and B folders and work from the A's every day. Generally, administrative people won't have many A's, B's, and C's, so you may not need a 1-5 to prioritize them. Remember, a To Do is anything that can be done that is important, a one-time activity, neither routine nor a maintenance task, is not urgent or doesn't have to be done on a specific date.

> *Successful people are those people who are willing to do those things that unsuccessful people are not willing to do.*

People ask me why I created this system. Quiet Time is the reason for the system. QT can really make a difference in your work life.

If you choose to do this, I can guarantee your success at being highly productive. I have worked with some pretty powerful individuals through the years, and the most successful are those who do this. There is an old saying in the insurance industry: "Successful people are those people who are willing to do those things that unsuccessful people are not willing to do." It is that simple and yet that difficult. Life is full of irony.

Remember These Concepts

- Create time from time you think you don't have.
- In order to get, you have to give.
- When you have a long time to accomplish a task, you tend to think of it as unimportant.
- If you don't know where you're going, you'll never get where you want to go.
- A way to get ahead is by getting a little behind.
- Take a QT every day at the same time, working on important rather than urgent tasks.
- Successful people are those people who are willing to do those things that unsuccessful people are not willing to do.

Things To Avoid

- Doing a Routine To Do or Tickler task in the QT.

3.6

Project Management

Projects

- My Husband Had His Project Cut Off And I Haven't Had Any Relief Since
- Projects
- Your Guide Today
- Slowly I Turn, Step By Step, Inch By Inch
- Support Can Be Beautiful
- Ladies And Gentlemen, Start Your Projects
- Setting Up A Project

What You Will Learn In This Chapter

- What a Project is
- How to break down Projects so you will do them

☀ <u>Myths of the Office</u>

I can always get a project accomplished more easily if I wait until the last minute.

Projects

My Husband Had His Project Cut Off And I Haven't Had Any Relief Since

Years ago, I was saving the world by working as a social worker in Virginia in the heart of the tobacco fields. We often received letters from our caseload of clients who were trying to explain their predicament. Sometimes what came out was pretty funny such as the title above. I felt it was a perfect way to head this section on Projects. In addition to the above, the following are also actual excerpts of that valuable type of information we received from them. What's their relevance to organization? None that I can think of, but at this point in the book, I thought you could probably use a laugh. You figure them out.

1. Mrs. Jones has not had any clothes on for a year and has been visited regularly by the clergy.

2. I am glad to report that my husband who is missing is dead.

3. Please find for certain if my husband is dead. The man I am now living with can't eat or do anything until he knows.

4. Unless I get my money soon I will be forced to lead an immortal life.

5. You have changed my little boy to a girl. Will this make any difference?

6. In accordance with your instructions I have given birth to twins in the enclosed envelope.

7. In answer to your letter I have given birth to a son weighing ten pounds. I hope this is satisfactory.

8. I want money as quick as I can get it. I have been in bed with the doctor for two weeks and he doesn't do me any good. If things don't improve, I will have to send for another doctor.

9. I am forwarding my marriage certificate and my three children; one of which is a mistake as you can see.

10. I am very much annoyed to find that you have branded my son illiterate. This is a dirty lie, as I was married a week before he was born.

Now you can see why I got out of that line of work.

Projects

We now come to the fourth Action Category, Projects. What is a Project? A Project is a series of steps or tasks to do over a period of time. Projects are slightly different from the other three Action Categories in that they are more of a holding area. Because of this, the steps of the Project have to go into one of the other Action Categories to be done: To Do, Tickler, and Routine To Do.

How is a Project different from a To Do? A To Do is a one-time task. To Do's usually can be completed in one sitting. Projects take time to finish. Many times they'll take more than a couple of hours, sometimes weeks, months, or even longer.

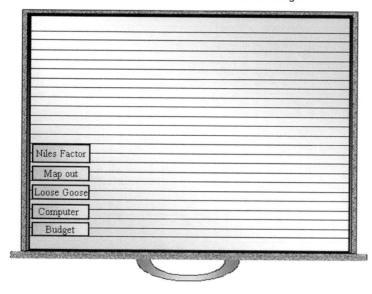

6-1
Projects

A Project consists of three areas: a guide sheet, step sheets, and Support information. The guide sheet gives you an overall view of what needs to be done and lists the steps to do. The step sheets contain each individual step from the guide sheet broken down on a separate sheet. When all the steps are completed, the Project is completed. The Support materials include information that you refer to regarding the Project and work that you have completed from the Project.

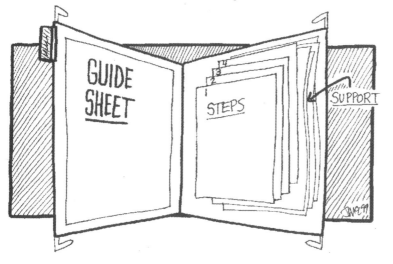

6-2
Guide
Sheet,
Steps, And
Support

Projects are hybrids. A hybrid has the properties of two or more items. Remember back when Gregor Mendell was experimenting by combining different varieties of flowers and attempting to create new ones? Those were hybrids. My favorite example of a hybrid is the broccoflower. A broccoflower is a vegetable composed of both broccoli and cauliflower. Great! Just what I need, another vegetable that I hate.

A Project has both Action and Support components in it. The guide and the steps are part of the Action. The reference materials and completed work are part of the Support. Even though there are Support elements in a Project, you still want to keep the file with your other Action Categories. Why? Leaving something in the Support area means you don't want to do anything with it; thus nothing will prompt you to do it. If any portion of any task is an Action, it always needs to go into the Action area.

Your Guide Today

The guide sheet gives you an overall view of the Project, a listing of all the steps, which step you are on, deadline dates, to whom a step was delegated. It provides the big picture as well as a visual outline of all the steps needed to complete it. The guide sheet is paper-clipped or stapled on the inside left of a yellow hanging folder. The format of a guide sheet can be set up many ways. The following diagrams show a few examples.

6-3
Project
Guide
Sheet With
Numbers

Project: _____ Target Date:_____

Due Date: Steps:

_____ 1. _____

_____ 2. _____

_____ 3. _____

_____ 4. _____

_____ 5. _____

_____ 6. _____

_____ 7. _____

_____ 8. _____

Project: _____ Target Date:_____

Due Date: Steps:

_____   _____

_____   _____

_____   _____

_____   _____

_____   _____

_____   _____

_____   _____

_____   _____

_____   _____

6-4
Project
Guide
Sheet
Without
Numbers

Project: _____ Target Date:_____

Due Date: Steps:

_____   1. _____

_____   _____

_____   _____

_____   2. _____

_____   _____

_____   _____

_____   3. _____

_____   _____

_____   _____

_____   4. _____

6-5
Project
Guide
Sheet With
Staggered
Numbers
And Spaces

6-6
Project
Guide
Sheet
Numbered
With
Object,
Results,
Contact
And Phone
Number,
And As-
signed To

Project: _____ Target Date:_____

Objective: _____

Results: _____

_____

Contact: _____ Phone #: _____

Assigned To: _____

Due Date: Steps:

_____   1. _____

_____   2. _____

_____   3. _____

_____   4. _____

_____   5. _____

6-7
Project
Guide
Sheet With
Delegated
To And No
Numbers

Project: _____ Target Date:_____

Due Date: Steps: Delegated To:

_____   _____   _____

_____   _____   _____

_____   _____   _____

_____   _____   _____

_____   _____   _____

_____   _____   _____

_____   _____   _____

_____   _____   _____

_____   _____   _____

_____   _____   _____

Typically there will be a space for the Project name and the completion date at the top of each guide sheet. Don't fill in the due date along the left side of the guide sheet unless you really have one. Other parts of the sheet can include your objective with the Project, the results you want to accomplish, a contact name and phone number, and to whom it is assigned or delegated.

Many times, additional steps are added to a Project once it has begun. Rather than completely number every step on the left side, intermittent steps are numbered with spaces under each to allow you to list the new steps such as in Diagram 6-4.

That way, when you need to add steps, you can write 4A, 4B, etc. You can also use the guide sheet as a way to monitor Projects you have delegated to others.

Slowly I Turn, Step By Step, Inch By Inch

On your guide sheet, you'll have all the steps, or as many as you know about, listed down the page. For every step that is listed on the guide sheet, you'll also have a separate step sheet or 3 x 5 card that will correspond to the step on the guide sheet. If you have ten steps, you'll have ten separate step sheets. They'll be paper-clipped together with Step #1 on top and the other steps following behind in descending order. Keep the entire batch of steps on the right side of your folder.

You'll need to number each step sheet. You can do this by writing a number next to Step # _____ on the left side of the sheet. Below the step number, write out the instructions for the step, which you copy directly from the guide sheet. Do this with each step on the guide sheet. The lines on the step sheet allow you to use it as a worksheet; you can save it and later reference it in the Support section of your Project.

Project: _____ Date Due By:_____

Steps #: _____

_____

_____

_____

_____

6-8
Step Sheet

Support Can Be Beautiful

So far we've talked about the guide and the steps which are part of the Action section. Now let's look at the Support information and materials that accompany a Project. Think about all the paper that you refer to when you are working on a Project. Where do you keep it? Where do you keep parts of it that you have completed? Contacts, statistics, and correspondence can all go into the back of the folder or, if the folder is opened up, the far right inside back of the Project hanging folder.

If you pulled out a Project hanging folder from your drawer and opened it up, you'd find the guide sheet paper-clipped or stapled to the left inside front of the folder. In the middle would be the steps clipped together and, finally, the Support materials on the far right side or inside back of the Project folder.

Normally you will use only one hanging folder per Project with the name of the Project on the tab all the way over to the left front side of the hanging folder. When working on a Project, the simplest and easiest way to keep track of pertinent reference materials is to leave them in other Support Categories rather than having a fat Project File.

If you don't already have an existing file for the Support materials you'll be using with the Project, and you have a considerable amount that won't fit into one hanging folder, use multiple hanging folders. Keep your guide and your steps in the main Project folder with the Project name tab on it. All Support information will then go into additional folders behind the first, main folder. The tabs will be one tab length over to the right in the second column (Diagram 6-9).

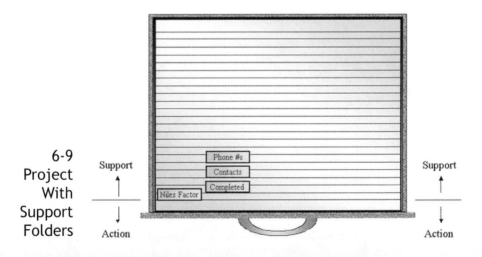

6-9
Project
With
Support
Folders

Breaking down your Support materials into separate files will give you breathing space. Possible Support File names are: Contacts, Completed work, Phone numbers, and any other names you choose to use. If possible, use the same Support File names over and over for various Projects. You'll become familiar with those names, making it easier to locate reference materials when you need to set up the files for a new Project.

Ladies And Gentlemen, Start Your Projects

How do you start the Project? Remember, Projects are a holding area for the steps and unless you move them into another Action Category, they'll stay in the Project folder forever or until your boss yells at you. Steps flow out from the main Project hanging folder like flying saucers do from the mother ship. They fly out, but they also eventually return.

Think about how you cheat on a diet. Take a piece of cake, for instance. You'll pick off just a little piece, justifying that you really aren't eating it. Then another itsy, bitsy piece. Then another. And another. "Hey, I'm not really eating it," you say. "I'm just having a little pick here and there." You can use this wonderful skill you have developed through the years to make working on a Project easier. Just like that gigantic mound of pure chocolate delight that vanished due to the cultivated art of being a skillful picker, so can your Project.

Most people hate to work on Projects because they are too big, too difficult or take too long to do. So, what do you do? Procrastinate, as any self-respecting employee would.

Anything that you procrastinate is a perfect candidate for becoming a Project. If that means the Project has only two or three steps, so what? At least this way you are getting your task done. If you utilize that same picking technique you'll be amazed at how easily those steps can be accomplished. The secret is to break the Projects down into very small and easy-to-do tasks—20 minutes or less so you get that high or buzz. By doing this, you are fooling your brain into believing it will get buzzed.

Let's talk again about a favorite American pastime, doing your taxes. Why would doing your taxes be a Project? Because most of us can't get our taxes done in less than a couple of hours. Of course, if you can use the short form, that would make doing your taxes a To Do A rather than a Project. It's a fairly simple process. I'm sure you have seen the form. List the money you have made and send it all in. So easy, isn't it! Come to think of it, that's pretty close to the long form too.

So the Project would be to do your taxes. Say the date you want to finish them is February 15th. The very first thing you need to do with any Project is to brainstorm it. Brainstorming is simply going into your right brain, which is the artistic, conceptual, idea side. There are no bad or wrong ideas in the right brain. Think about all the different tasks that you need to perform with your taxes. Take a blank piece of paper and list every thought and action that comes to mind. Write them all down anywhere you want on the paper!

Once you have listed them all, come back to reality and shift from your right brain to your left brain—the structured, logical side. Look at all the ideas you wrote on the sheet and eliminate any that won't work or don't make sense. A few might be: Getting the forms; Interest earned; Receipts; Calling your accountant; Bank statements; Mortgages; Investments; W-2's; Expenses; Offshore accounts; Moving out of the country to the North Pole because you can't take it any more. Then list the steps in the order that you'll do them.

> *The smaller and simpler the task is, the greater the chance of doing it.*

Break down the tasks into the simplest and smallest components you can. Say it took you 15 hours to do your taxes. If from January 1st to April 15th you only spent one hour each weekend (15 weekends) on them, you'd have them done. The best way to motivate yourself to accomplish a task is by making it very simple to do and rewarding yourself with a buzz. If a task is simple, you'll have a greater chance of doing it. If you get a buzz, you'll be that much more ready to do it.

Your Projects will be much easier to complete if you do this. The smaller you can make the steps, the more you'll get done and the quicker you'll get them done. You can always create five-minute tasks. I personally would rather do 20 five-minute tasks than one large, lengthy task.

Once you have established the steps on the guide sheet, set up a step sheet for each step. Let's say there are ten steps to doing your taxes. On each step sheet you will list the Project name: Taxes. Where it says Step # ___, you'll fill in the blank with 1 on the first sheet, 2 on the second, and so on.

If you have deadlines, list them on the guide sheet on the left and on the top right of that particular step sheet. The due date on the step sheet will correspond with each of the steps on the guide sheet.

Grab a yellow hanging folder and label the tab Taxes. On one side is your guide, in the middle clipped together are ten step sheets, and any tax-related reference materials are in the back of the file.

How do you get started? Go to the Project folder and pull out step sheet #1. Drop it into your In Box and you're on your way.

Setting Up A Project

The following are all the steps in setting up a Project:

1. Try to get out of it. (The sensible thing.)

2. Try to delegate it back to your boss. ("I know you are very skilled at... Could you help me with...?") Caution. Doing this too much may cause you to be delegated to another company.

3. Delegate it to one of your employees who have been slacking off lately. (There are so many to choose from.)

4. When you can't get out of it, find someone else who is crazy enough to do it. (Some people like to do things you don't like. Can you believe that?)

5. Having failed at the above attempts, name the Project and write it on a tab.

6. Attach the tab to the front of a yellow hanging folder all the way to the left.

7. List the objective you want to accomplish on the guide sheet. (Optional)

8. List the results you want on the guide sheet. (Optional)

9. Decide if you want a completion date. If you do, or if you have a target date, list it on the top right of the guide sheet.

10. Go into your right brain. Brainstorm on a separate sheet of paper. Come up with as many thoughts and ideas you can on what needs to be done.

11. Shift into your left brain. Eliminate any unnecessary steps from the list.

12. Number the steps in the order you want to do them.

13. Transfer the steps onto the guide sheet in the order that they'll be done.

14. Set up a step sheet for each step on the guide sheet listing the step number on the sheet.

15. Paper-clip or staple the guide sheet to the left or inside left front of the hanging folder.

16. Paper-clip the step sheets together. Place them behind the guide sheet in the hanging folder.

17. Drop in any materials you'll be referencing for that Project behind the step sheets in the hanging folder.

18. Pull out step sheet # 1 and drop it into your In Box.

You're now ready to start the Project. Remember if you don't pull Step #1 out, the Project will just sit there and will never get done. Where does the step go? Stand, Action, To Do, A. Why A instead of B or C? Because you always want to be working on at least one step of a Project. The steps of a Project that are in the To Do Category will always be an A. If you constantly feed the steps into To Do A, you will daily be moving your A's into your 1-5's which you work on in your QT. Hopefully, you'll always be working on a step of a Project. If you have three Projects, you probably will have three step sheets in your To Do A's. Put Step #1 into a yellow hanging folder and drop it in behind the A guide folder in your To Do A section.

Where else could the step sheets go? If you had a call to make on a specific date or information to take along to a meeting, it would go into the Tickler.

After you have finished Step #1, throw the step sheet away, go to your Project folder, check off #1 on the guide sheet and pull out Step #2. Or if you have worked on the step sheet, perhaps written information on it and want to keep or reference it, take the step sheet and place it in the back with the completed work in the Support area. Check off #1 on the guide sheet and pull out Step #2.

Remember when you come up with the idea of a Project, it is not a Project until you have completely set it up with a guide sheet and steps and Step # 1 is in one of your Action Categories.

Until it is a Project, the card or sheet signifying that it will be a Project goes into To Do A where you'll set it up to be made into a Project.

Remember These Concepts

- The smaller and simpler the task is, the greater the chance of doing it.

Things To Avoid
- Not starting.
- Doing it perfectly.
- Making the steps of a Project too big or too long.
- Always putting the steps of a Project into the Tickler.

3.7

Another Kind Of Action Category

Flow With The Show

- A Producer, An Estimator, And A Realtor

What You Will Learn In This Chapter
- How to approach work using a different type of system

💣 <u>Myths of the Office</u>

My employees can't do it as well as I can.

Flow With The Show

A Producer, An Estimator, And A Realtor

An additional approach to the four Action Categories is to create a Flow System. A Flow System is a way to streamline and simplify a set of similar and repetitive tasks. Certain jobs require repeating the same steps for each job or customer. Examples would be a TV producer, an estimator for a mechanical contracting company, and a real estate agent.

I once worked with Marika O., a TV producer for a major news channel. When she was producing a show, we discovered that each shoot was pretty much the same. She wanted to learn a way to streamline her operation. We set up a seven-step Flow System sheet she could use whenever she was working on a show out on location.

The following are examples of Marika's Flow System form, her Support Categories, and her Action Categories.

Marika uses this same form for every shoot. Whenever you can identify repetitious work patterns, create and use a Flow System

> *A Flow System form will always keep you on track.*

form. When you are ready for a new job or customer, simply grab the form and fill in the blanks. Listing all your steps on a form saves you from doing them from memory. And you don't have to reinvent the wheel each time. The following is the front page of her form.

Marika's Show Itinerary

Show:

Segment:

Air Date:

Shoot Date:

Return Date:

Correspondent:

Crew:

Initial Meeting At:

7-1 Itinerary

The following is on the back of her itinerary form.

❏ 1. Travel Agent
    ❏ Airline Tickets FF #
        ❏ Call
        ❏ Pick Them Up
        ❏ Give To Crew
    ❏ Rental Car
        ❏ Directions
    ❏

❏ 2. Expense Money
    ❏ Put In Request
    ❏ Pick Them Up
    ❏ Give To Crew
    ❏

❏ 3. Hotel   Date:
    Phone:
    Address:

    Directions:

  ❏ Hotel   Date:
    Phone:
    Address:

    Directions:

❏ 4. Articles Enclosed
❏ 5. Questions To Be Asked About Sheet
❏ 6.

❏ 7. Characters
    Name:
    Phone:
    Address:
    Directions:

    Name:
    Phone:
    Address:
    Directions:

7-2
Flow
System
Check-Off
Form

The way to use the form is to start at the top left and work down. Work on #1 first. Check the boxes that you'll be using under #1. If you're renting a car and you need airline tickets, check both boxes. The boxes below and to the right of them list the various options of actions that you typically take. The idea is to have as many options listed as you can so all you have to do is check off a box or write in a date rather than write a lengthy narrative for each step. It's also a good idea to leave empty boxes like ❏ 6 in case you need to add in other steps. When you have completed a number (❏ 1- ❏ 7), check off the box ❏.

When you come back to the form to find what your next step is, scan down the left side of the form to the first unchecked box. This will indicate the next step you need to work on.

The following are her Support Categories with its hanging folder color in parenthesis:

- Reference (Gray)
- Personal Life (Pink)
- Scripts (Burgundy)
- Experts (Aqua)
- Health (Red)
- Office (Blue)
- Computer (Navy)
- Proposals (Orange)
- B-Roll (Black)
- Personal Job (Purple)
- Personal Finance (Green)
- Software
- Mementos
- Articles
- Magazines
- Binders
- Books
- Office Supplies
- Personal Drawer

Besides using a Flow System sheet, Marika created another Action Category called Shows. Notice Shows is not in alphabetical order. Rather the files are in the order she does them. The following are her Action Categories:

Important (Value)

(Proactive)

- <u>To Do </u>(Do It 1 Time)
  - 1-5 My Top 5 To Do A's
    which I do in my QT
  - A   Very Important
  - B   Important
  - C   Somewhat Important

- <u>Projects </u>(A Series of To Do's
  Over Time)
  - Names of Projects
    Consist of:
  - The guide
  - The steps
  - Reference and completed
    material
- <u>Shows</u> (Ones she produces)
  - Idea
  - Blue Sheet
  - Proposal
  - Research
    - Articles
  - Experts
    - Call for Interview
      - LM today
      - LM 1
      - LM 2
    - Interviewed
    - Characters
    - Proposals
    - B-Rolls
    - Logs
    - Itinerary
  - Script

Time (Urgent)

(Reactive)

- <u>Tickler </u>(Reminder)
  - 1-31
  - January-December
  - Pending
    - Pam
      - Blue Sheet
      - Proposals
      - Scripts
    - Senior Producer
- <u>Routine To Do </u>(Batched)
  - Bills
  - Blue Sheets
  - Call
    - Left message
  - Copy
  - Read
  - Send
  - Story Ideas
  - Talk with:
    - John
    - Legal
    - Pam
    - Senior Producers

Here is a Flow System for estimators from a mechanical contracting company in Pontiac, Michigan.

Project name: _____ #: _____

Phone: _____

Address: _____

❏ 1. Book the job

❏ 2. Permits
    ❏ Give info to Chris
       ❏ Received permit

❏ 3. Inspection called
    ❏ Date _____

❏ 4. Order materials/equipment _____
    ❏ Pull purchase agreement
    ❏ Fill out information agreement/Give to Chris
    ❏ Shipping date _____
       ❏ Received submittals
    ❏ Submitted

❏ 5. Subcontracts
    ❏ Awarded
    ❏ Write subcontract/Give to Chris

❏ 6. Job hand off
    ❏ Documents
    ❏ Labor goals
    ❏ Job #

❏ 7. Billings
    ❏ Month 1
    ❏ Month 2
    ❏ Month 3
    ❏ Month 4
    ❏ Retention

❏ 8. Close-out documents

And, finally, a Flow System for Kellum S., a real estate agent who works with buyers.

Overall Kit Sheet

Client:

                                    Date Done

❏ Manila folder
❏ Contract obligation
❏ Active client sheet
❏ Sale and processing form
❏ Earnest money deposit sheet
❏ Referral card for gift   /   /
❏ Home warranty brochure   /   /
❏ Copy of contract   /   /
❏ Lead-based paint disclosure   /   /
❏ Lender shopping article   /   /
❏ Lender information sheet   /   /
❏ Orientation letter   /   /
❏ Buy closing gift   /   /
❏   /   /
❏   /   /
❏   /   /

7-4
Real
Estate
Agent

Preclosing Checklist

❏ 2 originals of contract
❏ Original signed disclosure
❏ Fax directions to closing attorney
❏ Call closing attorney to verify package
❏ Review settlement statement from lender
❏ Take closing gift
❏
❏ Remind buyer:
    ❏ Change utilities and alarm system
    ❏ Certified check
    ❏ Photo ID
    ❏ 1 year home hazard insurance

Active Client

Information

Name:
Address:
Work phone: Work location:
Home phone: Fax #:
Referred by:
Working with other agent: ❑ Yes   ❑ No
                                            Who: _____

Current Home Status

❑ 1. Desired move date: _____
❑ 2. Desired neighborhoods:
❑ 3. Living status:
   ❑ 1. Owns
      ❑ Needs to sell to buy
         ❑ Yes
         ❑ No
      ❑ Needs contingency contract
         ❑ Yes
         ❑ No
   ❑ 2. Rents
      ❑ Lease
         ❑ Lease end date: _____
      ❑ Month to month
❑ 4. Desired close date: _____

Lender Information

❑ LENDER
   ❑ Yes
      ❑ Name:
      ❑ Phone:
      ❑ Call lender:
         ❑ Yes   Called on /   /
         ❑ No
   ❑ No
      ❑ Sent lender names and articles.   Sent on /   /
      ❑ Pre-qualified or approved
         ❑ Yes
         ❑ No

Contract Obligation

Property address: Binding date:

Buyer: Phone:

Buyer: Phone:

Seller: Phone:

Seller: Phone:

Listing agent: Phone:

❑ 1.   Get signed Seller's Disclosure and Survey   /   /
❑ 2.   Lead-Based Paint Disclosure   /   /
❑ 3.   Deposit Earnest money by   /   /
❑ 4.   Sale and Processing sheet   /   /
❑ 5.   Book inspector   /   /
❑ 6.   Book closing   /   /
❑ 7.   Loan approved by
        ❑ Loan approval   /   /
        ❑ Property appraisal   /   /
❑ 8.   Inspection amendment to Seller by   /   /
❑ 9.   Final acceptance period   /   /
❑ 10. Home warranty verification   /   /
❑ 11. Miscellaneous stipulations   /   /
        ❑   /   /
        ❑   /   /
        ❑   /   /
❑ 12. Final walk-through   /   /
❑ 13. Closing   /   /
❑ 14. 1 week follow-up call   /   /
        ❑   /   /

Seller

❑ 1.   Termite letter
❑ 2.   Home warranty
❑ 3.   Miscellaneous stipulations
        ❑   /   /
        ❑   /   /
        ❑   /   /

Client Meeting

❏ 1. Set appointment
❏ 2. At meeting:
  ❏ 1. Give them the Orientation letter
  ❏ 2. Pre-approval
    ❏ Yes
    ❏ No
  ❏ 3. Establish price range: $ _____
  ❏ 4. Establish neighborhood:
  ❏ 5. Give them a copy of the Contract, Lender information, and Lead-based paint brochure.

If you can create a standardized process for any repeated action in your company or organization, do it. It will save you many hours of time, which will allow you to spend more in your QT.

Remember These Concepts

• A Flow System form will always keep you on track.

Things To Avoid

• Reinventing your system each time you repeat the same action.

4.1

Your Daily Schedule

Your Day Blocked Out
- You're In The Army, Mr. Jones

Steps Of The System
- Your Daily Steps
- The Action Categories
- The Shift

What You Will Learn In This Chapter
- A system to run your day
- The steps of that system
- How to make a necessary shift

💣✳ <u>Myths of the Office</u>

Your entire day should be blocked out.

Your Day Blocked Out

You're In The Army, Mr. Jones

It's 04:00. Up and at 'em. If you've ever been through basic training in the military, you know 24 hours of your day have been carefully blocked out and planned. You don't have much choice about how you spend your day. But, your workplace is not basic training. You shouldn't want every minute of your work day blocked out with an activity, yet that's what many people do.

When you completely block out your day, hour by hour, you set up yourself for failure: being late to your next appointment; falling behind in your work; feeling overworked, rushed and bewildered as to why you aren't getting more done. What happens to your schedule when emergencies pop up? It falls apart. Just like you eventually will do.

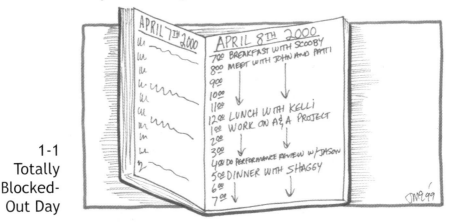

**1-1
Totally
Blocked-
Out Day**

The trick is to leave time open to work and to block out key times during the day such as your QT or a call time if you are in sales. The more you can keep your day open, the greater the chance of your day working. Keep as many slots open as you can throughout the day for emergencies, impromptu meetings, spill-over time, and general work. Your day will run much better if you only have a few blocked-out times a day, rather than trying to block out the entire day. Besides, you'll actually have a life if you do it this way. Leave time open to work.

Leave time open to work.

There are certain activities that you must do every day to keep a relatively normal work life. The way to accomplish these is by following a basic schedule of Processing and Producing. Don't worry about too much unscheduled time; it will be filled up in ways you can't imagine.

The basic schedule for your day revolves around Processing and Producing.

1. PROCESS (Information)

1. Three times a day
   - E-mail
   - Voice mail
   - In Box (Do last)

2. Once a week
   - On the last day of the week, review everything in all of your Action Categories so you know what you need to do.

2. PRODUCE (Work)

1. Tickler – Today stuff. Work on those tasks that must be and can only be done today.

2. Routine To Do – Maintenance stuff. Work on those tasks that you do continually or repetitiously, either daily, every couple of days, weekly, or monthly. Batch similar tasks together and do them at the same time.

3. To Do – Important and impactful stuff. Tasks that you can do ahead of time, before they are due, or items that, when you work on them, cause you to move from point A to point B more effectively. Work on these very important and highly impactful tasks in your QT.

Remember. The urge is to do it (Produce) first when presented with a lot of things to do rather than to be aware of and see everything (Process) that needs to be done. In summary, Process information three times a day and Produce work by working from your To Do, Routine To Do, and Tickler Categories daily.

Steps Of The System

Your Daily Steps

The following are the steps you need to do daily or, in one case, weekly.

Step 1. All paper, etc., always goes into your In Box first.

Step 2. Process your voice mail and e-mail three times a day. Go through your In Box three times a day. When finished, distribute the contents of your Out Box.

Step 3. Check and do your Tickler.

Step 4. Look at all the files in the Routine To Do and pick out the ones that you've decided to do.

Step 5. Before your QT, look at all your To Do A's, pick out the top five most important To Do A's, and place them in your 1-5 files.

Step 6. Work on your 1-5's during your Quiet Time.

Step 7. On your last work day of the week, review all your Action Categories to assess where you are and where you want to go.

Take as look at the following example. It gives you a sense of what your day might look like. There's plenty of open space to schedule meetings or appointments. Notice the arrows below Routine To Do. The time you spend doing Routine To Do's can vary. Many times you'll be working in your Routine To Do when you need to attend a meeting or go on an appointment. When you return to your office, simply go back to working on your Routine To Do's.

Example

A Typical Day

9:00	Voice mail, e-mail, In Box.	(Process)
	Tickler	(Produce)
9:30	Routine To Do	(Produce)
10:00	↓	
10:30	↓	
11:00		
11:30		
12:00	Voice mail, e-mail, In Box.	(Process)
	Tickler	(Produce)
12:30		
1:00		
1:30		
2:00	QT	(Produce)
2:30	QT	(Produce)
3:00	QT	(Produce)
3:30	QT	(Produce)
4:00	Voice mail, e-mail, In Box.	(Process)
	Tickler	(Produce)
4:30		
5:00		

Perform the following every day:

✔ **Step 1.** All paper, etc., always goes into your In Box first.

This first step will keep your office clean and centralize your incoming paper. Everything, including paper, cards, notes, loose files, calls to make, things handed to you, papers from appointments or meetings, books, binders, food, and videos, will always go into your In Box first.

✔ **Step 2.** Process your voice mail and e-mail three times a day. Go through your In Box three times a day and distribute your Out Box contents right after going through your In Box.

The first thing you'll do daily will be to go through your voice mail and e-mail. Right after processing your e-mail and voice mail, process everything in your In Box using your five-step In Box system. You go through your In Box after your e-mail and voice mail because you may have printouts of your e-mails and 3 x 5 cards with names and numbers from your voice mail. When you have finished going through your In Box, distribute the contents of your Out Box to wherever it goes out of your office or cubicle, including items to others, to the Central Files, and to the long-term storage area. Do it three times a day. Good times to do it are first thing in the morning, around lunch time, and late afternoon.

If you have an assistant or a administrative person, have him/her bring in your In Box contents five minutes before your scheduled time to go through your In Box. On the way out, your assistant takes out your Out Box contents and places them in his/her In Box to process. You'll then go through your In Box at your regular time three times a day: in the morning, lunchtime, and late afternoon.

✔ **Step 3.** Check and do your Tickler.

Next do everything in your Tickler. Why everything? Because everything in it must be done today. The amount of work in your Tickler should be greatly lessened since you are now aware of what really goes into it.

When do you do the Tickler and how often? Whenever you choose to as long as it's at least once a day. Many people do their Tickler immediately after going through their In Box first thing in the morning. They get it out of the way so it doesn't hang over them during the day.

The second time you go through your In Box, which is usually around lunchtime, there are often a few maintenance items in it, such as returning calls, responding to queries, or checking on routine business.

Many people do their Tickler three times a day, immediately after processing their In Box. This allows them to handle all items that are for that date including: urgencies; date-driven tasks that can only be done on that date; calls; follow-ups; tickets; reminders; and materials for meetings or appointments.

✔ **Step 4.** Look at all the files in the Routine To Do and pick out the ones that you decide to do.

Look at all the files in your Routine To Do. Why all of them? So you know what's on your plate. Awareness is control! You must Process first, then Produce.

The Action Category drawers are nothing more than three-dimensional to do lists and you want to know all the tasks that are on the list.

Most people have the biggest challenge with Routine To Do. Why? Because there is no set number of files to do. It's up in the air and a lot people have a very hard time with that. You can do one or all of them depending upon your available time and the number of tasks in each file. Remember to batch as many similar tasks together as possible and do them at the same time. Using this assembly-line approach, you'll crank them out that much quicker. If you can hold out for doing them only once a week, hold out. If you can't get all your reading done in one day, then spend some time every day knocking the reading out.

> *Awareness is control!*

You don't necessarily need to do every file daily, but you must look at all of them. Some days when I have a very busy schedule, I am only able to do a few of the files. Am I going to "Call" anyone today? Who did I "Call" yesterday and leave a message with? Did I get any calls from those people? Am I going to "Read" today? No. I'm going to "Type." Am I going to "Write?" I've only got one thank-you note in there, so I'm not going to "Write" today. I'll wait until I have a few more. If I have a lot of time today, I'll do all of them.

Look at all the files in your Routine To Do Category and select the ones you'll do. These are routine and repetitive activities that you do daily, every couple of days, weekly, monthly, or quarterly.

✔ **Step 5.** Before your QT, look at all your To Do A's and pick out the top five most important tasks and place them in your 1-5 files.

Before your QT, look at all your To Do A' s and pick out the top five most important ones. Take them out of their yellow hanging folder and place them into your 1-5 files which are in the front of your To Do Category. Place your empty yellow folder in front of your 1 File with the other empty yellow folders. What you're doing is looking at your three-dimensional to do list with all of the most important and impactful folders to choose from. Pick the top five most important tasks.

During your QT, if you complete all of your 1-5 files, pick out the next top five most important files from the rest of your To Do A's and place them in your 1-5 files in your To Do Category.

✔ **Step 6.** Work on your 1-5's during your QT.

Work on your 1-5 files from your To Do Category during your Quiet Time, which you take at the same time every day. Ideally, your QT is 20 percent of your day. You'll be totally uninterrupted during this time, with the door closed and no phone calls, working on your most important items.

This is the most important aspect of your system! This step allows you to work on important tasks that you never seem to have time to do, yet are the ones that need to be done the most.

This is why the training was created. Your QT and 1-5' s will get you out of the overwhelmed state you are in now. Following this step may be one of the most difficult things to do in your life, but if you choose to do it, your life will change in a way that you never could have imagined.

✔ **Step 7.** On your last work day of the week, go through all your Action Categories to assess where you are and where you want to go.

It's been a long, tiring week. Today is the last work day of the week. You are fried. That is why they call it Frieday.

On your last work day of the week, check the status of all your Action Categories. Take a few minutes (usually not more than ten) to plan what you need to do next week.

This is a necessary and important step. Some people choose Monday. Any other day works fine also. Friday seems to work best for most people since it's at the end of the work week. The current week is over and you want to get a feel for next week.

Instead of taking concerns and uncertainties about work home with you, check your Action Categories on Friday. You can take a well-deserved rest from work over the weekend and, come early Monday morning, be ready to begin work immediately rather than trying to figure out what you will be doing for the day.

Check each Action Category once a week to determine:

✔ **What's in it**

Looking at all of your Action Categories once a week keeps you current on everything in them, which puts you in control.

✔ **What you still need to do with it**

Remember your system is a like a three-dimensional to do list. Looking at it will instantly alert you to what needs to be done.

✔ **Items to trash**

Just because you've put it into one of your Action Categories doesn't mean it must be done. Remember the To Do I left in my A section for three months? After checking it week after week and finally coming out of my daze, I realized it wasn't really an A.

> *Once a week, look through everything in your Action Categories.*

Items from your To Do C's often become trash, as will Left messages after you call repeatedly without a return call.

✔ **If it should be moved to another file**

Remember, the game is to move as many A's into your 1-5 and do them in your QT. Once a week you will look at all of your To Do A's, B's, and C's and possibly move them.

The Action Categories

Let's look at each Action Category you will review the last day of the week.

📌 To Do

Look at each file (yellow hanging folder) behind your A, B, and C guide file. Reprioritize the folders behind each guide and decide if they'll stay where they are or need to be moved to another letter (behind an A, B, or C). The idea is for all the files to progress to become A's, which then move into the 1-5's. C's move to B's. C's move to A's. B's move to A's. But sometimes A's move to B's, B's move to C's, and C's become trash. Don't let any A's stay in the A section too long. If an A stays in the A section for more than three weeks, the following may be true:

1. You are procrastinating it by not moving it up to the 1-5's. Move it into the 1-5's that day and do it in your QT.
2. It's not really an A. You just thought it was. Move it to B or C.
3. It's trash. Throw it away. You just thought it was important.

Any of you're A's, B's, and C's may also go to another Category. Today (the last day of the week) is the only day to check your B's and C's, since they are not as important as your A's, which you check daily right before your QT.

📌 Tickler

Look at the next seven days and see what's in them. This gives you an idea of what must be done on those days. If you are going out of town or will be away from your office for a while, this is an ideal time to be aware of what's in your Tickler so you can handle it ahead of time or take it with you. Plus, if you check it on Friday, you can spot anything in Saturday or Sunday that shouldn't be there.

Check your Pending file or files. Again, items in the Pending file are items that you are waiting to receive from someone else. If you are content to wait another week, simply leave them in the file. If you want to call the person or take action on the items, place the items into your Call File in your Routine To Do Category.

📌 Routine To Do

Look at every file in your Routine To Do section. Check for any files that you might not have done in the last week so you can be aware of them at the beginning of the next week and do them.

📌 Projects

Generally, you'll only look at your Project files when you pull steps from them to put into another Action Category or when you refer to them. Once a week you need to assess how you're progressing with the Project in order to see if you're on schedule with it. Check the guide sheet in the Project File to see what your progress is.

The Shift

There are two shifts that will enhance your productivity:

1. **Changing your outlook from the "day" to the "week" mentality.**

   Most of us define "how much we got done today" as the unit of measure for our work.

   Instead of focusing on the day, start thinking about work in terms of the week. This ties in with the mechanics of the system.

2. **Having your day revolve around your Quiet Time.**

   "I don't have enough time" usually means that you choose to do something else. It's vital that your Quiet Time be the main focus of your day. So many people say they never have enough time to complete their important tasks. Why? First, they completely block their day out with appointments, giving them no free time to work. Then they allow themselves to be constantly interrupted with intrusive beeps, rings, and quacks.

> *Work your day around your Quiet Time.*

   Work your day around your Quiet Time. If you use the system, you can transfer the time you save to Quiet Time.

Remember These Concepts

- Leave time open to work.
- Awareness is control!
- Once a week, look through everything in your Action Categories.
- Work your day around your Quiet Time.

Things To Avoid

- Abandonding the rest of the system if you miss a step during the day.

4.2

Interruptions

Pardon Me

- Constantus Interruptus
- Well Excuse Me
- How Can I Interrupt Me? Let Me Count The Ways
- Solutions

What You Will Learn In This Chapter
- Who causes most of your interruptions
- Common items that will interrupt you

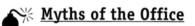 ## Myths of the Office

Other people cause all my interruptions.

Pardon Me

Constantus Interruptus

Think how many times during the day you're working on something when someone stops by, says hello, or hands you something. Or think about those times you're working on something, the phone rings, you answer it, and then after hanging up, you stop what you were working on and begin to work on whatever the phone call was about. Or simply, there are times you're working on something, you think of something else, and you start working on that.

Example

Take a look at the following:

- You've just finished a big report. You are very proud of it. You walk over to your boss's office to drop it into her In Box. Your boss just happens to be sitting there so you start gushing over the incredible job you did.

- You're an administrative assistant who is dropping off a file to another administrative assistant. As you drop the file off, you say hello and ask them how they are. A brief history of the last year of your life ensues.

- You're working at your desk when someone hands you something of low importance to do. You immediately stop what you're doing and start working on it.

- You're working at your desk which has yellow sticky notes and paper all over it. While working, you're distracted by one of the many yellow stickies reminding you of something you need to do. You stop what you're working on and start working on one of the yellow sticky notes.

What's wrong with these scenarios? The answer is *you* and your Constantus Interruptus problem. You are the problem.

One of the biggest complaints I hear is that of being constantly interrupted during the day. Many people feel all their interruptions are caused by external sources. If your whole day consists of being interrupted, something's wrong. It can mean a couple of things. Something is wrong in your industry, the culture in your company is screwy, or you are a reactor. As a reactor, you may not be preparing, planning, or acting to handle situations before they occur. Or you may simply be caught up in the reactive, urgent times.

> *You are the cause of over 50 percent of all your interruptions.*

In this day of everyone being a victim and blaming everyone else for their troubles, most people don't want to believe they are the ones causing over half of their interruptions. Sometimes being constantly interrupted comes with the job—most of the time it doesn't. There are legitimate exceptions: administrative positions, receptionists, secretaries, and positions that require constant interruptions, such as customer service reps.

Sometimes in a workshop I'll hear "Greg, please tell me how I won't be interrupted at all during the day." I respond that they are going to be interrupted part of the time no matter what they want; that's how we do business. We are social beings; we like breaks during the day. We like to socialize. If we don't want any interruptions, we can try sitting on a mountaintop.

You can take 50 percent of your interruptions and eliminate them. If you have 50 interruptions a day, it's likely that 25 of them are controllable and the other 25 aren't. Focus on eliminating the 25 you can control. Your day will be that much easier when you do.

Well Excuse Me

If you constantly are interrupted, locate the interruption before it begins. Analyze the pattern of the interruptions—who initiates them, what time they occur, what they're about. If the same person interrupts you every day, find out when and why they do it. If it's your boss, suggest, "May I meet with you every morning and every afternoon for a couple minutes so we can batch all our questions together? It will save us both some time by collecting all the things we need to speak about."

If you find recurring interruptions, go to the boss and say, "I've seen that this type of problem over and over again. Here's a solution to change it." If you know of a problem that constantly occurs, jump ahead and handle it beforehand. When I work with companies, I often notice recurring patterns. The idea is to identify those patterns and squelch them before they become fires. A great time to identify and work on them is in your QT.

How Can I Interrupt Me? Let Me Count The Ways

The following are guaranteed ways of interrupting yourself:

✔ Desk
Have paper and clutter piled so high on your desk, floor, and credenza that you can't see more than three feet in front of you. Make sure you have all the things you need to take Action on interspersed with your Support stuff.

Solution
Always keep your desk, floor, and credenza totally paper-free. Every piece of paper will distract and interrupt you if it's out where you can see it.

✔ Noises
Ask to be moved next to "Bull," the person with the loudest voice in the company. Or, sit next to a loud, droning, distracting noise, perhaps the copy room or, better yet, be situated across from the desk of the company gossip.

I just worked with a client at a TV station. She shares an office with a guy who has two TV sets going at the same time on two different channels. Can you imagine the poor woman trying to get any work done! She asked for help—I left cable cutters with her.

Solution
If you have a case of ADD, a mosquito buzzing a mile away will distract you. Imagine what all that noise will do to your already minute attention span.

- If possible, telecommute and work at home.
- If you have an office, work with the door closed. If that's against your company's ridiculous culture, cheat by closing it as often as you can get away with it. At the very least, beg to keep it shut during your QT.
- Use a white-sound device, especially if you work in a cubicle. It's a great way to block out distracting noises, particularly the sound of the obnoxious top producer closing yet another sale while you try to figure out how to make your quota. No humming to it please. Ohmmmmmm.
- If you work in a cubicle, work in the deserted conference room whenever you can.
- If you are in an administrative position, ask to work in your boss's big, beautiful, plush office with the door shut when he or she is gone. Just don't sit in the lush Corinthian leather chair.

✔ Yellow sticky notes
Redecorate your office walls with them. Yellow is such a nice, bright color. You never really liked that drab wallpaper anyway. While you're at it, see if you can plaster the little suckers over everything else in your office: your desk, credenza, phone, book

shelves, and computer. They do have a Yellow Room at the White House, don't they?

Solution

I hate yellow sticky notes. My goal in life is to see people use them only for two things: communicating information to others and for directions on something they themselves need to work on.

✔ The wall

Tape every memo you have received in the last three months onto your wall, especially the important ones, such as the company's holiday schedule for the year.

Solution

Hang pictures, decorations, and memorabilia on the wall. Keep business information or things to do off the wall and filed in your drawers. If they are on the wall, they'll distract you when you look up. If you are a right-brain, artistic, creative type who believes you must have stuff on the wall, place them on only one wall (not the wall you face at your desk) and keep the others free. If you have a wall with a bulletin board, be careful of what you put on it and don't overload it. The exception to paper on the wall would be frequently called phone numbers or extensions, especially for administrative people or customer service people.

✔ Urgencies

Treat everything as an urgency or better yet as an emergency. The rule is to always stop whatever you are doing and start on something else. When you are handed something, immediately stop what you're doing and work on it no matter how insignificant it is. In fact, the less significant the more points you earn.

Solution

The tendency today is to treat everything as an urgency and do it immediately. Qualify. Qualify. Qualify all so-called urgencies. Most things are not an emergency. Instead of reacting in panic, simply drop whatever it is into your In Box and finish what you were working on. Success is measured by what you have accomplished not on how much you have started.

✔ Meet with the boss

As an administrative person, the very minute you finish a task or find something out, stop what you're doing and let your boss know. Never collect more than one thing to talk about with her at a time. See how many times a day you can interrupt her. Go for a record.

Solution

Save everything except emergencies or real urgencies until the morning stand-up meeting.

✔ Meet with your assistant

Give your assistant something to do. Ten minutes later give her another task to do and then ask if she has finished the first one. You can interrupt her six times an hour using this technique. Better yet, repeat it all day long. It's a tremendous morale booster. She'll never get done and be forced to work longer hours. Longer hours means overtime. Overtime means more money. More money means better morale. Does this qualify as the raise she was asking for?

Solution

Save everything you want to talk about with your assistant. Meet with her first thing in the morning in a quick stand-up meeting. If you need to talk periodically, do it when she brings in your In Box contents.

✔ Desk to desk

Whenever you drop something off at someone else's desk, make sure you say hello, ask her how she is and tell her what's new. Then proceed to fully explain in detail what she needs to do with the paper that you are handing her. Never mind that the directions are already written on a yellow sticky note attached to the sheet, fully explaining what needs to be done. She'll love the attention. Now do this 20 times a day with everyone else in your office too. Let's see. If everyone else in the office does this to them, 30 times 20 equals...

Solution

The practice of dropping off and saying hello/giving directions is insidious. It happens all day long. Not only are you interrupting someone else, but you're also interrupting yourself. Two interruptions for the price of one. Such a deal!

Instead of talking to someone and interrupting her, simply write what needs to be done on a yellow sticky note and attach it to the upper right corner of the sheet. Drop it into your Out Box and distribute it only when you distribute your Out Box contents, which will be three times a day. When you drop it off don't say anything.

If you can't just drop it off and you need to talk with her, put it in your Action/Routine To Do/Talk with/Michelle (person's name) file (Part 3, Chapter 4). If it's an emergency, which it shouldn't be very often, then of course, interrupt her.

People often complain that they are interrupted all day long. What they don't want to acknowledge is they are allowing the interruption to occur. They don't want to appear rude or offensive by saying something to the person for fear of being branded as unfriendly. Simply tell the person interrupting you who is dropping off/chatting/giving direction that you appreciate her saying hello but every time someone drops something off and says hello, it causes you to stop what you are doing. Every time you're interrupted, you have to stay an extra 15 minutes at night and you may already be getting out fairly late. Ask her if it happens to her. Ask her if you can have lunch with her and catch up that way.

✔ Open-door policy

Always maintain an open-door policy. "Come on in any old time. Feel free to talk with me and interrupt me when the spirit moves you. Your time is more important than mine is. My people can never say that I'm not always there for them." You've got to love American managers. "Can do" is their motto. Unfortunately, doing it correctly isn't always what they do.

I found a perfect example of this when working with agency managers for a major insurance company. They believed they should be totally available to their salespeople at all times. It didn't matter if they were in a meeting or on a call, the salesperson could barge right in. Sales, I was told, was the driving force. It was why they were in business. How could you ever dare to tell your salesperson you couldn't talk with him? What if he had a blockbuster of a deal and he needed to talk with you immediately to close it? Yet, strangely, those same agency managers complained of having very little time to plan sales strategies or anything else, for that matter.

Solution

I once ran a $36 million sales district, so I am somewhat familiar with selling. There's a big difference between being accessible and being a revolving door for rampant, egotistical whims, even if sales are a company's number-one priority, which I believe it is. If you train your people to be able to interrupt you at any time, you are teaching them a bad habit. Select a QT for yourself. Do not budge from it. Explain it to your salespeople.

Sell them on the benefits that they'll receive when they set up a QT and honor their own time boundaries. If you take an hour every morning and an hour every afternoon and ask your sales people to observe that time, they'll soon learn how to work around your schedule.

✔ Technology

Buy every new-fangled, modern device you can get your hands on. As soon as a new one comes out, stop what you're doing, and run out and buy it. Set up your life in such a way that you will either be called, beeped, vibrated, rung, whistled at or quacked at every five minutes. Welcome to Technology Hell! More is not always better!

Solution

Take your time with the technology. Learn one piece of equipment or program fully before buying a new, better one. Less is more. Don't fall into "the most toys wins" syndrome or "keeping up with the Joneses mentality." Realize each new piece of technology that you use will be another information source that you'll need to Process and that will interrupt you.

✔ Phone calls

Working with trial lawyers was also a riot. Some would complain that they were constantly being interrupted all day long. Yet when I suggested they use an answering service for a couple of hours they thought I was crazy. When a potential client called, I was informed, they needed to be available to talk with them immediately. If they weren't, the client might call someone else. They would lose all that business. Hey, you can't have your cake and eat it too! Just how much do you guys want to make, anyhow?

Solution

Contrary to popular belief, you don't have to be sitting by the phone 24 hours a day and answer it every time on the third ring. Who came up with the third ring, anyway? This belief of instantaneous customer service is causing a tremendous waste of effort in businesses today. Don't get me wrong; I truly appreciate good service. But people often go way overboard in this practice.

Take your phone off the hook for an hour; the world won't come to an end. If the world will come to an end, have someone cover the phone for you and then do the same for them.

Solutions

The following are ways to eliminate interruptions:

- Realize in many cases that you are allowing the interruption to occur.

- Be available to receive phone calls at the same time every day in your office. Let people know when you'll be in your office.

- If you are in a cubicle, work in an office with a door (and close it) whenever possible.

- Assistants can cover other assistants' phones for an hour, which will give them one hour of uninterrupted time from phone calling.

- Take 20 percent of your workday and spend it working without interruption on your important rather than urgent activities.

- Have everyone in your office utilize a QT where everyone works at their desks alone, taking no calls. The receptionist handles the calls.

- Close your door.

- Schedule a time to meet with your people before it is needed.

- Meet with your administrative person when they first bring in your In Box.

- Meet with people in their office, not yours.

- Identify who is constantly interrupting you. What are their habits? When do they come to see you? What do they specifically want?

- Stand up and go around the desk when visitors drop in.

- Make time daily or weekly to meet with your people.

- Ask others if it is a good time to talk.

- Can you say "no"?

- Use your telephone answering machine or voice mail.

- Screen your calls and visitors.

Remember These Concepts

• You are the cause of over 50 percent of all your interruptions.

Things To Avoid
• People who will interrupt you.
• Allowing youself to be interrupted.

<h1>4.3</h1>

Administrative Assistants

We Know Who Really Runs The Show

- My Secretary Promised That She Could Organize Me
- My Assistant Normally Handles That
- Bosses' Boo-Boo
- Helpful Hints For Assistants
- Communication From The Boss
- A Letter To Our Bosses

What You Will Learn In This Chapter
- How to communicate with your assistant

☀ <u>Myths of the Office</u>

My secretary can organize me.

We Know Who Really Runs The Show

My Secretary Promised That She Could Organize Me

It's crucial for a manager and an assistant to be on the same wavelength. If you use the same system, life can be a lot easier. For example, if a red hanging folder file is missing from your drawer, you'll know who has it and where to find it, since your assistant's Categories and colors will be the same as yours.

If you believe that you both think alike, try this exercise. Have both of you list all the Categories you can think of that you have in both offices. When you have finished, compare your lists. Surprise! The odds of you both having the same list are a million to one.

It's rare that an assistant or administrative person can organize her boss. She can run his life and tell him what needs to be done, but not organize him—not all by herself. What is needed is a combined effort by both to create and agree on a list of Categories and a set of procedures.

My Assistant Normally Handles That

I'm always amazed at the amount of time wasted by long and lengthy notes from the boss explaining where to file something. If you both use the same system, you can simply write where you want it to go in the upper right corner of the sheet of paper.

Say you want a paper filed into a client's folder. Here's what you would write:

Client/Lessard

Client (Category)/Lessard (File)

The Category is Client and the File is Lessard. File the paper in the Client Category and the Lessard File.

Or say a Category/Subcategory/File is needed. You want the paper in a client's file that is broken down by the type of company it is.

Client/Construction/Lessard

Client (Category)/ Construction (Subcategory)/ Lessard (File)

Writing this in a brief note on the upper right corner is a simple, effective way of communicating information to your administrative assistant without having to interrupt her. It saves your time and hers.

By using this concise directive instead of a lenghty note, your new system gives your assistant a greater chance of deciphering your writing. This means she can drop out of that night course, "Deciphering Ancient Hieroglyphics," you made her take.

If you want your assistant to take action on something, simply write your directions on a yellow sticky note without writing her name (Did I say yellow sticky? Gulp!) and stick it on the upper right-hand corner. No name on the sticky means it's for her since she's the only person picking up your Out Box.

If it goes to someone else, use the same procedure: a yellow sticky in the upper right-hand corner. But this time write their name and sign yours. They both are dropped into your Out Box.

Bosses' Boo-Boo

One of the biggest boo-boos bosses can make is to not meet or talk with their assistants daily. The assistants can tell you it's loads more fun when their bosses are traveling and they haven't called in for days. They just adore making million-dollar decisions on their own. What many bosses don't understand is how this limits their assistant's productivity.

Of course, as a boss, if you are wonderful enough to call, never give your administrative person any time to ask questions. You are, after all, the boss. You do not have time to waste with your lowly assistant. You have much more important things to do than squander away your valuable time in such a meaningless way. You, after all, are leading the company!

Wrong, boss! Management mortal sin (MMS), as the nuns would say. Your secretary or executive assistant is an extension of you. Unless she's a mind reader, you need to

> *Your assistant's productivity is directly proportionate to the amount of quality time you spend with him/her.*

work with her very closely. How do you feel when you're out of the loop or left wanting for information? You hate it. Why would it be any different with her?

Helpful Hints For Assistants

The following will help you communicate better with your boss:
1. Your first In Box delivery and Out Box pick up is the ideal time for you to meet with your boss in order to get clarification and answer questions.
2. Align your Category names and colors with your boss's.
3. When your boss wants something filed, have him use the Category/File system.
4. You need to keep the majority of your boss's bulk paper in your filing system or in the Central Files so you have easy access to it.

> *Everything needs to go to the administrative assistant before going to the manager.*

5. Keep your boss's calendar. Have people call you in order to set up appointments for him.

6. Have an Out Box for your boss on your desk and have everyone drop off information for your boss into that rather than dropping it off into your boss's office.

Communication From The Boss

Ditto with your assistant:

- Meet or talk with your assistant at least once a day, possibly two or three times. (Ask them how many times they need.) If you don't talk with your assistant, imagine how your life would be without them. Now that you've recovered from a mild heart attack, get up off the floor and go meet with them.

- The assistant goes first in the one-on-one meeting, when they bring in your In Box materials.

- Use one another to create energy when you're bogged down. Make time to do this. This is especially valuable for Project brainstorming and filling out the guide sheet.

- Use yellow stickies in the upper right hand corner for directions.

- Use the following system written on yellow stickies to convey information:

Written down	Meaning
• Category/File	Your assistant creates the file you want and keeps it.
• Category/File with your initials	Your assistant creates the file you want and gives it back to you.
• ©	A copy of it comes back to you. Perfect for following up when you delegate a task. The task goes to them—you get a copy.

A Letter To Our Bosses

I found the following memo in one of my client's offices. Please pay attention, bosses.

TO: Our Bosses

FROM: The Secretaries

RE: Office Procedures

General:
1. Never give us work first thing in the morning...we prefer a terrific rush in the late afternoon.
2. Whenever possible, please endeavor to keep us late. We have no homes to go to and are only too thankful for somewhere to spend the evening.
3. Should work be required urgently (a most unusual occurrence), it aids us considerably if you will rush in at intervals of 30 seconds to see if it is done.
4. When we stagger out carrying a pile of files, please do not open the door for us; we should learn to crawl under it.
5. Send us out to cash your checks, buy your cigars, etc.., in all weather—walking is exhilarating and, since we sit down all day, the exercise does us good.
6. Do walk out of the office without telling us where you are going or how long you might be. We enjoy telling people who wish to contact you urgently that we have no idea where you are.

Use Of Dictaphone And General Writing Procedures:
1. When dictating, please parade up and down the room and practice your golf strokes. We can understand what is said much more easily that way.
2. Please lower your voice to a whisper when dictating names of people, places, etc., and under no circumstances, spell them to us. We are sure to hit on the right way of spelling sooner or later, and we know the name and address of every person, firm, and place in the world.
3. Should a letter require a slight alteration after it is typed, score through the words heavily about four times and write the correct word beside it, preferably in ink or heavy pencil. Always make the alterations on the original or top copy.
4. Please dictate a paragraph and change your mind, with the corrected version following. It adds variety to our typing.

5. Hours for dictation: (a) during the lunch hour, (b) anytime between 4:30 p.m. and 5 p.m.
6. Should you wish to write out a letter or report, please write with a blunt pencil in the left-hand margin and use plenty of arrows, balloons, and other diagrams. If figures are altered, please write directly over those previously inserted.

Use Of The Telephone:
1. Remember, when asking us to place a long distance call, you must be very fast on your feet to get out of the office before the call comes through.
2. If possible, always pick up your calls on your secretary's phone. This makes sure that we cannot pick up calls for any of our other people. It also helps to keep us company—we miss you during the day.
3. When you have given us a rush project, be sure to use your intercom line frequently, at intervals of 60 seconds or so, to ask us to get minor items, such as coffee. Also, stop by every few minutes to tell us what you're doing that night, what you did the night before, your plans for the weekend, etc.
4. If you are paged, please ignore it. We usually have no particular reason for wanting to locate you and enjoy hunting you down or taking messages.
5. Do interrupt us while we're speaking on the phone. We've got two ears, so we might as well use them.

The next section, Part 5, deals with how to set up your system. Rest assured, it's not theory but rather a step-by-step set of directions.

Remember These Concepts

- Your assistant's productivity is directly proportionate to the amount of quality time you spend with him/her.
- Everything needs to go to the administrative assistant before going to the manager.

Things To Avoid
- Not meeting with or talking with your assistant daily.

5.1

Office Layout

Layout Of Your Office

- Stuck In The Middle With You
- Ladies And Gentlemen, We Are Preparing To Land
- Ergonomically Correct

What You Will Learn In This Chapter
- How to set up your office

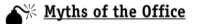 **Myths of the Office**

Keep the phone behind you on your credenza.

Layout Of Your Office

Stuck In The Middle With You

Walk into almost any office and where do you find the desk? Three-quarters of the way back in the room facing the door with two chairs in front, a bookshelf to the side, and a credenza directly behind the desk. Chances are that when you moved into your office, you changed everything except the layout. You probably left it arranged the same way that everyone before you had—and the same way the next 20 people after you will keep it as well.

Think of your office as a workshop or factory. Imagine how difficult it would be to maneuver around pieces of wood, tools, and machinery on the floor, almost tripping over them as you dodge them. My dad, Jack Vetter, who owned a construction company, used to always tell us to keep the floor clean and free from any objects. If items were left scattered on the floor, chances are that we'd trip over them—and if we didn't trip and hurt ourselves, it meant we were wasting time trying not to.

Many people try to successfully work in an office that's filled with paper and clutter on the floor. It works the same as a workshop. It just slows them down. They try to overcome this handicap by blazing a trail to their desk. For some people, getting to their desk is one of their main tasks during the day. They have to weave around corners of their L- or U-shaped desk or turn sideways just to slide through a narrow gap to their chair. Remember the concept: "If it's easy to do, you'll do it"?

Ladies And Gentlemen, We Are Preparing To Land

How your office is set up will dictate how productive you'll be. Imagine being in the cockpit of an airplane. Think what would happen if, when the pilot said, "Gear down," he had to unbuckle his seat belt, get up, and walk over to flip a switch. If you were a passenger, you'd be wondering why the plane was doing loop d' loops since no one was at the controls.

> *Set up your office with the efficiency of an airplane cockpit.*

You want to set your office up as ergonomically as a cockpit in an airplane. The more you have to move, twist, turn, and walk around in your office, the less you get done. Precious time is wasted when you have to stand up and walk across the room to retrieve something or turn around to your credenza to make a call.

Ergonomically Correct

What is ergonomics? It's the science of equipment design with the intent to reduce fatigue and increase productivity. To me that means a simple, stress-free, pain-free, comfortable, convenient office space, one that allows you to maximize your actions with minimum effort. Wearing jeans that are comfortable and not wearing a stupid collar that chokes you are perfect examples of good ergonomics. So much for professional definitions.

After reading each of the following, check to see how your office is set up.

🪧 Phone

If your phone is behind you, think how many times you turn around to use it. The more you're paid, the more each of your movements is worth. That reminds me of a few of the many overpaid baseball players in the game today. With the amount they're making, each hit they get is worth thousands.

Exercise

For a week, put a bowl on your credenza. Every time you turn around to use the phone throw a quarter in it. Then multiply the amount in the bowl by 50 weeks. That will give you an idea of what you are throwing away in lost time.

As we said before, if you are a righty, your phone goes on the left side of your desk. This allows you to pick the phone up with your left hand and write and dial with your right, or dominant, hand. If you are a lefty, the setup is the opposite.

> *The less you have to turn around in your office, the more you'll get done.*

🪧 Desk

One of my first clients was John H., a stockbroker. His office consisted of two regular walls, an outside window, and a glass wall separating him from the rest of the office. His desk was situated facing the glass and the rest of the office. When I first met and talked with him, I noticed he continually looked at three places: my eyes, the screen on his computer for stock prices (which is normal for someone in his business), and over my shoulder, which puzzled the heck out of me. After concluding our appointment, as I got up and turned around to go out, I couldn't help but notice the beautiful women who were working just on the other side of the glass wall. The first thing I did was turn his desk into the wall. Voila! Instantaneous productivity on his part! His wife was happy too!

All offices are not that easy, but you get the point. There are a lot of distractions waiting for you, especially if you face the door which, unfortunately, most people do.

To create a more intimate or cordial environment when meeting clients in your office, consider butting your desk up against your window away from the door. This way, when someone comes to visit, you can swing your chair around to him or her without a big desk coming between you. This works extremely well with lawyers and financial planners to enhance their "trust" factor with their clients. Their big desks don't cut off the rapport they're trying to establish. I always think of the movie *It's a Wonderful Life* with George Bailey stuck in that low chair looking up at Mr. Potter sitting behind his massive desk.

I know this means your back is to the door and the bogeyman will be able to sneak up on you, but you'll be amazed at how many fewer distractions and interruptions you'll have. You will also almost double the amount of space in your office by butting up against the wall.

📌 Wall

I know, now I'm picking on your walls too. Is nothing sacred in the office? Nope! Walls can distract you as much as cluttered desks. Keep them paper-free and keep those darn yellow stickies off them. The only thing that should go on walls are decorations, pictures, fun stuff, and memorabilia. Business items that you refer to all the time can go into your Tool drawer. The only exception would be a list of phone numbers, if you were in an administrative position, and a wall calendar.

📌 Chair

Probably the most overlooked tool or piece of equipment in your office is your chair. One of the easiest ways to tire yourself out is by working in a poor chair.

📌 Computer

The ideal place for a computer monitor is eye level up off the desk, on a shelf, with the keyboard sliding out from under the middle of the desk where that middle drawer always seems to be. The next spot is on your desk. Having the computer behind you keeping the phone company is definitely a Bozo no-no.

📌 Keyboard height

The more forward your wrists are bent, the more problems you'll have with them. The best position for your arms is at a level location with a pad under your wrists and your elbows at a 90-degree angle.

File Cabinets

Everything that can go into a file drawer should. I am a firm believer that it's easier to access information from a file drawer than any other way. The more places you have to look to find something, the longer it will take. Keep your file cabinets together if possible.

Where do Categories go in relation to your file drawers? Some people set them up alphabetically from the top file drawer to the bottom, with the "A" Category in the top drawer at the front and the "Z" at the end or bottom. Mine are set up so the ones that I use the most are closest to me and at an easy-to-reach level when I'm in my chair. Categories that are seldom used go into the top drawer and are the farthest away.

Your Action Categories need to be in separate drawers from your Support Categories. Never combine the two. Having all your Action Categories (To Do, Routine To Do,

> *Everything that can go into a file drawer should.*

Tickler, Projects) in one or two drawers allows you to be able to always go to this one area to know exactly what needs to be done. The place to keep your Action Categories, if possible, is in your desk. You'll probably need two and sometimes three drawers in your desk for them since you'll want plenty of room to move files around in each drawer.

Bunch your Support Category drawers together if possible. You'll probably have drawers with two or more Categories in them. On the other hand, some Categories may take up a couple of drawers. When you have a lot of file cabinets, a color sample of each Category can be placed on the outside of each file drawer.

Drawers

Each drawer can be used as a Non-paper Category in your desk if you have enough Categories. The more drawers, the more you can break down your Non-paper Categories. If you have two drawers, one can be for Office Supplies and Personal or Office Supplies and Tools. If you have a third drawer, you can break them down into Tools, Office Supplies, and Personal. Some people have Food drawers, Banking drawers, Maintenance Tool drawers, and on and on.

Shelves

Put Books, Binders, and Memorabilia on shelves. Books stay with Books, Binders with Binders, and Memorabilia with

Memorabilia. Every Category stays with their own kind. Not a very friendly shelf.

🖈 Proximity to your administrative person

When I look at how an office is set up, I'll always ask where the administrative people are located in relation to their people. I just love to see them walk all the way to the other end of the building to talk with their bosses.

🖈 Credenzas

If you choose to use one, use them for Memorabilia with files such as plants, photos, and awards. These items, though an important expression of who you are, are too much of a distraction on your desk and take up space (on your workbench).

🖈 Cubicles

If you're about to be evicted from the luxury of your very own quiet and spacious office to a miniscule cubicle, which many people are today, you have my deepest sympathy. If you have ADD (Attention Deficit Disorder), you're in for a wild, loud, and distracting time. When I was in sales I worked from a cubicle. It drove me crazy. All I could hear was a bunch of other salespeople yammering away on the phone. All I wanted to do was get out of the office. Hey, maybe that's why they had us set up like that, to get us out of the office and sell. I now work in my house where it is so quiet I can hear a tree fall in the woods. If you can, find a quiet place to work, such as the conference room, someone's office, or your home.

🖈 Office Layout

How should your office be set up? It depends upon how much space you have, your position in the company, the prestige needed, and how productive you want to make it. Consider whether productivity is more important than appearance.

Exercise

Look at Diagram 1-1. Can you pick out what's wrong with the layout of the office and what's missing?

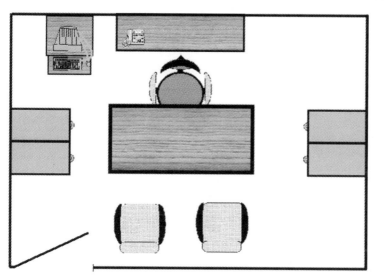

1-1
Office
Layout
Before

There are seven things that are wrong. They are:
1. The phone is on the credenza.
2. The computer is too far away and inconvenient to access
3. The file cabinets are split and too far away.
4. There are no In and Out Boxes.
5. There is no appointment book.
6. The desk is in the middle of the room.
7. The credenza can be eliminated.

Diagram 1-2 shows you a better way to set up your office.

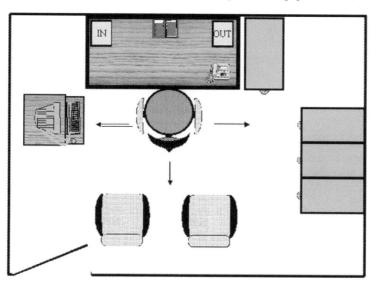

1-2
Office
Layout
After

Exercise

Draw a diagram of your office to see if you can make it more productive after changing the layout. First measure the dimensions of your office, the length and the width. On a piece of paper draw the length and width you just measured. Scale down the drawing so that one-half inch equals one foot.

Say your office is 10 feet by 14 feet. On your ruler draw a line 5 inches long. That would represent the 10 feet since each foot would equal a half an inch. Do the same with 14 feet. That would equal 7 inches on your sheet. You now have the outline of your room.

Now measure the length and width of your desk, credenza, file cabinets, bookshelves, and chairs. Adjust them to scale. Some people like to draw each piece, cut them out, and place them in their "to scale" room to see how well they fit in a new layout. "Honey, would you move the desk over there just one more time?"

Remember, there are only so many hours in the work day and the way to win the game is by getting as much done as you can in those hours. Saving time wherever you can, even if that means using the little ways, will add up in the long run.

Remember These Concepts

- Set up your office with the efficiency of an airplane cockpit.
- The less you have to turn around in your office, the more you'll get done.
- Everything that can go into a file drawer should.

Things To Avoid
- Items on the floor or credenza.
- Your desk facing the door.

5.2

Standardization

Culture

- I Am The Culture

Standardizing Your Company, Department, Or Group

- Everyone Together Now
- My Way Or The Highway
- Setting Up Your Company Categories
- Central Files To The Rescue

What You Will Learn In This Chapter

- How to standardize your department or company using one system

---

 Myths of the Office

I can't stay organized when I travel.

Culture

I Am The Culture

One thing I have learned through the years is if you can get the people on top to buy into a change, the battle is practically won. When they're willing, the first and most important issue that needs to be covered is the culture of the organization or company. What is culture? You know. The unwritten way things are done. The behind-the-scene way you do business. Those interesting quirks, those things that get in your way that you can choose to change.

The following is an actual list of the elements of one of my client's culture that they came up with.

- In Box Chatter. (When you drop something off with someone, always fully explain what he or she needs to do with it, especially if you have already written the directions on the paper. Never just drop it off without saying something. That would be rude.)

- Hallway Interruptions. (Talk to as many people as you can while you pass them in the hallway. If possible, start a major conversation.)

- Meetings. (When in doubt, call a meeting. Hide out in one if you can.)

- E-mailing Everyone. (CYA or CYB. Never offend anyone. Include everybody possible in each and every e-mail you send.)

- Routing and Circulating of Stuff. (Route anything and everything that can potentially be of any interest to anyone and everyone. They have a big hole of time at night to fill.)

- Open-Door Policy. (Anyone, anytime can and should walk right in. Make yourself at home. Come on down!)

- Pop-In Visitors. (No appointment is necessary. Hey, they probably don't have anything on their calendar anyway.)

- Social-Working Your People. (It is, after all, my duty to fix you.)

- Travel. (How much time can I be on the road?)

- Unsaid Processes. (Even though I am an adult, I will not confront you and deal with the problem. I will tell someone else about it.)

- The "We vs. Them" Mentality. (It's us against them, baby.)

- The Nonprofit Mentality. (After all, we aren't a business, are we?)

- Phone Calls. (I could never not answer a ringing phone. Whatever would they do?)

- "Decide Not To Decide" Mentality. (I can't do that. I can't decide. I won't decide. It's not the way we've done it.)

- Make 'Em Happy. (The unit's fee entitles them to speedy service, even if I don't get anything done.)

- Hoard It! (I should get five extra of these pens while I'm here in the storeroom; you never know when I might run out and need them.)

- Keep a Copy of Everything That Comes Into Your Office. (You never know when you might need to refer to it.)

Any sound familiar? "Everything is urgent" is another example of an element of certain cultures. If you truly want to shift into high gear, you must identify your culture and change it.

Standardizing Your Company, Department, Or Group

Everyone Together Now

When I work with a company, I will inform them that there are three things that they can do to literally double their productivity.

1. The first is to institute a company QT.

2. The second is to clearly define each person's job responsibilities and their real job priority, both of which need to be written down and reviewed.

3. The third is to standardize as much of their operations as possible, including their work systems and processes and their information storage. The key to information storage is creating company Categories.

Company Categories need agreement by management and a representative sample of the workers. This means a group gets together and comes up with the same names, terms, definitions, and color codes. Watching a company attempt this is like being in a session of Congress. Participating in it is like being a gladiator in the Roman circus. Normally, you need a ringmaster to conduct the session. It's pretty challenging, but the rewards for the company are outstanding.

Some of the benefits of company Categories are:

☺ Everyone will have the same information system.

Think about the time when someone is out of the office. They call in for you to find something, generally a life-and-death document that they need immediately. You have a greater chance of having your salary doubled on your next review than finding what they want. With company Categories, you're using the same system they are so you know exactly where it will be. Finding things in seconds when someone is traveling or out sick will be simple.

> *Standardize every system that you can.*

☺ New employees are productive more quickly.

When a new employee starts working with your company, they'll learn a set way to do things and a system for them to follow. Instead of spending time reinventing the system, they can immediately contribute. It's a whole lot easier when everyone is on the same system. New employees want to be shown a way to do things when they first start. Unfortunately, very few are.

☺ You can have individual Categories.

When you create company Categories you can also create individual Categories. Let's face it, there are a lot of rebels out there, and they won't be constrained no matter what you try to do with them. Having this additional option allows each person to create their own unique Category selection as long as they don't create Categories with files that can already go into one of the existing company Categories. Doing this will create duplication.

Example

Let's say your company has a company Category called Corporate, which includes the company's policies and procedures. An individual has a file in their Reference Category called Policies. Bozo no-no. It would have to go under the company Category called Corporate. However, if there were not a company Category called Corporate, it would be okay to keep it under Reference. Or, using the same example, say an individual created a Category called Administration and put all the files that would normally go under Corporate under Administration. Nope. They would be duplicating a Category (Corporate) with their own (Administration) Category.

☺ A temp's training is shortened.

I have used departmental Categories for an entire staffing department. The department was broken down into managers and recruiting assistants. Each group had their own set of Categories. When a temp was brought in after a short orientation, she instantly understood everyone's system. This saved incredible amounts of time by eliminating repetitive training and countless questions as the temp tried to figure out the different systems. Departmental Categories work for both the Support and Action Categories.

☺ It allows you to set up a Central Files area.

The object is to get as much paper out of your office as possible, except those items you use. Once it is out of the office, where should the paper go? Onward to the Central Files, that area in the hall or in a room by itself where the one copy that everyone needs is stored.

Many companies use Central Files or have a central filing room. Unfortunately, it's usually set up by one person and very few people understand how it works. When that person is sick or on vacation, the search-and-find operation also takes a vacation. That's why getting input and involving the entire group when creating the company Categories is so important. Everyone owns and understands it.

When someone pulls out a file from Central Files, simply have them drop in an $8 \frac{1}{2}$- by 11-inch replacement card with their name and the date it was removed. "Borrowed file sheets" are available in office supply stores. Using hanging folders will ensure the integrity of the order and contents of your system. A master list stored elsewhere is a way to back up your system.

My Way Or The Highway

A retention system makes managing your paper easy over the long haul. It provides guidelines for what information to keep, as well as where and how long to keep it. If you don't have one, set one up as soon as possible. Check with your accountant and lawyer to determine specifics.

Your long-term storage needs to be set up the same way that your paper files, computer files, e-mail, and Central Files are set up. Do you see a pattern here? You're processing, storing, and accessing all information the same way, using the OATS system.

The flow of paper and information can go from:

Your office (file drawers and computer) to
⇩
The Central Files (books, binders, files, disks, tapes) to
⇩
The long-term storage area (boxed Categories of stuff) to
⇩
Paper heaven (wherever that is)

Below are examples of centralized locations you can use:

The area	What is stored in it
• Storage room	Long-term storage and records.
• Office supply room	A back-up area where office supplies are stored.
• Central Files	Commonly shared file cabinets in a separate room or hallway. The color of each Category is on the drawer for easy locating.
• Central library	Books, periodicals, cassette tapes, videotapes, and binders.
• Departmental Files	Could also be in the Central Files. Department files normally are kept in the hallway or near the department for quick accessibility.

Setting Up Your Company Categories

When you round up the group to create company or departmental Categories, allow no interruptions. That means cellular phones, pagers, or other toys are conveniently, thoughtfully, and intentionally left far away from the room. Decide who will facilitate the session. This is the key to a successful exercise. Many times it shouldn't be the boss. This gives el

> *Everything must go into a Category.*

bosso an opportunity to be one of the gang and interject his/her input, the same way everyone else does. Set up guidelines for running the session or all heck will break loose. The goal is to come up with all the Category names for your paper and non-paper items. Remember, everything must go into a Category.

Exercise

Start by asking everyone what he or she thinks the Category names should be. As the names are flung and flailed at you, get them written down as quickly as possible on a flip chart or a blackboard so everyone can see them. Have someone do the writing for the facilitator so they can stay sane. List every name that is yelled out or mentioned. The last thing you want to do is alienate a member of the group by scoffing at their suggestion. (You can scoff later once the thing is done.) Remember this is a right-brain activity, i.e., creating and brainstorming. There are no wrong answers yet. (They come later.)

Then the good part comes. You get to do a reality check. Check to see if any of the Categories are similar. If they are, have the group go into their left brain and weed out the names that don't work. This is the fun part. (Of course, any name that a person comes up with is the best name, or so they think. The others are obviously all wrong.) After the battle for Category names is over, you get to come up with definitions for each name. That is even more fun. Try having a group define Reference or Forms.

Another way to start the process is to ask everyone to grab a few files from their desk. Go through as many people's files as you can. Pick up a file and ask the group what the Category is. Believe me, you will hear a variety of names. The idea is to get input from everyone and come up with a name that everyone likes and agrees on. Agreement is the key. The Category names that you come up with will be geared toward what your company does and the language it uses.

Finally, decide on the colors. Associate colors with the Categories whenever you can. Choose the color of your company logo for your Category called Corporate. If there is no color association, use whatever tickles the group's fancy. The colors of the company Category hanging folders and tabs are the same.

Example

Say the company Category for Forms is blue. That means both the hanging folder and tab are blue. The way to differentiate individual Categories from company Categories is for individual Categories to use white or clear tabs. When you look in a person's drawer, the clear or white tabs will indicate individual Categories. I know there are exceptions to this; gray and standard green hanging folders have clear or white tabs, but most people already know them. Hanging folders work well and long outlast manila folders.

Once the names have been agreed upon, engrave them in stone. Type up a list with the Category name, a definition, and a color.

A way to reinforce the colors and Categories is with a listing of all the Categories, their colors, and a definition of each Category on the side of one of the file cabinets in a plastic sheet. This simplifies locating files in the great Central File abyss.

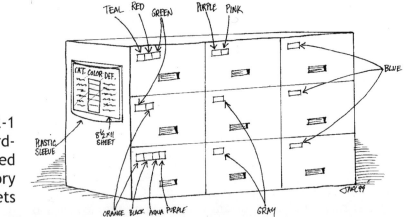

2-1 Standard-ized Category Sheets

Example

Category	Color	Definition
Reference	Gray	Any miscellaneous files that do not easily fit into one of the other Categories.
Clients	Red	Anyone who pays for your services.
Forms	Blue	Sheets of paper with blanks on it that need to be filled out. If they're filled out, they're no longer Forms.

Central Files To The Rescue

If you choose to set up your Central Files with company Categories, you need the whole group to participate in the process. Doing this on a weekend, holiday, Friday, or slow day will eliminate the interruptions.

Exercise

Before doing this, each person needs to have organized their office. From his or her organizing session, everyone should have stuff that goes into the Central Files. Have them put it into the Central Files room. Write the Category names on 3 x 5 cards spreading them on the floor around the perimeter of the Central Files room. Generally the file room or the hallway will work. An easy way to do this is with one department at a time. This eliminates total chaos and keeps your business from closing for that day. Have someone pick up a file, ask the group what the Category is and place it on a pile in front of (but not on) the card with the Category name. Do this until every file is on a Category pile.

Go through each Category pile and sort the papers into a colored Category hanging folder. Have someone write the file name on a sheet. Get the tabs typed up from the sheet and put them on their respective folders. Keep the file folders in order, placing the latest one on top of the other. This way, when putting the tabs on, the folders on the top of the pile will be coordinated with the last file name on the bottom of the sheet. Simply work back up the list to the top or first name, which will coincide with the first or bottom folder.

Finally, arrange the Categories in the file cabinets alphabetically from top to bottom and left to right. Place a small square from a hanging folder of the color of each Category on the drawer that Category is in. Place a typed sheet with the Category names, definitions, and colors in a clear plastic sheet, with the plastic sheet open end up, and attach it to the side of the first file cabinet as a reference for everyone who needs a reminder.

With everyone pitching in and categorizing the old files and typing the tabs, you'll be finished before you know it. At the end of the year, you'll be amazed at how many hours you have saved by doing this. I know what you are saying: "We don't have time to do this or we can't afford the lost wages and time. We are too busy. We've got too much to do." This will save you big time in many ways. It's well worth the time spent up front. It's a proactive activity, which you'll soon discover is the secret to success.

Remember These Concepts

- Standardize every system that you can.
- Everything must go into a Category.

Things To Avoid

- Having employees keep information locked up in their offices that others could use.
- Having everyone use a different system.
- Duplicating systems using different tools.

5.3

Setting Up Your System

Getting Started

- What You Need
- Setting Up Your System
- Traveling Folders
- Setting Up Your Home
- Afterwards

What You Will Learn In This Chapter

- How to get your system up and running
- How to set up your system in your office

☄ <u>Myths of the Office</u>

The more information I have, the better.

Getting Started

What You Need

The big moment has arrived. You've read the book, now you get to set up your system.

What do you need to do to get started? Make sure you have the following supplies.

✔ **Hanging folders**

You will need them for both your Action and Support Categories. Pendaflex hanging folders last the longest, plus they have a place to put your 3 x 5 cards—a pocket on the inside back.

   • **Action Categories**

   Use yellow for all your Action Category folders. Yellow is a bright and cheerful color. Besides, a client of mine, Cindy Dougherty, who happens to be part American Indian, has told me that yellow means "illuminated thought." Hey, how can you go wrong with that? Maybe the color will help inspire you.

Generally you'll want to buy four boxes of yellow, letter-size, one-fifth-tab hanging folders. Twenty-five folders come in each box. Of course, if you work with legal-size papers, buy legal. If at all possible, buy the letter size, since they're a lot easier to work with.

In your To Do Category, you'll need eight folders for your 1, 2, 3, 4, 5, A, B, C Files, plus around 25 for your empty folders that are in front of your 1 File and for all the tasks you will have in your A's, B's, and C's. Total 33.

In your Routine To Do, you'll probably have around 15 files. Total 15.

In your Tickler, you'll need them for your 1-31, January-December, and Pending Files. Total 44.

In your Projects, you may need around five folders. Total five.

Which brings you to a grand total of 97 hanging folders. The above is an approximation that will get you started. If you're working on 25 projects, obviously you'll need more folders.

• Support Categories

Each Support Category will get its own color. Colors to choose from are gray, red, blue, purple, pink, light green, orange, black, teal, aqua, burgundy, navy, green (standard olive color), earth brown (natural), earth red, and earth blue. Save the receipt when buying them so you can return unused boxes.

✔ Tabs

• Action Categories

Use a different color tab for each Action Category.

Action Category	Tab color
To Do	Red
Routine To Do	White or clear
Project	Blue
Tickler	Yellow

An easy way to remember the color tabs for your Action Categories is red, white, and blue. Red is most important; white is routine, day to day; you are blue when you have a Project to do; and yellow for the Tickler, since you're chicken because you're not working on the important stuff.

Buy one small pack (25) of red, blue, and clear letter-size, one-fifth tabs. You don't need to buy any yellow tabs since you won't be using them with your To Do, Routine To Do, or Project Categories.

> **• Support Categories**
> Use the colored tabs that come in each box.

✔ Cardboard Boxes
You need around ten cardboard boxes. Use them for loose item Categories such as Office Supplies, Tools, Personal, Books, Binders, Memorabilia. You'll need a couple of boxes to transport items home or to another area, plus one for your Out Box.

✔ An In Box and an Out Box
Perish the thought if you don't have both of these.

✔ Polish, cleanser, and rag
A clean office is a happy office. Use a furniture polish and a cleanser. Move all that old energy out.

✔ A big garbage pail
Hopefully this baby will be filled many times.

Setting up your system up

Round One.

1. Set some days aside to set up your system. Pick a day that you won't be interrupted, say a Saturday or Sunday. Or shoot for a Friday and have your receptionist take all your calls. It is important that you not be interrupted or it will take a long time to finish. The best way to do this is as quickly as possible. Dragging it out over a month is a lot harder. Knocking it out quickly allows you to benefit from the system immediately. The sooner you benefit from using the system, the more you'll continue to use it.

2. You'll be setting up your system and doing this exercise in your office. Move your chair and any other large items on the floor, such as floor plants, out of the room so you'll have a clean, open space to work in.

3. Review your Action and Support Category lists. Then write each Category name on a 3 x 5 card and place all the cards in

a semicircle away from you on the floor or lean them against and along the walls so you have an open center space to move around in. Keep the Action Categories together and the Support Categories together. Place the colored hanging folder for each Paper Support Category next to the 3 x 5 Category card. This will visually help you when you look for the pile to place the items on.

4. Use the boxes for your Office Supplies, Tools, Personal drawer, and Memorabilia Categories, plus one for your Out Box.

5. Stand and work on the other side of your desk if possible. Generally there is more room to spread out on the other side. Warning! This is difficult to do if you are in a cubicle.

6. Create a 3 x 5 card with the five steps of your In Box on it. Keep it out on your desk for you to refer to. Have some 3 x 5 cards, some paper clips, a yellow sticky pad, and a pen or pencil out on your desk.

7. You'll be going through everything in your office. This includes books, personal items, files, papers on bulletin boards, everything. Every drawer needs to be emptied. Every bookshelf needs to be emptied, your briefcase, which hasn't been emptied since your first day of work years ago, needs to be emptied. The goal is to move everything from its original space, which will change the energy of the entire room.

8. Put everything that's in your office on your desk.

9. Pick up the first item and treat it as if you're going through your In Box. Use the five-step In Box system for each item. This is crucial. You are creating a new habit. Instead of filing it away as you normally do, place it on the appropriate Category pile or box on the floor. When placing pieces of paper on each Category pile, make sure that you place each piece perpendicular to the last one. When you go through your pile a second time to place them into folders, it will be a lot easier to sort through them.

10. Go through and do this with every item and piece of paper that you have in your office. This may take a couple of days to do, depending on how much stuff you have. You will be training yourself with each piece of paper. It's important that you use all the steps when you go through everything. When you are finished, everything will be on a Category pile on your floor or in a box on the floor.

11. When everything is off its original spot and in a Category pile or box, clean and polish your desk, credenza, and file cabinets. You want to completely eradicate all that old energy. Plus you will have a nice, clean office too.

You're now ready for round two.

1. Create your Action Categories folders using the yellow hanging folders with the different color tabs. You can buy January-December and 1-31 tabs in an office-supply store. Print or type the file names on the white paper tabs for the other ones you'll need, such as Pending. Remember, do not make tabs to identify the Categories. The yellow hanging folder will indicate it's an Action Category and the red, white, blue, and yellow tabs on the yellow folders will indicate the specific type of Action Category (To Do, Routine To Do, Projects, Tickler). You will know the Categories by viewing them within a week.

2. In your To Do Category, staple your A, B, and C folders shut. Each task in your To Do will go into a separate, yellow, hanging folder behind either A, B, or C. You want each task in a separate folder; otherwise, they would all be mixed together in one folder and it would be hard to find the one you are looking for. Plus, when you wanted to move a task, for example from a C to an A, you'd have to dig it out from all the other tasks in that one folder. It doesn't work, believe me.

3. Go through all your Action Categories again. Pick up your To Do pile. Go through it again using your five-step In Box system—except this time, put them into the files that you have set up. The reason you go through all your piles twice is there is a good chance your first decision might not be your best decision.

4. Next, pick up your Routine To Do pile. Go through it using your five-step In Box system except, again, put them into the files that you have set up. Do the same with your Tickler and Projects. Keep your Action Categories together in one location, typically in two or three desk drawers if possible.

5. When all of your Action information is neatly filed away, jump into your Support. Pick up your Reference pile. Grab a box of the hanging folders you will be using (gray) and go through the pile. Use the five-step In Box system again. This time, put them into a colored hanging folder while you are saying: Stand, OATS, *Do not use Category labels. The color will tip you off.* Category, and File. When you are finished, go back and label each of the tabs and files. Do not use Category labels. The color will tip you off.

6. Do this with each Category. Generally, after going through both your Action and Support Category piles, you will notice

that you have put items in incorrect Categories. This is typical. In fact, the more changes you make the second time around, the more consistent and true your decisions will be. Your paper Support Categories will go into many more drawers than your Action. Alphabetize each Support Category. Then locate each Support Category according to how frequently you use it. Some people alphabetize their Support Categories in their file drawers; I don't. I set them up according to use. Do not keep any Support in the same drawer as Action.

> *Action Categories are always kept separate from Support Categories.*

> *Everything that can go into a file drawer should.*

7. When you are done putting away your last Paper Support Category, start with your Non-paper Support Categories. Grab a box and use your five step In Box system again. Non-paper Categories go into drawers and shelves, generally one Category per drawer, unless you only have a couple of drawers. If anything can go into a file cabinet, store it that way. (See page 202.)

Congratulations! You are set up. Tomorrow morning you can start using your system.

Traveling Folders

Traveling is already trying enough without having to worry about staying organized. Whether you are in sales, spend a good amount of time in the field, or work from two locations, you want to be able to use your system wherever you go.

When you're on the road, where do you stick all that paper and information you somehow pick up? Anywhere in your briefcase you can. Instead of cramming it in and then needing a pry bar to get it out, create a portable In Box.

Label three manila folders: Out Box, Action, and Support. (You don't need a Trash folder. Trash goes into the garbage pail.) Assign colors for the Out Box and Support folders. Make the Action folder yellow. Keep them in your briefcase. When you happen to pick up information, simply drop it into the correct folder. In your Out Box folder, take the back off a yellow sticky pad and stick the entire pad on the inside front cover. When you have something that will be going into your Out Box, write the message on a yellow sticky and then put it on the paper. When you get back to your office, pull out your three folders. They, of course, go into your In Box. From your Out Box folder, drop everything into your Out Box. File away the contents of your Support folder, then your Action. It makes that massive pile of stuff you need to go through much easier. Or you can continue to cram it into a section of your briefcase. Either way, other than the items that stay in your briefcase, you always need to empty the contents into your In Box.

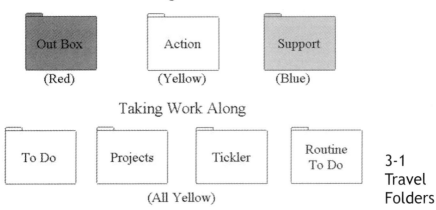

Collecting Information

Out Box (Red)   Action (Yellow)   Support (Blue)

Taking Work Along

To Do   Projects   Tickler   Routine To Do

(All Yellow)

3-1
Travel
Folders

• Travel and out in the field

Travel and out in the field are similar to working from two locations except you have one home base. Some people create a Mobile Milk Carton Car File (MMCCF). A MMCCF is a portable version of a few of your Action Categories and a few of your Support Categories. When I was in sales, I used to take my Forms and Brochures Support Categories in my car. When I needed a packet, out it would come.

• Working from two locations

First, decide which location will be your home base. The majority of your Action and Support Categories will be situated here. Your second location needs to have the same Action Categories and Files as your home base. Simply duplicate them in the second location.

You want to keep as much as you can of your Support information at your home base. If you need to take Support information with you, either take the hanging folders and place them in your second location file drawer or slip the contents into a manila folder that you can carry with you. The number of folders depends on the length of your stay.

If you plan on working at your other location, you need to create four yellow manila folders. Label them with each of your Action Categories: To Do, Routine To Do, Tickler, and Project (Diagram 3-1). Before you leave your home base, go through each of your Action Categories, pull out and place into the folders what you want to work on while you are at your second location. When you arrive, simply empty the contents of each folder into the appropriate Category and File. Simple.

When returning home, follow the same procedure. Go through your Action Categories and pull out what you want to take home with you. Initially, it may be a bit tricky, but after you do it a couple of times, you'll know exactly what to take and what to leave.

Setting Up Your Home

The new system you learned at your office can be used at your house too. A few changes are necessary, but overall the same concepts will be used.

Use an In Box and an Out Box. All mail, paper, etc., goes into your In Box. Go through it at least once a week.

Go through your entire filing system at the end of the year. Separate everything into Categories storing each Category in a big envelope or manila folder. Box and date everything.

Use an Out Box at home. Every time you leave your house or apartment, check it. That means you can put things into it such as your car keys or items you need to take with you. Simply drop them into your Out Box next to the door and check it every time before you leave.

Put a basket at the top of your stairs and one at the bottom. This will save you trips up and down the stairs. When something needs to go upstairs drop it in the basket. When you do go upstairs, pick up what's in the basket and drop it off into your upstairs In Box.

Some examples of Categories and Files you can use at home.

Action Categories	Support Categories
• To Do	• Reference
• A	• Car
• B	• Health
• C	• Receipts
	• Singles
	• Travel

- Tickler
  - 1 - 31
  - Jan. - Dec.
  - Pending

- Routine To Do
  - Buy
  - Call
  - Left Message
  - Pay
  - Read

- House
  - Appliances
  - Landscaping
  - Monthly Services
  - Repairs
  - Warranties

- Accounts Paid
  (Subject or Title)
  - Cable
  - Charity
  - Doctor
  - Gas
  - Phone

Afterwards

Once a week, pick out your fattest file, put it into your In Box and go through it and clean it out. This will keep any files from becoming too big. Or, go through it once a year at the end of your fiscal year.

Six months after you initially set up your system, go back through all your files again and clean them out. What you may find is that some of the Categories and File names may change after you have used the system a while. Some of the files may have accumulated too much stuff.

Warning

Do not be concerned if your office gets cluttered after you initially set it up and everything falls apart. Or you stop using the system for a while. Congratulations! You are human. Change takes time. It's typical for most people to goof up once in a while. The secret is to get back on the system as soon as you become aware that you are not using it. The greatest benefit with the system is no matter how far you stray from using it, whether it be a week or months, you can get back on it almost instantly. Gather all the loose paper on your floor, desk, and credenza and dump them in into our friend, the In Box. Then, go through your In Box. Once the system is set up, you will always have a basic system in place.

I truly hope you use the system. It has helped many people throughout the United States for many years. Don't let this be just another book you read and then store on the shelf. Set the system up. I can guarantee you it will definitely change your life for the Vetter.

Concepts To Remember

- Do not use Category labels. The color will tip you off.
- Action Categories are always kept separate from Support Categories.
- Everything that can go into a file drawer should.

Things To Avoid

- Putting off setting up the system because you still aren't absolutely sure how it all works.

Appendix A

Organizational Concepts

Part 1

Chapter 1
- Be a fire marshal, not a firefighter. Spot the fires before they start.
- If you continue to operate in a time-based tickler mentality, you will never be able to stay up with the flow of information.
- Ways to work in the information age:
  - Learn a whole new way to work.
  - Be proactive 20 percent of your day.
  - Learn and limit the amount of technology in your life.
  - Understand the difference between Processing and Producing.
  - Use one system.
  - Learn how to process information.
  - Limit your choices.

Chapter 2
- The more information sources you have, the more interruptions you will have.
- Your day is broken down into Processing and Producing.
- Process before you Produce.
- Processing includes:
  - Checking voice mail, e-mail and In Box, three times a day.
  - Reviewing all your Action Categories, once a week.
- Producing includes:
  - Working your To Do, Tickler and Routine To Do Action Categories every day.

Chapter 3
- Organization = A System + Decision-Making.
- Everything we do is for a payoff. Payoffs can be both healthy and unhealthy.

- The definition of insanity is doing the same thing over and over and expecting different results.
- The outside cannot fix the inside.
- There are reasons and results. Only one of them matters.
- The best way around something is always through it.
- The more right decisions you want to make, the fewer decisions you'll end up making.

Part 2

Chapter 1

- Everything always goes into your In Box first.
- When you are interrupted and given an item, simply drop it into the In Box and finish what you are doing.
- Every loose piece of paper on your desk represents a decision not made.
- From your In Box there are only four places a piece of paper can go: To your Out Box, Action, Trash or Support (OATS).
- The faster I move my paper from my In Box to my Out Box, the more I get done.
- The goal for every piece of paper that comes into your office is to get it out of your office.
- Whoever initiates and writes it keeps it.

Chapter 2

- The secret is to understand the status of everything in your office.
- No matter when you intend to work on something, the task is always an Action.
- Everything in your office is either an Action or a Support.

Chapter 3

- It takes more work to evade a task than to accomplish it.
- The more decisions you make, the less trash you will have.
- Your ability to throw out trash is directly related to your ability to make a decision.
- The more secure you are, the less you will want.

- Eliminating emotionally charged paper will free you up psychologically.
- The main reason to save anything is because you are going to use it.
- Less is more.
- At the end of every fiscal year, go through everything in your office, including your computer and e-mail files.

Chapter 4

- If it's easy to do, you'll do it. If it's hard to do, you probably won't do it.
- The five items that stay on your desk are your:
  - In Box.
  - Out Box.
  - Telephone.
  - Appointment book or calendar.
  - Computer.
- The less you have out on your desk, the less you will be distracted.
- The only other item on your desk should be the one thing you're working on.

Chapter 5

- Process your In Box. Don't "do" it.
- You spend more energy avoiding doing something than just doing it.
- Action creates energy.
- There's a fine line between deciding and doing when going through your In Box.
- The key to going through your In Box is in your ability to make decisions.
- Habits create needs.

Chapter 6

- A Category is a grouping of similar or like things.
- You already know how the Category model works.
- A form is a form is a form.
- The first way you organize anything is visually.
- Less effort creates more results.

Chapter 7

- All Support Categories originate from the Reference Category.

- All Support Files that don't easily fit into an existing Category always go into the Reference Category.
- A Category has five or more files in it.
- Unlike Paper Categories, you don't need five or more items to create a Non-paper Category.
- Everything in your office needs to be in a Category.

Chapter 8

- Colors are an easy way to remember Categories.
- Left to right, big to little, general to specific, front to back, A to Z.
- Whenever you want to break a file down, create a tab to the right of and behind the existing tab.
- To the right, ever to the right.
- You don't have to have five files when you use a Subcategory.

Chapter 9

- This is a subject-based system.
- If an item will fit into a hanging folder, file it there.

Chapter 10

- Using Windows Explorer is the quickest way to find anything.
- Left to right, big to little, general to specific.
- Front to back (file drawer), top to bottom (computer).

Part 3

Chapter 1

- The key is to work in all four quadrants rather than just the time-based one.

Chapter 2

- When the thought hits you, write it down.
- Use the actual file or paper to remind you of a task rather than writing it on a to do list.
- Write only one Action per card.
- Let the 3 x 5 card do the remembering for you.
- Separate Actions from Supports.

Chapter 3
- The less you put into your Tickler, the more you will get done.
- Pending = Passive.
- Remember, you're the one who determines how far to the right your tabs will go.
- Don't put those things to do about which you are undecided or unsure in the Pending.

Chapter 4
- Batch and block similar activities together.

Chapter 5
- Create time from time you think you don't have.
- In order to get, you have to give.
- When you have a long time to accomplish a task, you tend to think it is unimportant.
- If you don't know where you are going, you'll never get where you want to go.
- A way to get ahead is by getting a little behind.
- Take a QT every day at the same time, working on important rather than urgent tasks.
- Successful people are those people who are willing to do those things that unsuccessful people are not willing to do.

Chapter 6
- The smaller and simpler the task is, the greater the chance of doing it.

Chapter 7
- A Flow System form will always keep you on track.

Part 4

Chapter 1
- Leave time open to work.
- Awareness is control!
- Once a week, look through everything in your Action Categories.
- Work your day around your Quiet Time.

Chapter 2
- You are the cause of over 50 percent of all your interruptions.

Chapter 3
- Your assistant's productivity is directly proportionate to the amount of quality time you spend with him/her.
- Everything needs to go to the administrative assistant before going to the manager.

Part 5

Chapter 1
- Set up your office with the efficiency of an airplane cockpit.
- The less you have to turn around in your office, the more you'll get done.
- Everything that can go into a file drawer should.

Chapter 2
- Standardize every system that you can.
- Everything must go into a Category.

Chapter 3
- Don't use Category labels. The color will tip you off.
- Action Categories are always kept separate from Support Categories.
- Everything that can go into a file drawer should.

Appendix B

Five Steps Of The In Box

1. Stand up
2. Ask OATS (Out Box, Action, Trash, Support)
3. Decide the Category/File
4. Use all your senses
5. File it away

Your Daily Schedule

1. <u>PROCESS</u> (Information)
- 3 times a day go through your e-mail, voice mail, and In Box.
- 1 time a week on your last workday, review all your Action Categories.

2. <u>PRODUCE</u> (Work)
Work on your:
- Tickler – Tasks that must be and can only be done today.
- Routine To Do – Look at all your files, pick out those files that contain multiple tasks that can be batched together and then do them.
- To Do – Work on your top five To Do A's in your QT.

The Category Models

- Category
- File

- Category
- File
- Subfile
- File

- Category
- Subcategory
- File

- Category
- Subcategory
- File
- Subfile
- Type
- Subtype

Index

M

About The Author

Greg Vetter

Speaker • Workshop Leader • Productivity Coach

The perfect choice for a highly interactive, fun and content-packed program.

Speeches

• **Staying Afloat In A Sea Of Information**
Do you find you're being driven crazy by constant interruptions? Does it seem to take forever to complete the simplest of tasks? People in the business world are drowning in a sea of information. Taken from a page in his book, *Find It In Five Seconds*, Greg introduces six new ways to work and get ahead in the Information Age.

• **Shredding The Myths Of The Office**
"A clean desk is the sign of a sick mind." "If I can't see it, I'll forget to do it." These and other myths about organization abound in the workplace. During this entertaining program which combines lecture with audience participation, this thought-provoking program will completely dismantle commonly held beliefs and teach you A Vetter Way™ to organize your office.

Workshops

A Vetter Way™ series including:
  • A Vetter Way To Organize Your Office
  • A Vetter Way To Manage Your Sales Day
  • A Vetter Way To Define Your Job Responsibilities
  • A Vetter Way To Lead Productive Meetings

For More Information, contact Greg Vetter at:
Web page: www.vetterproductivity.com
E-mail: greg@vetterproductivity.com
Phone: 1-887-534-6348 (5FINDIT)

Order Form

Qty.	Title	Price	Can. Price	Total
	Find It In Five Seconds	$19.95	$26.95	
	Shipping and handling (US orders add $3.95 for first book, $2.00 for each additonal book)			
	Sales tax (GA residents only, add 7%.)			
	Total enclosed			

Telephone orders:
Call 1-877-534-6348.
            (5FINDIT)

Fax orders:
Fax completed order form
to (404) 303-8850.

Postal orders:
Send completed order
form to:
Vetter Productivity, Inc.
100 Maryeanna Drive
Atlanta, GA 30342.

E–Mail orders:
E–mail your order request
to greg@vetterproductivity.com

Payment: Please check one
    ❑ Check
    ❑ Visa
    ❑ MasterCard

Name on Card: _____

Card #: _____

Expiration Date: _____

Name _____

Address _____

City _____ State _____ Zip _____

Daytime Phone (_____) _____

Quantity discounts are available.

Thank you for your order!